MARGARET THE FIRST

1. Margaret Lucas. By Sir Peter Lely.

Margaret the First

A BIOGRAPHY OF
MARGARET CAVENDISH
DUCHESS OF NEWCASTLE
1623–1673

BY

Douglas Grant

RUPERT HART-DAVIS
SOHO SQUARE LONDON
1957

TO

Stella

AND

Abigail

Contents

Illustrations

Preface

MARGARET CAVENDISH, Duchess of Newcastle—the name at once brings to mind two famous and contradictory opinions: 'a mad, ridiculous, conceited woman', Pepys noted irritably; 'the thrice noble, chaste, and virtuous,—but again somewhat fantastical, and original-brain'd, generous Margaret Newcastle', declared Charles Lamb, in love with her singularity. To which side does the truth incline? Sir Charles Firth considered the question and wrote: 'What fame she has is with the few, and not with the many, with the best and not with the most. To some she is still the 'incomparable Princess', as contemporary panegyrists termed her, and Lamb delighted to style her. But to most she is and will be merely the fantastic figure which flits for a moment across the pages of Pepys.'

I have tried in this biography to show why Margaret Cavendish should be better known than Sir Charles thought likely. She is certainly fantastic—and one would not wish her otherwise—but her character has a solidity and her writings an interest which could not be guessed from Pepys's remark, or, for that matter, from Lamb's. I hope I have avoided equally Pepys's contempt and Lamb's sentiment.

There are five important studies of Margaret. Sir Charles Firth's introduction to his edition of her *Life* of her husband, first published in 1886, is as much the work of an excellent literary critic as of a great historian. The standard account of both Margaret and her husband is by Henry Ten Eyck Perry: *The First Duchess of Newcastle and her Husband as Figures in Literary History*, 1918. I have not attempted to follow Perry's example and write a double-biography. Newcastle had passed fifty when he married Margaret, and I could see no way of doing justice to his early career and still letting my emphasis fall where I wished it to, on Margaret. I have introduced Newcastle himself only when I considered his presence or personality essential to an understanding of her. This remark is not intended as covert criticism of Perry: his intention was different from mine and was thoroughly carried out. His work will not be superseded by this present study. Virginia Woolf's essay on Margaret in *The Common Reader*, 1925, is only an essay, but an essay typical of Mrs. Woolf: an essay which delights with its exact perception, and felicitous expression, of Margaret's qualities. R. W. Goulding, sometime librarian at Welbeck Abbey, published a brief but useful account of Margaret in 1925, *Margaret (Lucas) Duchess of Newcastle*, and printed papers inaccessible to Perry. The fifth work is by another historian, A. S. Turberville. His account of both Margaret and her husband in *A History of Welbeck Abbey and its Owners*, Volume One, 1938, is admirable. I have not drawn directly on Turberville and his work is not cited in my notes, but I am nevertheless indebted to him in several ways.

The matter of quotations may need some explanation. I have tried hard not to quote too much; but, apart from the temptation to let Margaret speak for herself, which she does inimitably, many of her works—in fact, all of them, with the exception of her *Life* of her husband—are extremely difficult to come by outside the great libraries, and I feel bound to provide the evidence in support of my own assertions. All the quotations, whether from books or manuscripts, have been modernized. I know the arguments against modernizing spelling, punctuation, and the use of capitals and italics, but I was not prepared to encourage Margaret's reputation for being fantastic by presenting her in the quaint frippery of seventeenth-century typographical style, particularly as the style varies from book to book; and having once begun with Margaret, I had to be consistent in my treatment of the other authors quoted. There is, however, one exception: I have given Margaret's love letters and Newcastle's love poems in their original dress—at least, in the dress in which they appear in my edition of them; something individual would certainly have been lost here by modernization.

I should like to think that this biography will make Margaret appear in future to be more than a fantastic figure flitting across the pages of Pepys. And I know that if there is a heavenly lodgement for Margaret's soul whence she can lean out to trace the fortunes of her fondest concern on earth—her reputation, I have an observer who trusts that Sir Charles underestimated the number of ' the best '.

DOUGLAS GRANT

13 *January* 1956.

Acknowledgements

I AM greatly indebted to the Duke of Portland, K.G., for permission to quote extensively from the Portland Papers, deposited on loan in the British Museum and in the library of Nottingham University. I must particularly thank Mr. Francis Needham for his unfailing kindness, advice and assistance. I must also thank Mr. A. G. H. Bachrach, Mr. M. F. Baudouin, Miss Jean Colquhon, Mr. N. J. Endicott, Mr. Rupert Hart-Davis, Mr. M. R. Trappes-Lomax, and Mr. H. S. Wilson; their occasional help has been invaluable. I wish to express my gratitude to the staffs of the libraries in which I have worked: the British Museum, Nottingham University Library, Leyden University Library, and the Huntington Library. The biography was materially helped forward by a year spent as a Nuffield Travelling Fellow, and I should like to thank the Nuffield Foundation for its generosity, and the University of Toronto, which granted me leave of absence to take up the fellowship and which has helped me in many other ways.

D. G.

1 A Visit to London

Though I cannot be Henry *the Fifth, or* Charles *the Second, yet I will
endeavour to be* Margaret *the* First.

On 11 April 1667, Samuel Pepys made his first attempt to see
Margaret Cavendish, Duchess of Newcastle. She and her
husband had just arrived in London from the north yet already
the town did nothing but talk of her eccentricities. Pepys had
heard how she rigged herself out in an ' antique dress ' and her
many footmen in velvet coats, and how at the end of a performance of her husband's comedy *The Humorous Lovers* she had
ostentatiously thanked the actors from her box. Wrongly
believing that she had written the play, Pepys had gone to see
it himself, and while dismissing it ' as the most silly thing that
ever come upon a stage ', he had been glad of the opportunity it
had given him of better understanding her character. His
insatiable appetite for personalities and oddities whetted by the
gossip, he set out for Whitehall on 11 April to see the lady, whose
whole history was ' a romance ', pay a visit to the Queen.[1] He
was not alone in his curiosity. The Court was crowded with
people who had come specially to see her, and as Pepys remarked,
an appearance by the Queen of Sweden could not have made a
greater stir.[2] But the spectators were badly disappointed;
Margaret Cavendish did not go to Court that night.

She did not go to Court until the night of 22 April, but her
arrival was worth waiting for. She drove up in a procession of
three coaches: in the first, of two horses, rode her gentlemen;
in the last, of four horses, her waiting-women; and in the

[The works of Margaret Cavendish are cited by shortened titles and unless
otherwise stated the edition is always the first.]

[1] Pepys, *Diary*, ed. H. B. Wheatley, 1949, vi. 233, 254.
[2] The reference is to Queen Christina.

15

second, of six horses, Margaret Cavendish herself. As she stepped out of her coach to enter the palace, her train was carried by a young lady dressed completely in white satin. She first visited the King and was then conducted by the Lord Chamberlain to the Queen, where the King himself came to her. A surprised newswriter remarked, ' This visit is thought extra-ordinary.' [1]

Four days later Pepys managed to catch a glimpse of her as he was driving into London from Westminster. He met the coaches in her procession and the footmen in their velvet and saw her from a distance looking, it seemed, exactly like her description. He noticed her velvet cap, her hair curled about her ears, the many black patches about her mouth—' because of pimples ', as he unchivalrously remarked—her ' naked ' neck, and her short black jacket, a *just-au-corps*; and the impression she made on him was of a ' very comely woman.' [2] Her apparent beauty confirmed him in his determination to see her close at hand, and on May Day he went to Hyde Park and braved the ' horrid ' dust and the dense traffic in the hope of watching her drive past. She did make the fashionable circuit, but was so crowded in by other coaches that he only saw that her own coach was large and black and ornamented in silver and hung with white curtains. He tried to intercept her on her way back from the Park to her mansion in Clerkenwell, but by stopping to have a drink to wash down the taste of dust, he missed her again. The afternoon had been wasted in learning no more than that the effect of her princely equipage was white and black.

A third chance to see her occurred ten days later when he almost overtook her on the road to Clerkenwell, but as she was surrounded by a hundred boys and girls running and scrambling about her coach to peer in at her, he had to give up the attempt. ' But I will get a time to see her ',[3] he noted, resolved that he would not be denied his share in the spectacle. His chance

[1] *Hist. MSS. Comm.*, 12 *Rep.*, *Pt. vii*, 1890, p. 47.
[2] Pepys, vi. 274.
[3] *Ib.*, pp. 282–3.

came on 30 May when she attended a meeting of the Royal Society; the climax of her London visit and, in a sense, of her whole extraordinary career.

Pepys was not the only diarist interested in Margaret Cavendish. John Evelyn, more fortunate in his acquaintance, visited the Newcastles at their house on 18 April. He was warmly received as an old friend, for twenty-two years earlier Newcastle and Margaret had been married in Paris in the chapel of Evelyn's father-in-law, Sir Richard Browne, then English Resident at the Court of France. Evelyn was delighted with his reception and especially by ' the extraordinary fanciful habit, garb, and discourse of the Duchess '; so much so that he hurried to wait on them again, taking with him his wife, whom they had last seen as his child-bride.[1] Margaret received Mrs. Evelyn, whom she used fondly to call ' daughter ' out of love for the memory of Lady Browne, in ' a kind of transport ', but her sharp visitor, watching her closely, condemned her out of hand. She disliked her fantastical dress, while reluctantly admitting that it suited her fine figure; she deprecated her attempt to disguise by a careful display of curls and patches that she was forty-four; she deplored her affected manner—' her gracious bows, seasonable nods, courteous stretching out of her hands, twinkling of her eyes, and various gestures of approbation '— and as for her conversation, it was ' airy, empty, whimsical and rambling . . . terminating commonly in nonsense, oaths, and obscenity.'[2]

Evelyn was not unaffected by his wife's opinion—at least his attitude to Margaret became less tolerant after this sharp summing-up—but he could not disregard the Newcastles; and after dining with the Duke on 11 May, he sat talking to the Duchess in her bedchamber until the Marquis of Dorchester and other company arrived, when he took his leave. The next time he met her was at the meeting of the Royal Society on 30 May.

Margaret Cavendish herself cannot have fully appreciated the

---

[1] Evelyn, *Diary*, ed. Austin Dobson, 1906, ii. 269, 271.
[2] *Ib.*, p. 271, n. 3.

17

disrespect and ridicule which greeted her appearance in London. Encouraged by an indulgent elderly husband, surrounded by sycophantic dependants, and meeting face to face in society only the exaggerated respect exacted by her rank, she was able to interpret the crowd's blatant curiosity as a tribute to her reputation as the first authoress of the age, whose example had given her sex ' courage and confidence to write, and to divulge what they writ in print.'[1]   And her reputation seemed to rest firmly on her many books—on her poems and opinions and plays, on her letters, tales, orations and philosophy, all written and published in the space of less than twenty years.   Should she at any time doubt the extent of her achievement, she had only to turn up the letters from her constant admirers, the Cambridge colleges, in which, to choose the style affected by Trinity, she was acclaimed as a ' Minerva and an Athens '.[2]   Of course she sometimes suspected that others did not see in her the image she had created of herself, but she was capable of defying their hostile opinion: ' I matter not the censures of this age,' she wrote, ' but am rather proud of them; for it shows that my actions are more than ordinary, and according to the old proverb, *it is better to be envied than pitied.*'[3]

The ' censures ' made upon her during her visit to London in 1667 were, with the exception of Mrs. Evelyn's, superficial, and had her critics read her books closely, they would have found that she had already anticipated them.   The ostentation with which she surrounded all her movements had been deliberately adopted as a mark of respect to her husband.   The wife of a nobleman who had been in turn governor to Charles II, general of all the royalist forces in the north during the Civil War, and an impoverished exile for fifteen years, having gladly sacrificed his immense wealth to the King's cause, could not be expected to allow the shiftless Restoration world to forget the honours

---

[1] *Sociable Letters*, p. 225.
[2] *Letters and Poems in Honour of the Incomparable Princess, Margaret, Dutchess of Newcastle*, 1676, p. 11.
[3] *Life*, p. (b).

due to the survivor from a greater age. 'I am so proud, or rather just to my Lord,' she affirmed, 'as to abate nothing of the quality of his wife; for if honour be the mark of merit . . . it were a baseness for me to neglect the ceremony thereof.' [1] But she did not attach an exaggerated value to such displays for her own sake: 'I should weep myself into water,' she exclaimed pathetically, 'if I could have no other fame than rich coaches, lackeys, and what state and ceremony could produce, for my ambition flies higher, as to worth and merit, not state and vanity; I would be known to the world by my wit, not by my folly, and I would have my actions so wise and just, as I might neither be ashamed nor afraid to hear of myself.' [2]

As for her appearance, she admitted that she took more pleasure in devising a fashion than in following one, dismissing the men and women of her age as 'nothing but mode; as mode-minds, mode-bodies, mode-appetites, mode-behaviours, mode-clothes, mode-pastimes or vices, mode-speeches and conversations.' [3] If she chose to wear a velvet cap decorated with long falling feathers, she wore it not because it was the fashion but because the feathers shadowed her face from the hot sun and cooled her with their fanning. Pepys and Evelyn might gossip and laugh at such harmless vanities, but she had already summed men up: 'in their dressings and fashions they are more phantastical, various and unconstant than women are,' she observed satirically; 'for they change their blocks for their hats—although they cannot their block-heads—forty times oftener than women change the shapes of their bags or hoods for their heads! . . . And do not men run visiting from house to house for no other purpose but to twattle?' [4] They might join with Mrs. Evelyn in ridiculing her curls and patches and other small tricks to save her beauty, but they should have known that women were judged largely by their beauty, and that once lost, there was

[1] *Natures Pictures*, p. 389–90.
[2] *Sociable Letters*, p. 167.
[3] *Ib.*, p. 131.
[4] *Natures Pictures*, pp. 111–12.

B 2

nothing more for them to do than to sink into the obscurity of domestic life. ' Beauty is the light of our sex,' she wrote, ' which is eclipsed in middle age, and benighted in old age, wherein our sex sits in melancholy darkness; and the remembrance of beauty past is as a displeasing dream.' [1]

Mrs. Evelyn's unkind summary of Margaret's character was the result of a complete opposition of temperament and of opinion. In spite of her intelligence, Mrs. Evelyn firmly believed that women were unfitted for an intellectual life; poetry, philosophy and scholarship were the prerogative of men and of no concern to women at all, and any time spent on them was time misspent. Women fulfilled their natures in their homes, by looking after their children, relieving the poor, helping their friends, and ' observing a husband's commands.' Such duties were ' of sufficient weight to employ the most improved capacities ' among them. [2] Holding these opinions, which were usual in her time, and admiring only a character which illustrated them, how could she be expected to appreciate an ardent feminist; one who eloquently denounced the servitude in which her sex was kept by men, and who explained that she wrote so much in order to win from posterity an ' extraordinary fame ', to be won in no other way—' all heroic actions, public employments, powerful governments, and eloquent pleadings ' being denied to her? [3] Mrs. Evelyn may have been amazed by her ' extravagancy and vanity ', and may have wondered as she heard her talk how she had escaped being confined in a madhouse, [4] but Mrs. Bathsua Makin, reputed to be one of the most learned women of the age, whose whole life had been devoted to the education of women, publicly cited her as an example to the sex. The Duchess of Newcastle, she wrote, 'by her own genius, rather than any timely instruction, overtops many grave gown-men.' [5]

[1] *Sociable Letters*, p. 2.
[2] Evelyn, i. p. lxv.
[3] *Natures Pictures*, p. ci.
[4] Evelyn, ii. 271, n. 3.
[5] Bathsua Makin, *An Essay to revive the Antient Education of Gentlewomen*, 1673, p. 10.

Disapproving so strongly of Margaret's opinions, Mrs. Evelyn easily extended her condemnation to her person and manner; but Margaret knew too well that the impression she made was often unfortunate. She had been afflicted with 'bashfulness' from her childhood and in spite of every effort had been unable to remedy the weakness; in fact, long before the meeting with Mrs. Evelyn she had despaired of a cure. She found it an acute embarrassment, 'for it hath many times', she remarked, 'obstructed the passage of my speech, and perturbed my natural actions, forcing a constraintedness, or unusual motions.'[1] Confronted across the room by Mrs. Evelyn, coldly eyeing her from behind the mask of a modest conventional housewife, Margaret's demon seized command, translating her into the affected, grimacing creature whom her guest was later to deride.

Mrs. Evelyn took her leave and returned to Sayes Court, to her children and domestic duties, and later heard without envy her husband's account of Margaret's visit to the Royal Society— an honour so far removed from the true interests of women as to seem highly ridiculous.

The Royal Society had its origins in the period of the Civil War but it was not formally established until after the Restoration; it received its royal charter in 1662. Its foundation illustrated the deep and widespread interest in science which Walter Charleton, an early member of the Society, attributed to that strange irresistible influence, the spirit of the age. The 'peculiar genius' of an age, wrote Charleton, 'inclines men's minds to some one study or other, and gives it a dominion over their affections proportionate to its secret influence.'[2] The spirit of the age was strongly abetted in England by the violence of the political and religious dissensions of the Civil War, which brought two traditional disciplines, theology and civil law, into disrepute. Charleton observed this development at the time and remarked that the 'major part' of the students at the universities

[1] *Natures Pictures*, pp. 381–2.
[2] Walter Charleton, *The Immortality of the Human Soul*, 1657, p. 49.

' addict themselves to physic ',[1] the only study above the national controversies.

The Royal Society became the centre of scientific research and discussion in England, serving as a channel of communication between scientists both at home and abroad, and, so far as it could, encouraging and co-ordinating investigation. Its terms of reference were wider and its aims more practical than would be the case to-day, and as the division between scientist and layman had not then been drawn, it was enthusiastically supported by a crowd of amateurs. It was expected to accomplish wonders. Natural history, let alone natural philosophy, ' is but in its rudiments ', wrote Joseph Glanvill to Margaret; ' the advance of it your Grace knows is the design and business of the Royal Society; from whom we may reasonably at last expect better grounds for general doctrines, than any the world yet hath been acquainted with.' [2]

Margaret had responded quickly to the spirit of the age. Her second book, published in 1653, entitled *Philosophicall Fancies*, had been her first attempt to set down in prose her opinions in natural philosophy; and since then she had developed and enlarged them in several other books, carried away by her enthusiasm for a study which, as she described it in her apology, ' is a great delight, and pleases the curiosity of men's minds; it carries their thoughts above vulgar and common objects; it elevates their spirits to an aspiring pitch; it gives room for the untired appetites of man to walk or run in, for so spacious it is, that it is beyond the compass of time.' [3] But her interest in science was not simply speculative; she was also aware of its practical importance, claiming that it was of use to every art of life, ' insomuch as it may be said, man lives merely by natural philosophy; so that natural philosophy is the light that God is pleased to give man to direct him in the course of his life.' [4]

---

[1] *Ib.*, p. 50.
[2] *Letters and Poems*, pp. 124–5.
[3] *Philosophical Opinions*, 1655, p. (a) 1ᵛ.
[4] *Philosophical Opinions*, 1663, p. b3.

Holding these opinions but debarred by her sex from direct participation in its activities, she admired the Royal Society from a distance; ' for certainly,' she wrote, ' were I empress of the world, I would advance those that have most learning and wit '.[1] The invitation extended to her to attend a meeting of the Society deeply satisfied her as an apparent recognition of her claim to be, in spite of her sex, a natural philosopher whose purpose was identical with and as serious as that of the Fellows.

The invitation, however, was not spontaneous. At a meeting of the Society on 23 May, Lord Berkeley mentioned that Margaret ' had expressed a great desire to come to the society, and to see some of their experiments; but that she had desired to be invited.' [2] Berkeley was seconded by the Earl of Carlisle and Dr. Charleton, and a motion that she should be invited to attend a meeting on the following Thursday was carried. At a meeting of the Council on the same day it was resolved that she should be shown some experiments, which were decided upon in a later resolution, and that Berkeley and Charleton should convey the invitation to her and attend her to the meeting. According to Pepys, the motion to invite her was warmly debated, many being against it; but as Margaret had several friends and connections in the Society—her brother, Lord Lucas, had been an Original Fellow—Pepys probably exaggerated the opposition. The reason behind the opposition seems to have been a fear that her visit would give the Society's critics a chance to mock at it; and as its aims were not yet widely understood, it was naturally sensitive to criticism, especially when such criticism threatened to take the form of ballads hawked about the streets.

At the invitation of Lord Henry Howard, the Society had met in Arundel House in the Strand ever since Gresham College, its original place of assembly, had been requisitioned by the City

[1] *Sociable Letters*, p. b2.
[2] Thomas Birch, *History of the Royal Society*, 1756, ii. 176.

after the Great Fire, and the mansion was crowded on 30 May in anticipation of Margaret's arrival:

> First in a stately room, I wis,
> As most within the city is,
>   Sate at a table long
> Nine lords, a duke of high degree,
> With all the crowd who came to see,
>   And I the rest among.

She was late in arriving and the business had already been begun before it was announced that she was at the gate in her coach. Lord Brounker, the President, went to the door of the meeting-room to receive her, and with his handsome mace of office carried before him, led her up to the table and seated her at his right hand. She came attended by all her waiting-women, six of whom were needed to carry her train, and the entrance of so large a party at first threw the meeting into confusion. Her dress and retinue were clearly designed to astonish the Fellows:

> But, oh, the hurry and the din
> To see this Dame to enter in;
>   No Lady of the May
> With all the ribbon of our parish,
> When at last wake our Nell did flourish,
>   As she was half so gay.
>   *   *   *   *
> But, Jo! her head-gear was so pretty,
> I ne'er saw anything so witty;
>   Though I was half afeared,
> God bless us! when I first did see her:
> She looked so like a Cavalier,
>   But that she had no beard.

As soon as she had taken her place the experiments, which had been entrusted to the capable hands of the Hon. Robert Boyle and Dr. Robert Hooke, were begun. The first was the weighing of air. A glass receiver of a capacity of nine gallons and three pints was placed in a scales and exhausted of air by means of Boyle's famous air-pump; and after it had been opened again and the air let in, it was found to weigh nearly two ounces heavier than it did exhausted. The other experiments were more spectacular: a piece of roasted mutton was dissolved in sulphuric acid and turned into a substance like thick blood; several transparent and coloured liquors were mixed together to produce strange hues and combinations; and a great lodestone, weighing sixty pounds, was shown 'driving away the steel dust at its poles'. As the experiments were being conducted, a 'very pretty black boy', probably a page to one of the company, ran excitedly up and down the room.

Pepys thought the experiments 'fine' but was more occupied in looking at Margaret, whom he was at last able to see after so many attempts. He had expected too much not to be disappointed. He was compelled to admit that she had been 'a good, comely woman', but her 'antick' dress and her 'ordinary' deportment so offended him that he confessed he did not 'like her at all'. He strained forward to catch what she was saying as the experiments were being performed but heard nothing 'that was worth hearing, but that she was full of admiration, all admiration'.

Among Margaret's women was a famous beauty, the Ferrabosco, who also had a reputation as a singer:

> The President before his mace,
> And at his right hand sate her Grace;
>> Behind stood Ferrabosco.
> So hight a pretty black-girl there,
> On whom philosophers did peer
>> Well skilled in Metaposco.

Being no philosopher, Pepys peered harder than the rest, having heard that if Margaret bade Ferrabosco show her face, she would 'kill the gallants'; but he was no more taken by the girl than by her mistress—she was 'indeed black' and had 'good black little eyes' but otherwise was 'but a very ordinary woman' in his expert opinion. The entertainment was not coming up to his expectations at all.

Other experiments included the mixing of two cold liquors

which grew hot upon infusion, and the swimming of a solid body in the middle of water; and a microscope was also produced for Margaret's inspection:

> But, oh! a stranger thing; this Dame
> A glass they showed with an hard name—
> I cannot hit upon 't;
> That made a louse to look as big
> As any sow that 's great with pig,
> Some swore an elephant.

At the end of the programme, Margaret, still crying that she 'was full of admiration', rose to leave and was led out to her coach by the Duke of Somerset, the Earl of Carlisle, Lord Berkeley and John Evelyn. After her departure the meeting returned to its business, and Dr. Hooke, the Society's maid-of-all-work, 'was put in mind of the experiment of measuring the earth in St. James's Park, to be tried there on the Monday morning following.'[1]

Evelyn went home to laugh with his wife at Margaret's conceit and eccentricity, and disappointed that no ballads were appearing in the streets to mark the occasion, set to work to write one to the tune of 'I'll tell thee, Dick', from which quotations have already been taken.[2] He addressed it to his friend Sir Joseph Williamson, the former Secretary of State and a Fellow of the Society. And Margaret herself, confirmed in her opinion of her genius for natural philosophy by the remarkable honour paid to her, prepared to return to Welbeck, where she could continue her meditations 'free from the entanglements, confused clamours, and rumbling noise of the world'[3]: a life suited to her temperament, for according to herself she had been a student even from her childhood.

[1] The account of Margaret's visit to the Royal Society is collected from the following sources: Birch, ii. 175–8; Evelyn, ii. 272; Pepys, vi. 323–4; *HMC*, 12 *Rep.*, *Pt. vii*, 1890, p. 49. The visit is also described by S. I. Mintz, 'The Duchess of Newcastle's visit to the Royal Society', *Journal of English and Germanic Philology*, April 1952, pp. 168–76.

[2] The holograph of Evelyn's ballad is in the Public Record Office (SPD 29/450).

[3] *Sociable Letters*, p. 56.

2 Early Life

My father was a gentleman, which title is grounded and given by merit, not by princes.

MARGARET CAVENDISH was the youngest daughter of Thomas Lucas, of Colchester, Essex. The family had long been settled in the eastern counties but the first to live in Colchester was John, the third son of Thomas Lucas, of Little Saxham Hall, near Bury St. Edmunds, who was Solicitor-General in 1503. John was probably born in the last decade of the fifteenth century and his life plainly illustrates the ambition of his class, which found its scope under the Tudors. The goal of that class of lesser gentry was to consolidate its social position by acquiring land, its financial security by allying itself with trade, and its political influence by following as its favourite profession the law.[1]

As he had been bred to the law like his father, John was attracted to Colchester by the opportunities which such a pleasant and thriving town could afford. It did not disappoint him. He was chosen Town Clerk, and served as Member for the borough in the Parliaments of 1545, 1547 and 1553. But his influence was more than local, and early in Edward VI's reign he was appointed Master of the Court of Requests, which had cognizance of all matters relating to small debts. His initiative is equally well shown in his shrewd handling of his private affairs. On his father's death in 1531 he succeeded to a share of the large estates and proceeded to add to his property by marriage. His first wife was Mary Abell, who came from a family which had

[1] The accounts of John and Sir Thomas Lucas are taken from the following sources: George Rickword, 'Members of Parliament for Colchester', *Essex Rev.*, 1895, iv. 113–15, 121–2, 242–3; Philip Morant, *History and Antiquities of the County of Essex*, 2 vols., 1768, *passim.*, and *History and Antiquities of Colchester*, 2nd ed., 1768, *passim*; *Visitations of Essex*, ed. Walter G. Metcalfe, Harleian Soc., vol. xiii, 1878, pp. 236, 437.

acquired great wealth in the clothing trade, Colchester's staple industry. His second was Elizabeth Christmas, and her family was comparable in wealth to Mary's and of considerable importance in Colchester. His wives brought him money and served through their connections to further his own investments.

The opportunities for acquiring land were enormously increased by the dissolution of the monasteries, and both Colchester's great religious houses, the Priory of St. Botolph and the Abbey of St. John the Baptist, were dissolved and their estates dispersed. In 1548 Lucas was able to buy the site of St. John's Abbey and part of its lands; and to provide his family with a seat suited to the importance with which he was endowing it, he proceeded to build a splendid mansion on the south side of the Abbey Church. There is nothing left now of the church or the conventual buildings, or of the mansion which marked Lucas's ambition for his posterity. The great gateway to the Abbey stands alone, leading nowhere.

Of the man himself it is hardly possible to gather any impression apart from the facts of his career, and these show him to have been shrewd, ambitious and acquisitive; qualities which are summarized in the character of Henry VII, the type of the age. One incident alone reveals the personality behind the conventional mask: it is recorded that being a great gamester Lucas won the wardship of Mary Roydon, daughter and heiress of Christopher Roydon, of Roydon Hall, Essex, from the Earl of Oxford at dice, and married her to his youngest son.

By his first wife, Mary Abell, Lucas had three sons. The first, Thomas, was born about 1531; the second is not known, even by name; and the third, John, probably died before his father's second marriage. By his second wife, Elizabeth Christmas, he also had three children, John, Margaret and Elizabeth. John was married to the prize, Mary Roydon, and had a large family of five sons and three daughters; Margaret married Thomas Penny, a doctor of physic, and died in 1587; and Elizabeth died unmarried.

John Lucas himself died in 1556 and was succeeded by Thomas.

Thomas also inherited his father's energy and ambition, and the extent to which he added to his fortune can be seen in the way he doubled the number of advowsons left by his father. John presented to the livings of Fordham, Mile End, Peldon and Shenfield; Thomas also presented to Great Horkesley, Langenhoe, Greensted and Mistley. And he married as carefully as his father. His wife was Mary, daughter of Sir John Fermor of Northamptonshire, a prominent Calais merchant. Fermor had his great wealth confiscated by Henry VIII for opposing Henry's church policy, but his losses were repaired by Queen Mary.

Thomas Lucas, after being educated at Trinity Hall, Cambridge, was bred to the law too, and engaged in politics. He was Member for Colchester in the Parliament of 1558, when his fellow Member was his relation, George Christmas. He did not sit again but served as High Sheriff of Essex in 1568, and became Recorder of Colchester in 1575. It was probably about this time that he was knighted. He paid extravagantly for recognition of his wealth and importance in September 1579, when Queen Elizabeth, on progress from Lord Darcy's seat at St. Osyth, visited Colchester. Sir Thomas welcomed her to the borough with an oration and entertained her for three days at St. John's Abbey. Seven years later, in 1585, he entertained the Earl of Leicester with comparable magnificence when he was passing through Colchester to take up his command as general of the forces despatched by the Queen to the Netherlands.

But Sir Thomas's public position was insecure, and in 1584 he was superseded as Recorder by Sir Francis Walsingham and retired from public life. The only plausible reason for his supersession is recusancy. His Catholic sympathies are strongly suggested by his marriage alliance with the Fermor family and his membership of no parliament other than Philip and Mary's, and possibly by his patronage of the High Anglican, Samuel Harsnett, afterwards Archbishop of York. Sir Thomas preferred Harsnett, who was at the time master of Colchester Grammar School, to the living of Shenfield and may have used his influence to further his later career.

Sir Thomas had five children, two sons and three daughters. All the daughters made good matches. Ann, the eldest, a lady-in-waiting to the Queen, married Arthur Throckmorton, of Powlesferres, Northamptonshire, against her mistress's wishes. In antagonizing the Queen by her marriage, she followed her sister-in-law, Elizabeth Throckmorton's example, who loved Sir Walter Ralegh 'not wisely, but too well'. Throckmorton became Member for Colchester in 1588, the result of Sir Thomas's influence. Constance, the second daughter, married Sir Rowland Lacy, of Skipton, Oxfordshire; and Mary, the youngest, Sir Gawain Harvey, of Marshall in Rumford, Essex. Of the two sons, John, the younger, died unmarried in 1615, and his estates were inherited by his brother.

Thomas, the elder son, was born about 1573, and was educated at Pembroke College, Cambridge. He, too, followed the law, being admitted to the Inner Temple in 1592, but he made a bad beginning. Sharing his father's irascible and imperious temper, he fought a single duel in 1597 with Sir William Brooke, a relation of Lord Cobham, and killed him. The only direct comment on the duel was made later by Thomas's daughter, Margaret: 'my father by honour challenged him,' she wrote, 'with valour fought him, and in justice killed him.'[1] The simplicity of the statement disguises the serious consequences to Lucas of his rash action. A sentence of outlawry was pronounced against him, and Cobham, in favour at Court, prevented any successful appeal for pardon and forced him to fly to France. His exile might have been considered little more than an enforced and prolonged Grand Tour had he not left the girl to whom he was betrothed expecting a child.

The girl was Elizabeth, the daughter of John Leighton of London, gentleman. She, too, had loved not wisely but too well, and in the months that followed her lover's flight she must have prayed desperately for his return before her child was born. Elizabethan society was tolerant of such mistakes but its tolerance was accompanied by jests broad and contemptuous enough to

[1] *Natures Pictures*, p. 368.

distress any girl with a consciousness of her equivocal position and clouded reputation. And the practical issue was alarming. If the child were a boy and born out of wedlock, his illegitimacy would deny him any right to succeed his father; a situation equally unfortunate and complicated whether the father returned to marry the girl after the child's birth or died abroad in exile. Lucas did not return in time—Lord Cobham blocked every appeal; and in due course Elizabeth bore her child *ante matrimonium* and named it Thomas, as though to fix its paternity.

Lucas's own situation was hardly more endurable. The years passed without any sign of Cobham's animosity weakening or being conciliated by the intercession of friends. As late as 1602 Lucas was writing dismally from Paris to Sir Robert Cecil, Cobham's brother-in-law, begging him ' to have compassion of my estate and of my misery endured these five years in desolate exile,' and entreating him to intervene on his behalf with the Queen. He offered at the same time to make Cobham ' any honourable satisfaction he shall demand.' [1] This appeal was also fruitless, but at last chance relieved him. Immediately after the accession of James I, Cobham was arrested on a charge of complicity in the ' Main ' plot to place Arabella Stuart on the throne, and after being tried and condemned, he was imprisoned in the Tower until his death in 1619. Once his influence was broken, Lucas could be pardoned and allowed to return home, and on 18 March 1604 the King issued a warrant for preparing a bill in Parliament to restore him to ' his blood and gentry.' [2]

On his return Lucas married Elizabeth Leighton and settled down to live with his father at St. John's Abbey. His early misfortunes had quieted him, and even after he had succeeded his father in 1611, he played a singularly small part in public affairs, except for serving as High Sheriff of Essex in 1617. He was content to stay at home among his growing family, which was admirably governed by his wife. John, his eldest legitimate child, was born in 1606, and after the birth of two daughters,

[1] *H M C, Salisbury MSS., Pt. xii*, 1910, pp. 450-1.
[2] *Ib., 11 Rep., Pt. vii*, 1888, p. 134.

Mary and Elizabeth, a third son, Charles, followed in 1613. Anne was the next child and then Catherine, born in 1617. The eighth and last child, Margaret, was born in 1623.

Thomas Lucas died on 25 September 1625, long before he could see any of his children finally settled, and was buried beside his father and mother, who had died in 1613, and his younger brother, John, in the family vault in St. Giles's Church, which stands outside the great gate to St. John's Abbey. He had drawn up his will two days before his death in an effort to settle his affairs, and by it he left the manor of Lexden, worth £600 a year, to Thomas, his illegitimate son, and charged his estates with £10,000 for portions for his five daughters.[1] Apart from this document, the only written evidence to his character is the scraps of correspondence relating to the duel.

The history of the Lucas family has so far been a jog-trot of particulars which would suit equally well any other rising family of the period. They simply show a family asserting itself by its acquisitive energy and multiplying its roots in every possible direction to ensure stability. In such a development a pause often occurs in the third generation, which, inheriting sufficient to blunt its ambition, relaxes to enjoy what has already been acquired; and the pause is either an occasion for rest before the direct movement forward is resumed, or the preliminary onset of exhaustion, which will reduce the family to nothing as quickly as it reached its peak. In rarer instances the pause is a preparation for the sudden appearance of the unusual; a flamboyant exaggeration of family traits earlier held in check. The family history is then worth bolting for premonitory signs; and the signs may be no more striking than gambling for a ward, disguised loyalty to a persecuted church, and violence carried to the point of killing in a duel.

After Thomas Lucas's return from exile such a pause set in, and until his death the family's history is the undistinguished round of any other ordinary county family: a history whose only

---

[1] A copy of Thomas Lucas's will is in Somerset House (Clarke 104). He was never knighted, as Morant and others assumed.

chronicle is the rentbook. Not that life on such a level is necessarily dull, but it is too close to its own ground to be remarked on later. It needs a figure to dominate the foreground if it is to seem more than an academic composition in style. Lucas died less than two years after the birth of his daughter, Margaret, and as she is the figure awaited, the family's history shifts immediately after her father's death on to another level, far above the flats which have necessarily had to be crossed.

On the death of her husband, Elizabeth Lucas comes into prominence, and is seen competently handling the many difficulties which he had inadvertently bequeathed. The principal one concerned the inheritance. The eldest son, Thomas, could not inherit, and as the legitimate heir, John, was a minor, the estate fell under the cognizance of the Court of Wards, an unhappy prospect. The practice was for the crown to regard such occasions as windfalls and to grant the wardships to its own immediate advantage. Did Elizabeth need a warning of how unscrupulously wards could be treated by their guardians, she had only to look back on the fate of Mary Roydon, won at dice and married out of hand. Nothing so dramatic could be expected in the case of John Lucas, but an avaricious guardian could cause sufficient damage and harassment in the two years that were wanting to his majority to frighten even the most equable and determined person. Elizabeth was saved from the more serious consequences of her husband's premature death simply by luck. Her eldest daughter, Mary, had won the affection of Peter Killigrew, whose family had influential connections, and on 10 September 1625 Lord Conway, Secretary of State, had written to Thomas Lucas recommending Killigrew to him as a husband for his daughter. The request was disregarded in the confusion of Lucas's illness but Elizabeth immediately turned it to advantage, using her daughter to bargain for the settlement of the wardship on the best possible terms. She was counselled in this emergency by Samuel Harsnett, now Bishop of Norwich, who was staying at St. John's, summoned there to administer the last offices to the dying man.

33

Harsnett wrote to Conway on 25 September, the very day of
Lucas's death, perhaps even in obedience to his last commands,
to lay at the King's feet Elizabeth's consent to the marriage of
her daughter and Killigrew, and to request on her behalf that
Killigrew might also be given the wardship. This haste may
appear unseemly, but it was essential if the crows were to be
forestalled who scanned the bills of mortality with an eye to
exactly this kind of business. Her appeal was favourably
received and quickly acted upon: on 5 October Conway wrote
to the Master of the Wards asking for all possible favour to be
shown 'to the ward of Thomas Lucas, the rather for Mr.
Killigrew's sake.'[1] The estate could not escape unbreached.
Elizabeth had to pay £1,700 in cash and £200 was charged on
the lands during the minority, but there was the compensation
of the King's granting a pension of £200 a year to Killigrew and
his wife and the survivor of them for life.

Elizabeth Lucas is to be admired for the astuteness she showed
on her second direct appearance in this history, and her behaviour
then requires a readjustment of the impression made by her unfortunate entrance. Her early imprudence now seems to have
been the result not of wanton silliness but of easy good-humour,
braced, on the evidence of her children's heredity, by a passionate nature; and the equanimity which allowed her to survive the
long separation from her lover and its attendant disgrace with
her temper unwarped, also enabled her calmly to assume responsibility for the family in its crisis. Once having undertaken
to manage affairs, she remained in control; and though she often
asked her son after he had attained his majority and had married
to take the management into his own hands, she was pleased to
be retained in power, being, as her daughter Margaret averred,
'very skilful in leases, and settling of lands, and court-keeping,
ordering of stewards, and the like affairs.'[2]

[1] Details of the marriage negotiations and of the settlement of the wardship are given in *Cal. State Papers Dom., 1625, 1626,* 1858, pp. 102, 111, 117,
152, 165.
[2] *Natures Pictures,* p. 377.

She gave another example of her competence in business two years later. The bailiffs of Colchester had rated her double the amount her husband had been assessed at and she at once petitioned the Council of State to right her grievance; protesting in her favour the sums she had already paid to compound for the wardship, her daily charity to the poor who came to her gates and her great gifts to them at Christmas and other times.[1] Whether or not the petition was successful, her promptness of application for redress to the Council itself further illustrates her shrewdness and her determination to defend her property at all costs, even at the expense of the family's popularity in Colchester.

Since Elizabeth largely moulded the characters of her children, especially that of Margaret, who could not even remember her father, her own personality must be viewed more intimately than is allowed by the light of formal documents. The more intimate view is given by Margaret herself; and though, in an age when children obeyed the command to honour their parents in their choice of epithets to describe them as well as in their deferential behaviour towards them, her remarks necessarily conform to the patterns of conventional praise, she does succeed in suggesting her mother's individuality.

Elizabeth's early indiscretion accounts for the hardness she showed in the handling of affairs. Once learnt, the lesson was never forgotten, that society is quick to take one at a disadvantage, and its effect was shown in her manner. Her mien was of such ' a majestic grandeur . . . that it would strike a kind of an awe to the beholders, and command respect from the rudest,'[2] and, in her children's opinion, who had no reason to be awed by it, enhanced her natural beauty of face and carriage. The attitude was, however, largely defensive; within the safety of her family her good nature had free play. She ruled her servants kindly but firmly, nursing them when they were sick and readily pardoning a fault, though preventing their undue familiarity with her children, for fear they should corrupt them with coarse examples.

[1] *C S P D, 1627-8*, 1858, p. 497.
[2] *Natures Pictures*, p. 377.

35

She was particularly anxious to keep the servingmen away from the maids in the nursery, 'lest their rude love-making might do unseemly actions, or speak unhandsome words in the presence of her children.'[1] And in return the children were trained to behave towards servants with a 'humble civility.' She treated her children with the greatest indulgence, denying them nothing that would make them happy, in the belief that children who were bred niggardly later discovered an analogous flaw in their characters. Had she been more economical she could have added to her daughters' portions but she preferred to spoil them rather than risk raising in them 'sharking qualities, mean thoughts, and base actions.' And her indulgence of them was corrected by her positive injunctions to avoid vice and pursue virtue, and by her own example of good temper. She taught by kindness, never by anger or blows, and consequently she won their affectionate respect.

When Margaret came to write about the breeding of children, everything she had to say reinforced her mother's practice; the rules she had laid down were above criticism. To breed a child in 'pinching necessity' was certainly to teach it 'to dissemble and shark', but to treat a child generously was to encourage in it a generous and liberal spirit; and the second course was all the more practical since it trained the child to handle in later life any inherited fortune discreetly, and not to riot it away. She also condemned out of hand the folly of using threats and blows, which might compel a child from fear into showing an outward respect for forms but could never awaken in it a genuine love of grace and knowledge, as kindness and persuasion do: 'for force breaks the understanding, destroys all ingenuity; for the fear of punishment confuses the brain, and disquiets the mind so much, as it makes them incapable of right impressions.'[2] And she, too, would have children preserved from the bad example of servants. Parents who allow their daughters to frequent the scullery, to have them danced 'upon

[1] *Ib.*, p. 370.
[2] *Sociable Letters*, p. 317.

36

the knee of every clown and servingman ', run the risk of their becoming ' like unto like.' [1]

Elizabeth's conception of her children's breeding is beyond reproach, but the same approval cannot be extended to her idea of education—and consequently to that of the age's in general—where her daughters were concerned. They were taught nothing that an ' ancient decayed gentlewoman ' [2], kept for the purpose, could not teach, and her attainments stretched no farther than elementary reading and writing. Margaret says airily in another place that she and her sisters had tutors ' for all sorts of virtues, as singing, dancing, playing on music, reading, writing, working, and the like ' ; [3] but all her verifiable accomplishments can be traced to the ' ancient decayed gentlewoman ' rather than to those ' virtuous ' tutors. She had no instruction at all in any subject other than two of the three rudiments, and the little she received in those can be described as cursory at the best.

In general, Margaret's education was no worse than that given to other girls of her class and time. The accepted opinion was that it would be a waste to give girls more knowledge than they could use; and beyond the rudiments all the instruction they were supposed to require was ornamental. Lady Fanshawe's description of her own education is—apart from French —practically identical with Margaret's; she had all the advantages, she wrote, that the time afforded, ' both for working all sorts of fine works with my needle, and learning French, singing, [the] lute, the virginals, and dancing.' [4] The exceptions were usually the girls raised in households sympathetic to Puritanism, where the more serious view of life led to a more thorough idea of education. Lucy Hutchinson, for example, claimed to have been able to read English perfectly at the age of four, and to have had at seven no less than eight tutors ' in several qualities, languages,

---

[1] *Worlds Olio*, p. 79.
[2] *Sociable Letters*, p. 367.
[3] *Natures Pictures*, pp. 370–1.
[4] *Memoirs of Anne Lady Fanshawe*, 1907, p. 22.

music, dancing, writing and needlework.'[1] She showed such aptitude for scholarship, moreover, that her father had her taught Latin, in which she easily outstripped her brothers.

All Margaret's later faults as a writer can be traced to her defective education, and as she herself became more acutely aware of them, she either attempted to justify them or attacked their cause. She often disclaimed any ability in learning, particularly in languages, but even if she had had the ability, she refused heatedly to regret the lost chance: 'I do not repent that I spent not my time in learning, for I consider it is better to write wittily than learnedly.'[2] But her attitude in her calmer, less defensive moods was very different. 'Let me tell you, Wife, that is the reason all women are fools;' she makes one of her characters say, referring indirectly to her own mother; 'for women breeding up women, one fool breeding up another; and as long as that custom lasts there is no hopes of amendment, and ancient customs being a second nature, makes folly hereditary in that sex.'[3] And she wished that she had been brought up like a song-bird in darkness, and had been instructed properly in poetry, history, moral and natural philosophy, and mathematics: 'Thus perchance I might have spoke as eloquently upon every subject, as birds sing sweetly several tunes.'[4]

Her mother's discipline was so light that Margaret was not even trained in the ordinary practical arts considered proper to her sex. She confessed she could not spin or sew or cook. In fact the only art she knew proves her to have been her mother's daughter; she understood 'indifferently well' how to keep sheep and order a grange.[5] But at least the freedom she was given allowed her unusual character to follow its own bent. Had she grown up in a more formal home, where the position of women was better understood and girls were bred in the 'old Elizabeth

[1] Lucy Hutchinson, *Memoirs of Col. Hutchinson*, ed. C. H. Firth, 1885, i. 24.
[2] *Philosophical Letters*, p. 2b.
[3] *Playes*, pp. 123–4.
[4] *Ib.*, p. 248.
[5] *Sociable Letters*, p. b^v.

way, which was for maids to be seen and not to be heard '[1], she would have been temperamentally incapable of stepping out later from the anonymity of domestic life to become the first literary woman of the age.

Margaret's passionate admiration of her family is one of her most delightful simplicities. Every one of her brothers and sisters was perfect in her eyes, conforming exactly to an ideal standard of physical beauty. They were all shapely in limb, of the requisite stature—neither ' dwarfish, or of a giant-like stature '—comely in feature, of the approved mean in complexion ; and, lastly, they all had ' sound teeth, sweet breaths, plain speeches, tunable voices : I mean not so much to sing as in speaking, as not stuttering, nor wharling in the throat, or speaking through the nose, or hoarsely, unless they had a cold.'[2] Seen through the eyes of this loving and imaginative child, St. John's Abbey was the retreat of the last Arcadians ; and to the extent that she shared their perfections and enjoyed their Golden Age, she wondered at her own felicity.

She knew her eldest brother, Thomas, least well of the three. Apart from the great difference in age, he had been bred to arms, after being educated like his father at Pembroke College, Cambridge, and later served as a captain of horse in the Low Countries—the great training-ground of young Englishmen, which prepared them for coming events. He must have been absent from home during most of her childhood. He was knighted in 1628, and was married on 27 January 1629 to Anne, daughter of Sir John Byron. The youngest brother, Charles, who was also educated at Cambridge, at Christ's, ' had a practic genius to the warlike arts . . . as natural poets have to poetry '[3], and began his military training under his brother, Sir Thomas. In a pass granted in 1637 to Sir Thomas to go into the Low Countries with his lady and servants, Charles, who accompanied him, is described as a cornet.[4] He was the most romantic of the

[1] Dryden, 'An Essay of Dramatic Poesy', *Essays*, ed. W. P. Ker, 1900, i. 47.
[2] *Natures Pictures*, pp. 376–7.
[3] *Ib.*, p. 371.
[4] *C S P D, 1637*, 1868, p. 138.

brothers, and the respectful admiration with which Margaret writes of him indicates how deeply his character affected her imagination.

The second brother and head of the family, John, was the closest to Margaret; she writes of him with less awe and more personal affection. He was not bred to arms like his brothers, though he was a more skilful swordsman than either, and was much better read than they were in both arts and sciences, ' being a great scholar, by reason he is given much to studious contemplation.' [1] His bent is shown by his early interest in the Royal Society. Margaret came to him with the difficulties she had encountered in her reading, and he helped to turn her interest towards science, which was later to engross her attention completely. He married on 17 December 1628 Anne, the daughter of Sir Christopher Nevill, of the Charterhouse, a younger brother of the Earl of Abergavenny, and brought his bride, who was seventeen, back to St. John's.

Elizabeth lost no time in marrying off her daughters, and can have met with little trouble if their attractions even approximated to Margaret's description. The eldest, Mary, had married Peter Killigrew, and the second, Elizabeth, married William Walter, the son and heir of Sir John Walter, Lord Chief Baron of the Exchequer, on 20 December 1632. Walter had been educated at Christ Church, Oxford, and following his father's profession, was called to the bar in 1630. He had also served as Member for Weobley in the Short Parliament of 1628. The third daughter, Catherine, was married next, on 7 May 1635, to Edmond Pye, of Leckhamsteed, Buckinghamshire, the son and heir of a wealthy London scrivener. Margaret loved this sister with a ' supernatural affection ', and her description of her childish passion is a touching illustration of her own emotional nature. She was constantly fearful of Catherine's life and health; watching her in the night if she breathed quietly to reassure herself that she had not died, studying every mouthful of food she took in doubt of its effect—a solicitude that earned her the epithet of ' Sancho

[1] *Natures Pictures*, p. 372.

40

Panza's doctor '—and even knocking on her closet door when she was at her prayers longer than usual to ask her how she did. These were a few of the many impertinences, Margaret wrote later to Catherine, when the happiness of her childhood shone the brighter for being remembered in the anxieties of exile, ' which my extraordinary love troubled you with, of which trouble you are now quit, living so far asunder.' [1] Only Anne and Charles died unmarried.

These marriages did not break up the family; instead of the daughters moving into the sphere of their relations by marriage, the sons-in-law fell under the attraction of Elizabeth's strong character and were taken into her family. She usually spent half the year in London, and though her daughters then lived in their own houses they met almost every day, ' feasting each other like Job's children '; and when she was in the country they lived with her the greater part of the time. They were all perfectly contented with one another's company, seldom mixing with or even visiting their relations by marriage, but always going about ' in a flock, together agreeing so well that there seemed but one mind amongst them.' [2] As for their amusements when they were in London, in winter they went to plays or drove about the streets in their coaches to see the sights and the crowds, and in spring they frequented fashionable Spring Gardens or Hyde Park, or took a barge and had supper and music on the river. When they were at Colchester they enjoyed the ordinary country pleasures. This was their idyllic way of life until the ' unnatural war came like a whirlwind, which felled down their houses.' [3]

Growing up in the comfortable cocoon of the family, and completely protected by it from any pressure towards conformity, Margaret could freely indulge her day-dreams—or, as she preferred to call them, her ' contemplations '. They were the day-dreams of any romantic girl, fostered on poetry. She would fancy that she was such a beauty ' as Nature never made the

[1] *Sociable Letters*, p. 423.
[2] *Natures Pictures*, pp. 372–3.
[3] *Ib.*, p. 372.

like ', equally famous for wit and wisdom. A picture must necessarily be made of such a paragon, and as it was passed round the world by the chain of her admirers, it caught the attention of the greatest of kings, 'such a one as Alexander or Caesar ', who fell desperately in love with the copy and promptly married the original.[1] This was the basic theme of her imaginings; spun endlessly and formlessly from the central situation of herself as a learned and beautiful princess capturing the adoration of a wise and powerful king.

The difference between her romancings and those of other green girls was the emphasis laid on her own learning and on the special character of her prince. Unlike the other dreamers, she was not content to be only beautiful, and her lover was not allowed to be simply charming; he had to be, at the ultimate evolution of the dream, one of three candidates, or, better still, a composite character who included the virtues of all three. The three were Caesar, Ovid and Shakespeare: Caesar, 'for his valour ', Ovid, 'for his wit ', and 'our countryman ', Shakespeare, 'for his comical and tragical humour.'[2] The fact that they were dead was of no matter; they would be revived to match her capacities. Another peculiarity was the length of time these 'contemplations' were continued. They were never checked by experience and consequently deepened by damming into a reservoir of potential inspiration, but ran with shallow purposeless facility to the end.

But if she was to be recognized as a wit as well as a beauty she must send a copy of her mind as well as of her face about the world; and to accomplish this she began to write early, scribbling in her childhood, in her loose hand and startling spelling, sixteen 'baby-books ', as she called them—babyish in all but size; the least of them covered no less than 'two or three quires of paper.' When she later unearthed them and forwarded them to a correspondent interested in her juvenilia, she described them ruefully as each one being like 'a frippery or broker's shop,

[1] *Playes*, p. 182.
[2] *Sociable Letters*, p. 338.

wherein is nothing but remnants, bits and ends of several things.'[1] What they were really about it is impossible to say, but to judge by her maturer work, they probably showed her seated enthroned in the centre of things with her prince by her side, darkly and erratically speculating on whatever chanced to catch her attention. All of them, she admitted, were 'as confused as the chaos'; a judgement which the unchivalrous have not hesitated to apply to her published work. The baby-books show her early attachment to writing, if only for the sake of realizing her dreams; and her ambition to excel in literature became more compelling as she grew older.

Another trait which appeared early in her childhood was her love of dressing-up. She had little use for toys and spent most of her time at her toilet or on the design of her own dresses, 'not taking that pleasure in such fashions as was invented by others', and delighting 'in a singularity'.[2] This extravagance, for which she later became notorious, was an attempt to lend reality to the part she played in her world of make-believe. It was easier to pretend to be another Queen of Sheba when her glass reflected her dressed in strange and striking attire, and the practice also prepared her for the day when she should at last confront and astonish her Solomon.

But would she dare to confront her Solomon even in the fantastic disguise of her own fashions? The curse of her childhood was bashfulness. In the family circle she felt no embarrassment, and in her day-dreams she addressed an admiring and subject world with authoritative eloquence, but when she was required on rare occasions to mix with strangers, she could hardly speak or move naturally for fear, and her consternation appeared in her blushes. At such moments she felt her self-confidence ebb away, and in an attempt to brave the imagined hostility of a world suddenly grown critical, her behaviour became exaggerated to the point of absurdity. Then she doubted and pitied herself, and to hide her weakness grew foolishly self-assertive.

[1] *Ib.*, p. 267.
[2] *Natures Pictures*, p. 387.

43

Her upbringing was entirely responsible for her being so out of touch with society, which might have disciplined and given substance to her imaginings, but at least it brought her into close association with one aspect of reality; one which unfortunately lacked the power to correct her tendencies. She always delighted in nature, and showed a true understanding of country matters. 'I was bred a private country life,' a character in one of her stories exclaims, but the voice is hers, 'where . . . the singing of the birds are the harmonious notes by which we set our innocent thoughts, playing upon the heart-strings of content.'[1] Her writings, especially her poetry, constantly illustrate her sensibility to nature; not only to its obvious graces, its hedgerow elms, springing cornfields and lively brooks, but to its creatures: how she felt for 'poor Wat', the hunted hare, and that nobler victim of the chase, the stag; her pity for their unnecessary sufferings making her speak out of turn in a century when cruelty to animals was all too common. The only domestic skill she herself claimed to possess was that of keeping a grange, and her claim is remarkably borne out by the knowledge she showed of the deceits practised by the labourer : the reaper would fling a sheaf over the hedge almost under the eyes of the master, seed would be tossed down in handfuls by the sower to be picked up after the master had gone home, and the shepherd would filch the twin lamb and the swineherd the tenth pig almost as a matter of course. Her description of the hare's mazy flight and her recital of the labourer's trickeries reveal her sharpness of observation and shrewdness of mind; and had these qualities been more developed by her early circumstances at the expense of her languorous self-indulgence in 'contemplations', she would have been better prepared for her later career.

As Margaret looked back on her childhood, she was conscious only of its calm happiness; a contented level unbroken by any excitement greater than a brother's or a sister's marriage. One incident happened in her late adolescence which must have made an impression on her romantic imagination, though she does not

[1] *Ib.*, p. 212.

refer to it herself in her brief autobiography. In November 1638, Maria de Medici, unwanted in France, or indeed anywhere else, arrived in England to visit her daughter and son-in-law. Neither Charles nor his wife was at all eager to entertain her, harassed as they were by the increasing difficulties of the experiment in arbitrary government; but as they could not stop her descent, they made hasty arrangements to receive her. She landed at Harwich and set out on Saturday, 6 November, for Colchester, where she was welcomed at the town gates by the Mayor and corporation and presented with a gold cup. Sir John Lucas lodged and entertained her at St. John's Abbey, and at the splendid banquet held there that evening the French visitors were particularly impressed by the civility of their hosts, who spoke in French for the guests' greater convenience. Margaret must have been completely tongue-tied, rising only to a rehearsed phrase at the moment of her presentation. Outside in the streets the enthusiastic townsmen lit bonfires. The next day being Sunday, the Queen passed the morning at prayer and the afternoon in strolling about the beautiful gardens, whose leafless walks had been prettily decorated with evergreens as a compliment to royalty. She left on the Monday for Chelmsford.

This account of her entertainment is taken from the enthusiastic account of Puget de la Serre[1], the self-appointed chronicler of the Queen's enforced peregrinations. He was so enamoured of his conception of her majesty that wherever she went he saw the people opening their hearts, the gentry putting on better behaviour, and even the trees doing their best, in spite of the inexorable laws of nature, to please her. In his eyes Maria de Medici's descent on England was attended by a beneficial shower of blisses, but in others' her arrival was yet another of the many portents which warned of disasters ahead—disasters which were to involve equally the King, the gentry and the people, all of whom were in Puget de la Serre's fantastic opinion in competition to pay his Queen homage.

[1] Puget de la Serre, *Histoire de L'Entree de la Reyne Mere du Roy Tres-Chrestien, dans la Grande-Bretagne,* 1639.

3 Civil War

*I neither heeded what was said or practised, but just what belonged to my loyal
duty, and my own honest reputation.*

THE year 1638 was, as Sir Henry Slingsby noted in his diary,[1] a
year of storms. The lightning seemed inspired to make churches
its special targets, firing them and melting the bells in their
towers. The worst disaster of the kind happened at Withicomb,
in Devon; there the church was struck on a Sunday in the
middle of divine service and many worshippers were hurt.
Surely such occurrences were not accidents but warnings directed
at the unrighteous? As Slingsby remarked darkly, they gave
' cause of speech to many which were better let alone, and their
cause rather maintained with the true foundations of verity.'
The godly were quick to see in these happenings a divine condemnation of all they disliked and a witness to the purity of
their objections. That heavenly fire should visit the churches
came as no surprise to those who viewed with abhorrence the
papistical tendencies of the ecclesiastical policy enforced by Laud
—yet another of the malignant ministers tolerated by the King,
whose eyes were blinded to the true interests of Church and State
by the wiles of his popish French wife.

Slingsby's own sympathies were royalist, and as he looked back
on the decade since 1629, when Parliament was dissolved and the
experiment in autocratic government begun, he saw a nation
which had lived in peace whilst war was mercilessly ravaging
the whole of neighbouring Europe. But those whose sympathies
were opposite received the very different impression of national
liberty and religion being smothered under an arbitrary reign
before the eyes of the people, who stood weakly by, not daring

---

[1] Sir Henry Slingsby, *Diary*, ed. Daniel Parsons, 1836, pp. 28–30.

46

like the heroes on the Continent to fight in defence of their rights. In their opinion the country was not enjoying a peace but rather a quietness, 'like the calm and smooth surface of the sea, whose dark womb is already impregnated with a horrid tempest.' [1]

Margaret Lucas was a royalist, and the decade preceding Maria de Medici's descent on St. John's Abbey was for her, too, an idyllic time; and not only because her memory of it was accompanied by the fond recollections of childhood. England seemed to her, as it did to Slingsby, a fortunate island, guarded by ministering seas from the troubles without:

> There was an island rich by Nature's grace,
> In all the world it was the sweetest place.

So she began one of her poems [2] on the theme of England's good fortune, and after celebrating in sincere though doggerel verse its beauties—its choiring birds, stately trees, temperate climate and rich pastures, 'Where grass grows up even to the belly high'—she ended,

> And in this pleasant island peace did dwell,
> No noise of war, or sad tale could it tell.

And Nature's partiality to the land was exceeded by God's, in His election of Charles I, a king, wise, beneficent, just.

But had Margaret grown up in a family like Lucy Hutchinson's, and had her eyes sharpened by puritanism to appreciate the signs of the approaching storm, she could have discovered them in her immediate neighbourhood. Few people in Colchester—'a ragged and factious town, now swarming with sectaries', as Evelyn later called it [3]—can have been surprised at the lightning's choice of churches; they could have been disturbed only by the

---

[1] Hutchinson, i. 4.
[2] *Poems*, pp. 116–18. I have preferred always to quote from the first edition of *Poems, and Fancies*. The second and third editions were greatly improved in the sense that the grammar, metre, and rhyme were revised; but it is almost certain that the revision was not Margaret's own but a secretary's, and the revision obscures her characteristic accents.
[3] Evelyn, ii. 113.

leniency of divine retribution. The town was one of the hotbeds of puritan sentiment, principally on account of its cloth industries, which bred a proletariat periodically distressed by fluctuations of the market. Its proximity to London also encouraged the local sectaries by allowing them to hold easy communication with the national leaders. Thomas Cotton, of Bergholt, the brother-in-law of Dr. John Bastwick, maintained ' some peevish intelligencer in London ' and read the news he received in the streets on market days, the zealots thronging about him ' as people use where ballads are sung.' Henry Burton himself, who was, like Bastwick, soon to be sentenced by the Court of Star Chamber, at the notorious trial of 1637, to lose his ears and suffer perpetual imprisonment, came down to preach a seditious sermon in Cotton's private chapel, and repeated it publicly in the city on a lecture day. And at a meeting called in 1634 by Sir John Lucas and two other commissioners to raise funds towards the national subscription for the repair of St. Paul's, a cause especially dear to Laud, William Ball, of Little Horsley, a wealthy puritan sympathiser, stepped forward while the rest ' were straining courtesy who should make a beginning ' and contemptuously tossed a shilling on the table, setting an example which the others felt bound to follow—out of good manners, Laud's correspondent added tactfully.[1]

The political opposition to the Government was more serious than the sectarian, since it roused the greater number of the gentry to resist the imposition of unparliamentary taxes. Sir John Lucas again courted unpopularity by his support of the crown. As High Sheriff of Essex he was responsible for rating the county under the writ of ship-money of 1637, and did his work so efficiently that some of the nobility and gentry lodged a complaint with the Council. Summoned before the Council to justify his action, he explained that he had taken care that the weight should fall upon those able to pay and not upon ' the poorer sort of people, wherewith that county abounded ' ; an

[1] William Lynne to Archbishop Laud, 29 Oct. 1634; *C S P D, 1634-5,* 1864, p. 252-3.

explanation so in line with Charles's own sentiments that the King personally thanked him for managing to assess the whole county for the first time, and urged him to continue as he had begun.[1]

Trying later to understand why the idyllic England of her childhood had been suddenly plunged into civil war, Margaret, disregarding like so many of her contemporaries what had been actually happening in the street, had no better explanation to offer than that the people had waxed fat and kicked. Burton conferring with Cotton in his study, the shelves lined with every seditious pamphlet—written in England, printed in Holland and smuggled back into the country; Bastwick inveighing from the pulpit against popery and its Anglican promoters; her brother journeying up to London to defend himself against the charges of his neighbours; the poor trudging in rags down every road: none of these was considered for a moment as a sign of the forces of dissolution working below the surface to destroy the image of England blest and at peace. And this blindness to the significance of events, which must have been discussed within doors, was not insensibility or stupidity on her part, or on the part of the greater number of her royalist contemporaries; it was due to a lack of a proper historical consciousness—an effect of viewing the past as a gallery of characters, each framed by events but otherwise unattached to circumstances. The present appeared permanent, subject only to unprepared violent change. The greater perceptiveness shown by Lucy Hutchinson is accounted for by puritanism, which, by teaching its adherents to look forward constantly to a renewed world, made them more aware of the workings of the past and of the unsatisfactory nature of the present. When the Civil War broke out it was to Lucy Hutchinson a storm that had long been brewing, but to Margaret it was sudden and unpredicted.

The entertainment of Maria de Medici marked the end of the last days in the sun. At the beginning of the new year Slingsby was watching military exercises on Bramham Moor, and the sight

[1] *Ib.*, *1637*, 1868, pp. 132–3.

caused him to reflect sombrely on what they portended. The reason for the exercises was the threatened war with Scotland, the effect of Charles's foolish attempt to impose the English prayer book on that country. The imposition outraged both the Scots' sensitive nationalism and their fanatical protestantism. Helped by the number of experienced soldiers returned from the Thirty Years' War, they were making ready to defend their independence, if need be, by force of arms. Incapable of diplomacy, Charles determined to enforce his authority, and calling upon the nobility for support, he moved a hastily organized army north. But the troops were inadequately armed, trained, and disciplined; their commanders were at odds, or were lukewarm in their support; and the first bishops' war ended ignominiously for Charles in mid-summer without a blow having been struck.

Charles could not accept his failure and prepared to renew the struggle; but as his ability to crush the Scots depended upon raising an army, and as his own revenues were unable to bear that additional expense, he was compelled to summon a parliament. While the country was getting ready for the election, an army was also being raised, and the Lucas family was involved in the military preparations from the start. Sir Thomas and Charles (now knighted) had returned from the Low Countries on the first hint of war, and on 7 February 1640 Sir Thomas was appointed Commissary-General of his Majesty's horse troops in Ireland. Sir Charles had been promoted by this time to a captaincy.

The Short Parliament assembled in the middle of April, and, drawing up a moderate list of grievances in church and state, demanded their redress before voting supplies. With incredible folly Charles simply dissolved Parliament on 5 May and proceeded to take action against the Scots himself, relying upon ship-money and various loans and levies to supply his army. None of his financial expedients was fruitful, and the state of the army is shown by Sir Charles Lucas's request to Sir Henry Wilmot, Commissary-General of Horse, before marching north in July, that two of his troops, one of which was wholly unarmed and the other without pistols, should be properly equipped as they were being 'sent near an enemy.' [1] One of the troops was commanded by his elder brother, John; all the Lucas brothers were thus under arms.

With the royal army in such physical shape and equally weak in morale, the pattern of the first bishops' war could only be repeated more disastrously. The Scots crossed the border and cannonaded the English at Newburn-on-Tyne, whereupon the greater number promptly threw down their standards and ran. The Scots occupied Northumberland and Durham unopposed, and co-operated with the opposition in England to force Charles to summon another parliament. The Long Parliament met on 3 November, 1640, and the preliminaries to the Civil War began.

Before a people can bring itself to accept the horrors of civil war, so much worse than those of a national war, it must have debated the opposing principles until the issues have become obsessive, transforming familiar faces into appearances so foreign and hateful that the blood rises and can find relief for its fever only in blows. The movement towards violence against the resistance of habitual loyalties, affections and decencies is slow at first, but quickens and becomes irresistible once the passions have corrupted ideas, concealing their compulsive disorder under the acceptable, because impersonal, disguise of ideals: to kill for the sake of truth and right is held no murder. The eighteen months that followed the assembly of the Long Parliament saw a progress of this kind. The attainder and execution of Strafford, the 'root and branch' bill, the Grand Remonstrance and Charles's attempt to arrest the five members: these and the like proceedings divided the nation into two menacing parties. By 22 August 1642, when Charles raised his standard at Nottingham, each was ready for the least provocation to strike.

The leaders on either side, however, were reluctant to move irrationally even then, being unable to see that the debate had come to an end; but the people, especially the city mobs,

[1] *Ib.*, *1640*, 1880, p. 481.

deliberately excited by the constant appeals made to them and exasperated beyond forbearance by the delaying arguments, instinctively sensed what was ahead, and showed by their spontaneous violence the real forces which underlay the formal rhetoric of both parties' proclamations and declarations. One of the first victims outside London was the Lucas family. On the very day that Charles raised his standard, a mixed mob of town and country, numbering about two thousand, attacked St. John's Abbey on the pretext that Sir John had arms and horses intended for the King's service. They were temporarily quietened when Major Thomas Wade agreed to commit Sir John and his mother and sister—who may have been either of the unmarried daughters, Anne or Margaret. Wade carried them to his own house, but once the mob learned that they were there and not in custody, they threatened to pull down Wade's house about his ears, and he was forced to lodge his charges in the Moot Hall to save both himself and them from injury. As they were being removed a countryman struck at Elizabeth Lucas with his sword, so violently ' that if a halbert had not crossed the blow, both her sorrows and her journey had there found an end.' The mob then set to work on the Abbey and plundered it of 'plate, money, books, boxes, writings and household stuff.' They spilled out into the gardens and defaced them, and then killed the deer and drove off the cattle. Their delight in destruction carried them at last to St. Giles's Church, where they broke open the Lucas vault and ' with pistols, swords and halberts ' transfixed the coffins of the dead.[1]

Wade wrote immediately to London to Sir Harbottle Grimston, Recorder of Colchester and Member for the town, for advice, and the House promptly sent down two Members to restore order. Sir John was carried up to London and committed a prisoner to the Gatehouse, but was soon released on bail. His horses and arms were confiscated for Parliament's use. He took

[1] This account of the happenings in Colchester is taken from the following sources: *H M C, 10 Rep., Pt. vi*, 1887, pp. 146–7; *5 Rep.*, 1876, p. 46; *Life of William Cavendish*, ed. C. H. Firth, n.d., p. 163, n.1.

advantage of his liberty, however, to join the King in time to fight at Newbury, and his loyalty was rewarded with a peerage; he was created Baron Lucas of Shenfield at the beginning of 1645. Elizabeth Lucas herself wrote indomitably to the House of Lords to protest against the outrage and to petition that she and her servants should be given the right to search those houses where she knew or suspected her goods were hidden. Whether or not permission was granted, it is unlikely that she recovered much.

Margaret may have been with her mother at this time, or she may already have been staying with one of her married sisters, probably her beloved sister Pye. Her sisters and their husbands were among the royalists who flocked to Oxford after the battle of Edgehill on 23 October when Charles set up his court in the city, and Margaret may have accompanied them, or joined them there shortly after their arrival. Life in Oxford was very different from what its guests had known before. The town was so crowded that accommodation was almost impossible to find, and Anne, Lady Fanshawe, counted herself lucky to have a bad bed in a garret of a baker's house in an obscure street. Few of the courtiers had clothes or money, food was short, and infection spread quickly through the cramped quarters; the only relief from tedium and discomfort was the constant talk of war, its pitch varying as news came in of the royalists' veering fortunes. Yet, in Lady Fanshawe's opinion, most of them bore the experience ' with a martyr-like cheerfulness ' [1]; and the place itself— its quiet colleges and shady gardens a reassurance that in spite of troops and courtiers the residing values were only temporarily overlaid—was a solace.

One person was missing without whom the court was incomplete—the Queen. Henrietta Maria was still in Holland, trying to raise supplies by the sale of her jewels, and she did not set out for England until 2 February 1643. She landed after a very rough and dangerous passage, which brought out her typically gay and effervescent courage, at Bridlington Quay, in Yorkshire, on 22 February under the eyes of four parliamentarian ships,

[1] Fanshawe, pp. 24–5.

which bombarded the harbour with dangerous accuracy until the escorting Dutch vessels, under the command of van Tromp, threatened to attack unless they stopped. During the bombardment the Queen risked her life by running from shelter to rescue her lap-dog: such gestures were at the bottom of her reputation. She was welcomed at Bridlington by one of her favourites, the Marquis of Newcastle, who commanded the royalist forces in the north. Her journey south was delayed until 4 June, when she set out under the escort of a large force detached from Newcastle's army. On 13 July she was met by Charles at Edgehill, and the next day rode into Oxford by his side. The bells rang out and the crowds cheered as she passed through the streets, smiling gaily and laying a hand on her husband's arm as she delightedly acknowledged the acclamations. She enjoyed her popularity to the full and was confirmed by it in her own romantic notion of herself as a ' she-majesty ', a ' generalissima ', holding victory in her hand. Her arrival fortunately coincided with the zenith of the royalist cause. It was her last triumph.

Henrietta Maria was lodged in Merton College but, though preparations had been made for her comfort, she could not possibly expect the style she had been used to. One of her principal wants was of attendance. Learning of this need, Margaret Lucas, irresistibly attracted by the romantic figure presented by the Queen, which so nearly corresponded to her own idea of herself as a princess famous for all heroic and feminine virtues, begged her mother to allow her to volunteer as a maid of honour. All the family were at first strongly opposed to the idea. They thought that her lack of experience of the world, she never having been out of their sight, would make her quite incompetent to navigate the dangers of a court, especially since her beauty would be an incitement to trade on her innocence. Margaret herself was fully aware of her own callowness and admitted that she relied on her family not only for confidence but for direction in the smallest matters; but unable to resist the Queen's attraction, or at least the fascination of her own image of the Queen, she persisted until her request was granted.

Her family need not have worried about her behaviour. Once released from their protection, she was so bashful and so uncomfortably conscious of the dangers to her honour that she explained later, ' I durst neither look up with my eyes, nor speak, nor be any way sociable, insomuch as I was thought a natural fool.' [1] Apart from this charmingly simple and direct statement of her predicament upon arriving at court, she has given a more dramatic account in one of her plays, *The Presence*, which, like all her imaginative works, is primarily autobiographical. There arrives at the court of Princess Melancholy—an idealization of Margaret herself—a new maid of honour, Lady Bashful, who upon her introduction by the mother of the maids is quite silent. ' Lord! ' exclaims Lady Quick-Wit, another of the maids, ' how simply she looks! ' ' Give me a simple girl ', Monsieur Mode returns, smelling an opportunity; ' I love to teach, not to learn.' The impression she makes on the rest of the maids is of ' a clod of dull earth ', and her later behaviour confirms them in their judgement, particularly since, as one of them explains, ' she shuns men as she would do serpents, and locks her chamber doors against them, and accounts it a crime to be seen undressed, and a sin not to be forgiven, to be seen in bed '—precautions which, in view of the aims of M. Mode and his fashionable friends, it would seem only natural to have taken. But Lady Bashful's reticence and modesty conceal a remarkable temperament: ' I had rather be a meteor singly alone,' she asserts in an unguarded moment, ' than a star in a crowd ': and the play is devoted to showing how far she transcends her appearance. Surrounded by strangers, fearful of committing the least indiscretion and troubled by the impression she was making, Margaret fell back for comfort upon daydreams of the kind represented by Lady Bashful's career, which showed her to herself fixed in a firmament of admiration.

While Margaret was trying to adapt herself to her new life and learning her duties, forces were at work under-mining the royalist cause. Compared with the parliamentarians, the royalists lacked

[1] *Natures Pictures*, p. 374.

three requirements for victory—money, discipline and thorough-ness. Charles's resources were inadequate to support a long war, his army, and especially his cavalry—brilliantly led though it was on occasion by Prince Rupert—was too undisciplined to exploit its initial superiority, and his counsels were rendered ineffectual by his own vacillation and the jealousies of his advisers, neither of which was helped by his wife's interference. Parliament had inexhaustible resources; it was prepared to enforce discipline on its troops; its policy was directed by principle and foresight; and these advantages must in time ensure its victory, could the King be prevented from seizing a quick decision.

Its victory was hastened by the Scots' second interference. Alarmed by the Irish 'cessation' of September 1642, which seemed to commit Charles to popery, Parliament concluded the Solemn League and Covenant with the Scottish presbyterians, and in accordance with its terms Leslie led his army across the border in January 1643. The Marquis of Newcastle, who had recently raised his unsuccessful siege of Hull, the only place to hold out against him in Yorkshire, hurriedly marched north to confront Leslie, whose forces greatly outnumbered his own. Before he marched he wrote to thank Prince Rupert for sending him cavalry reinforcements under the command of Sir Charles Lucas—particularly as Lucas 'is so much in your Highness's favour', he added.[1] The northern campaign had now for Margaret the additional seriousness of her idolized brother being involved, and each rumour reaching Oxford brought her personal alarm.

As the Scottish army made its way slowly down the coast, Newcastle successfully harassed its communications with his cavalry in spite of the bitter weather, and tried desperately to bring it to battle; but its weighty and cautious advance could only be slowed not checked without reinforcements, and on 25 March Newcastle wrote to Rupert from Durham begging him to come to his aid: 'if your Highness do not please to come hither, and that very soon too, the great game of your uncle's

[1] Newcastle to Rupert, 4 Jan. 1644; quoted by Eliot Warburton, *Memoirs of Prince Rupert*, 1849, ii. 356, n.1.

will be endangered, if not lost; and with your Highness being near, certainly won '[1]—an ironic comment when the effect of Rupert's later arrival is considered. Newcastle was handling the difficult campaign with considerable skill, and the outcome was still undecided when disaster overtook his rear. Lord Bellasis, who had been left in command of the Yorkshire royalists, was suddenly overwhelmed by Fairfax at Selby on 11 April, and Newcastle had no alternative but to retreat hastily into York, where he was blockaded by Leslie and Fairfax, who were joined six weeks later by the army of the Eastern Association under Manchester and Cromwell.

During the campaign which ended with the retreat into York Sir Charles Lucas had had a chance of studying the character of his general, one of the most controversial of the royalist commanders. The popular image of the cavalier—an image of a man leisurely confronting the world with the elegance shown in his portrait by Van Dyck, and disguising a melancholy serious temperament under a mask of levity whenever it threatened his pose: a man luxurious in dress, refined in taste, witty in verse, amorous by nature, loyal by instinct, religious by impulse, courageous by habit—this image owes greatly to Newcastle: ' a very fine gentleman,' as Clarendon called him, [2] acknowledging the attraction which his manners, affability and intelligence exercised upon all who came into his company. He had made himself particularly popular in Nottinghamshire, where he constantly resided, his seat being Welbeck, after succeeding in 1617 to his father, Sir Charles Cavendish, a younger son of the famous Bess of Hardwick. He had ' so endeared ' the gentlemen of the county to him, an impartial observer wrote, ' that no man was a greater prince in all that northern quarter.' [3]

His popularity did not depend solely on his character. He entertained lavishly and was enabled to carry the expense by great

---

[1] Quoted *ib.*, p. 397.
[2] Clarendon, *History of the Rebellion and Civil Wars in England*, ed. W. Dunn Macray, 1888, iii. 381.
[3] Hutchinson, i. 164.

additional wealth inherited in 1629 from his mother, Katherine, the younger daughter and co-heir of Cuthbert, Lord Ogle. He also added to his inheritance by judiciously marrying in 1618 Elizabeth, widow of the Hon. Henry Howard and daughter and heir of William Bassett, of Blore, Staffordshire. The extravagance of his hospitality, and of his taste, was shown to perfection on the two occasions when he entertained the King, at Welbeck in 1633 and at Bolsover in 1634. The first entertainment cost between £3,000 and £4,000, and the second between £14,000 and £15,000. Clarendon's comment on the second was acid: 'which (God be thanked), though possibly it might too much whet the appetite of others to excess, no man ever after imitated.' [1]

Ben Jonson wrote masques for both these occasions, *The King's Entertainment at Welbeck* and *Love's Welcome at Bolsover*. He had already found in Newcastle a generous and deeply appreciative friend and patron—'your truest beadsman and most thankful servant', is the subscription to one of Jonson's letters—and had written epitaphs on both his father and mother. The epitaph on Lady Cavendish is bold in its praise:

> She was the light (without reflex
> Upon herself) to all her sex!
> The best of women! her whole life
> Was the example of a wife!
> Or of a parent! or a friend!
> All circles had their spring and end
> In her! and what could perfect be,
> Or without angles, it was she!

Jonson was only one—though the favourite—among the many poets and dramatists patronized by Newcastle: Richard Brome, John Ford and James Shirley were the most notable to dedicate to him; 'Great both in peace and war, thus fame Did honour Sidney', was Shirley's tribute to his place in the tradition of patronage: and he wrote verses and plays himself as well as

[1] Clarendon, i. 167.

encouraging others. But his interest in all the arts and sciences was wide and sympathetic. He was devoted to music and to painting, addressing Van Dyck in the most affectionate and admiring terms, and showed an intelligent interest in science, encouraged by the enthusiasm of his younger brother, Sir Charles Cavendish, who was unusually competent in the subject and the correspondent of many leading mathematicians and philosophers. The arts Newcastle excelled in himself were swordsmanship and especially horsemanship. He was reputed to be more versed in the art of manège than any contemporary, and Jonson amusingly confirmed his reputation in the finest of the poems he addressed to him:

> When first, my Lord, I saw you back your horse,
>   Provoke his mettle, and command his force
> To all the uses of the field and race,
>   Methought I read the ancient art of Thrace,
> And saw a centaur, past those tales of Greece;
>   So seem'd your horse and you both of a piece!
> You show'd like Perseus upon Pegasus,
>   Or Castor mounted on his Cyllarus;
> Or what we hear our home-born legend tell,
>   Of bold Sir Bevis and his Arundell.
> Nay, so your seat his beauties did endorse,
>   As I began to wish myself a horse:
> And surely had I but your stable seen
>   Before, I think my wish absolv'd had been.
> For never saw I yet the Muses dwell,
>   Nor any of their household half so well.
> So well! as when I saw the floor and room,
>   I look'd for Hercules to be the groom;
> And cried, Away with the Cæsarian bread!
>   At these immortal mangers Virgil fed.

Newcastle was at first content to live at Welbeck, travelling in progress from time to time between his many houses and castles scattered about the north, and to enjoy the great honours which his wealth and distinguished loyalty brought him. He was created Viscount Mansfield in 1620, Earl of Newcastle in 1628, and served as Lord Lieutenant of Nottinghamshire from 1626 to 1642; he held the same office in Derbyshire from 1628 to 1638 during the minority of his cousin, the Earl of Devonshire. But growing jealous of the reputation of lesser men about the court and being anxious to prove more immediately his intense affection to the crown, he began to intrigue for one of the highest court offices, the governorship to the Prince of Wales. He met with many delays and disappointments but was at last successful. He was appointed on 4 June 1638, after a preliminary two months as Gentleman of the Bedchamber to the Prince.

Lucy Hutchinson, who praised his earlier residence in the country, contemptuously remarked on his translation into a courtier, that ' a foolish ambition of glorious slavery carried him to court, where he ran himself much into debt, to purchase neglects of the king and queen, and scorns of the proud courtiers.' [1] Mrs. Hutchinson's brevity and bias led her into exaggeration. Newcastle was trusted as far as their natures would allow by both the King and Queen. His religious loyalty to their persons was accepted, though perhaps too casually, as an invaluable support, particularly when the opposition to their policy became acute; and his relations with the Prince were excellent, and need no other confirmation than these verses—lame though they are, and not the first example one would have preferred to offer of Newcastle's poetry—addressed by him to his pupil [2]:

> Sir, I was sick, and you were with me; since
> I thought to thank you, not as you are prince
> Or my loved master, but as you enroll
> Good Nature's subjects to your monarch soul.
> Know your immortal sweetness such a thing,
> Though but a prince, makes you a little king.
> Your love and judgment, without flatt'ry, can,
> Though you're but young, now stile you justly man.

[1] Hutchinson, i. 164.
[2] *A Collection of Poems by Several Hands*, ed. Francis Needham, 1934, p. 42.

It was probably on the occasion of this sickness that Charles wrote wittily and affectionately to his governor: 'I would not have you take too much physic: for it doth always make me worse, and I think it will do the like with you. . . . Make haste to return to him that loves you.' [1] Though he was later to acquire the habit of forgetting old obligations, Charles never entirely lost his affection for Newcastle and retained the 'sense of those good principles he instilled' into his pupil. [2]

Newcastle held the governorship until his implication in the Army plot of 1641; and as soon as war broke out he raised the royal standard in the north, relying upon his tenants to provide the nucleus of his army and upon his own fortune to support it. His generalship was successful until the fatal intervention of the Scots which drove him into York, but his caution and his jealousy of the independence of his command gave his many enemies at court grounds for complaint, particularly since he himself was critical of the court's interference in military matters. His personal courage in battle was beyond reproach; in every action 'he gave instances of an invincible courage and fearlessness in danger; in which the exposing himself notoriously did sometimes change the fortune of the day when his troops begun to give ground'; but his behaviour after an engagement had ended gave offence. He would then retire, according to Clarendon, 'to his delightful company, music, or his softer pleasures, to all which he was so indulgent, and to his ease, that he would not be interrupted upon what occasion soever', and would leave the administration of his army entirely to his lieutenant-general, James King, Lord Eythin, a Scottish professional soldier trained in the Thirty Years' War. [3] His conduct did not impair, though it may have lessened, his success, but it was used by his enemies to disparage his achievement. The King, however, showed his appreciation of these services by raising him to a marquisate on 27 October 1643.

[1] Quoted by Henry Ten Eyck Perry, *The First Duchess of Newcastle and her Husband as Figures in Literary History*, 1918, p. 20.

[2] *Life*, p. 128.

[3] Clarendon, iii. 382–3.

The siege of York showed Newcastle at his best. His personal bravery inspired the defence to repulse all attacks, and his careful management of supplies enabled the city to hold out until relieved. Relief was long in coming, however, and not until 1 July did Prince Rupert's army arrive within sight of the city walls. The beleaguering armies at once raised the siege and moved off in the direction of Tadcaster. Newcastle promptly despatched a gentleman to welcome Rupert, but instead of turning aside into the city to consult with Newcastle, who might have been expected to have much better intelligence of the enemy, Rupert disregarded him and set out immediately in pursuit of the retreating parliamentarians. Newcastle was deeply insulted by the affront and equally alarmed by Rupert's precipitancy. He had learnt from his intelligence of disagreements among the parliamentarian generals and of bad feeling between the English and Scottish troops, whose morale and condition had been seriously weakened by the long leaguer; and his own plan was to allow the enemy to retire freely and to attack their divided armies separately, once his own had been strengthened by the large reinforcements daily expected. Rupert's haste seemed folly to him. His irritation and exasperation at Rupert's incivility and strategy were quickly heightened by rumours that he had been superseded in his command.

Rupert's conduct has never been satisfactorily explained, though the attempts at justification have been many. His disregarding Newcastle upon his arrival at York may have been due to a professional contempt for the older man's reputation for caution and dilettantism in war, but common sense should have suggested the wisdom of consulting with the commander on the spot, whose intelligence of the enemy should have been at least useful. But to pursue and immediately defeat the enemy would have had such a disastrous effect upon the parliamentarian cause, and would have redounded so greatly to the commander's honour, that the temptation to seize such glory for himself alone may have been the cause of Rupert's marching recklessly ahead. He might not have made the attempt, however, though

LA BATAILLE GAIGNEE

2. William Cavendish, Marquis of Newcastle.
By Abraham van Diepenbeke. Engraved by Peter Clouwet.

the strategy was in line with his character, had it not been for the letter of instruction he had received from Charles before moving north; this he wrongly glossed into a direct order to engage the enemy at once.

The following morning, 2 July, the York garrison, including Newcastle's famous regiment of White Coats—known as Newcastle's ' Lambs '—joined Rupert's army, which had earlier been reinforced by the cavalry under Sir Charles Lucas, sent away into Lincolnshire before the siege of York began. The vanguard had already made contact with the Scottish and parliamentarian armies, which had taken up positions on Marston Moor. Newcastle had been urged by his friends, playing on his jealousy and anger, not to serve under Rupert, and it is to his credit that he replied, ' that happen what would, he would not shun to fight, for he had no other ambition but to live and die a loyal subject to his Majesty.' [1] When Newcastle and Lieutenant-General King came up with Rupert, the Prince said, after the usual salutations, ' My lord, I hope we shall have a glorious day.' They asked ' whether he meant to put it to a day, and urged many reasons against it.' But Rupert would not listen to their strategy, which was to allow the enemy to retire and attack the divided armies separately. He was temperamentally incapable of caution, and trusting in the magic of the heroic gesture and in his interpretation of the King's letter, he was determined to force the issue. His answer to their objections was typical: ' Nothing venture, nothing have.'

Later in the day when the army had taken up positions, Rupert showed them his order of battle. ' By God, sir,' King exclaimed, ' it is very fine in the paper, but there is no such thing in the field!' The parliamentarians, who outnumbered the royalists, occupied the crest of the moor, and a wide ditch, held by Rupert's musketeers, alone separated the armies. Rupert brushed aside King's criticism and vigorously defended himself. Newcastle then asked him when he intended to engage? ' We will charge them tomorrow morning,' Rupert replied. By this

[1] *Life*, p. 47.

time Newcastle had had an opportunity of studying the troops on the ground, and his next question proves him to have been a competent tactician: was Rupert certain, he enquired, that 'the enemy would not fall on them sooner?' Rupert's terse answer—'No'—ended the conference.[1]

It was a chill damp day; the rain-flurries that beat across the moor drove the troops to take what cover they could; and as soon as the conference ended, Newcastle returned to his coach for shelter and called for a pipe of tobacco. But before he could light up, the enemy, seizing advantage of the obvious weakness of Rupert's disposition of his troops, began the attack. Hastily buckling on his armour, Newcastle mounted and rode towards the front, accompanied by his brother, Sir Charles, and his equerries, Major Scot and Captain Mazine, the famous horseman. The first assault had broken the royalists' right wing and Newcastle at first tried to halt the fleeing cavalry; but failing to rally them in their panic, he put himself at the head of a troop of gentlemen volunteers. 'Gentlemen, you have done me the honour to chuse me your captain,' he cried, 'and now is the fittest time that I may do you service; wherefore if you'll follow me, I shall lead you on the best I can, and show you the way to your own honour.'[2] His exhortation was probably shorter in practice than this piece of remembered eloquence, but he at once led his troop into action against a Scottish regiment and routed it, killing three of the enemy himself with his page's half-leaden sword, taken to replace his own.

The cavalry of the royalist left wing, led by Goring and Sir Charles Lucas, was brilliantly successful, but neither its victory nor such gallant actions as Newcastle's could win the day against superior generalship, particularly the generalship of Cromwell, whose calm was in direct contrast to Rupert's impetuosity; and the royalists were quickly broken into rout, suffering heavy casualties. Only Newcastle's infantry regiment, the 'Lambs', held its ground, and in spite of repeated offers of quarter, fought

[1] Clarendon, iii. 376, n.
[2] *Life*, p. 49.

64

on until it was cut down almost to a man. If the spirit of his troops is a judgement on a commander, then the conduct of the 'Lambs' vindicates Newcastle's character from some of the slighting criticisms thrown on it. Newcastle himself was among the last to quit the field, and escaping under cover of darkness caught up with Rupert outside York.

The success of Goring and Lucas had been so great that it was misinterpreted as a complete victory, and a dispatch to that effect was sent to Oxford; but the court's rejoicing was cut short by a later dispatch announcing defeat. Charles had to face the disaster alone. Henrietta Maria had retreated to Cornwall in readiness to escape to France, and when Charles sent the news on to her, Margaret Lucas learnt that her brother, Sir Charles, had been taken prisoner. As she stepped on the ship to sail into exile, she had her personal grief to bear as well as her fear for her mistress's safety and her alarm at the future.

4 Escape to France

Glad was this ship that she safe harbour got.

After Newcastle had escaped from Marston Moor and had caught up with Rupert, both commanders entered York to sleep, and both decided independently in the course of the night to abandon the city—though, as Clarendon severely remarked, their armies had not been completely destroyed, nor their chances of regaining the initiative irretrievably lost, had they been prepared to co-operate; but co-operation was impossible in the frenetic aftermath of defeat.

There is no certain account of what really occurred between them; but according to one report, which favours Rupert, the following conversation took place between them, and King, in the morning: 'Says General King, "What will you do?" Says the Prince, "I will rally my men." Says General King, "Now, Lord Newcastle, what will you do?" Says Lord Newcastle, "I will go into Holland," looking upon all as lost. The Prince would have him endeavour to recruit his forces. "No," says he, "I will not endure the laughter of the court," and King said he would go with him.'[1]

The dialogue makes Newcastle appear merely frivolous, but certainly fear of what his enemies at court would say when once they learnt of his defeat contributed to his decision to quit the country. He had been too cautious in action, too reluctant to jeopardize his independence and too critical of the court's interference in military affairs to avoid giving his enemies an opportunity of venting their personal animosity in justifiable criticism; and his defeat meant that they would inevitably urge his failure to prevent him from regaining his former position, were it ever

[1] Warburton, ii. 468.

in the nature of things possible. Even before the battle, it had been rumoured that he had been superseded in his command. If the defeat had lost him the power of rebuilding his army, as he sincerely believed, to have stayed in England would have ended in his becoming a hanger-on of the court, an object of contempt to those whom he despised.

But the conversation explains his conduct only in part. Clarendon asserted that he was too passionately distressed by Rupert's reckless dissipation of his forces to compose himself ' to think of beginning the work again, and involving himself in the same undelightful condition of life, from which he might now be free.' [1] This condemnation shows him in furious disgust simply refusing even to contemplate rebuilding his army, and interpreting the situation to exonerate himself from such a laborious task, ill suited to his easy nature. But such a reading of his character, though by no means entirely false, reduces his decision to a whim and does not take account of his inherent pacificism, which made him the most humane of the generals on either side: no brutalities or atrocities can be laid to his charge. He had raised his original army largely by appealing to personal allegiances, and the strength of its attachment is proved by the conduct of his ' Lambs '. He could build up another only by a similar appeal, and rather than repay his troops' loyalty by offering them to be sacrificed to the rashness of any other commander who might be appointed over him, he thrust it out of his power to betray them by accepting the ignominy of retreat. He acted instinctively in the heat of his justifiable anger with Rupert, and as he would not have done had there been time for deliberation; but though those instincts unsuited him for a soldier, they were not trivial but deeply rooted in a complex character.

When his wife came to write his life, she simply repeated his own sincere conviction that as he was of no more use to the King, he had no other immediate course open than to retreat abroad. We see his action as a prelude to sixteen years of exile and give it a finality it was not intended to have; but his

[1] Clarendon, iii. 384.

contemporaries, however bitterly they blamed him, saw it as an expedient rather than as an absolute rejection of responsibility. The King wrote to him after receiving news of the battle to thank him for his past services, particularly his ‘ late gallant defence of York ’, and to assure him that on his return from abroad he would ‘ be sure to be received and ever entertained with that favour and estimation ’ which he might expect from his ‘ most assured constant friend ’.[1] Even Clarendon, whose attitude is really one of tolerant contempt, praised him for ‘ his readiness and alacrity again to have embarked himself in the King’s quarrel upon the first reasonable occasion.’ [2]

This extenuation is not an attempt to disguise the serious flaw in his character, nor to reduce the charge that his defection dealt a serious blow to royalist morale. His example encouraged many to quit the country who might otherwise have stayed and helped to rally the scattered forces. John Constable may have been trying to excuse his own flight when he wrote from Amsterdam, ‘ I must tell you if the Marquis of Newcastle had stayed in England neither I nor any else had thought of coming over, but his going lost his army and all those that depended on him ’; [3] but his remark is enough to support an indictment.

Once the decision to leave had been taken, Newcastle and his company were escorted by a troop of horse and a troop of dragoons to Scarborough, where they embarked in two vessels. Newcastle’s wife, Elizabeth, had died in April of the preceding year, and he was accompanied by his two young sons, Charles and Henry, both of whom had fought beside him at Marston Moor. He left his three daughters behind at Welbeck under the protection of a garrison, which capitulated on terms to Manchester in August. Sir Charles Cavendish was also in his brother’s train, and among the rest were General King, who was suspected of treason by the royalists on account of his nationality, and unfairly charged by those partisans of Newcastle who

[1] Warburton, ii. 477–8.
[2] Clarendon, iii. 385.
[3] *C S P D, 1644*, 1888, p. 379.

wished to excuse his flight of persuading him to take that course; Lord Widdrington, a connection of Newcastle's, and one of the most heroic characters of the age; and the ardent royalist, John Bramhall, Bishop of Derry and later Archbishop of Armagh.

During the four days at sea Newcastle had time to consider quietly his broken life, and, his passions having cooled, the prospect must have filled him with dismay. He had lost his power, he had left the King's cause dangerously threatened, he was proscribed by Parliament as a grand delinquent, and his flight had left his great estates open to sequestration. What else had he to hope for but to die an impoverished exile, unless his natural resilience supported him and luck played into his hands? His despondency was increased by his sons' sickness. Charles went down with smallpox in the course of the voyage, and shortly after Henry suffered a dangerous attack of measles. Newcastle must have made a melancholy crossing.

They landed at Hamburg on 8 July and took up quarters in the city, which for some reason appeared a better choice than Holland as a refuge. Newcastle had £90 in hand, sufficient to tide him over the first weeks; but, unable to meet the continued heavy expense of his numerous retinue, he was forced to send several servants back to England to find credit. As soon as he had found it he bought a coach and ' nine horses of an *Holsatian* breed ',[1] thus establishing at the start the characteristic pattern of his exile—the constant search for credit and, once it was found, the immediate purchase of horses.

The manège of horses, however, could not distract his attention from the hopelessness of his situation. The stay in Hamburg must have been intended at the beginning as temporary, but he was still there in February 1645, when he wrote to his pupil, Prince Charles, to congratulate him on being made a general: ' And it is no small comfort to me and mine,' he continued, ' that we have lived to see you a man; and could I see but peace in our Israel, truly then I care not how soon death closes my eyes. But whilst I crawl here in this uneven world your Highness must

---

[1] *Life*, p. 54.

be troubled with me as my first master, and now it is your turn to take care of me.'[1] But if the Prince was to be given a chance of caring for him, and if he was to play a further part in royalist counsels, he must move closer to the centre; and the Continental centre was Henrietta Maria's court in Paris.

He began to move south shortly after he had written to Charles, sailing from Hamburg to Rotterdam and calling at Amsterdam on the way. From Rotterdam he sent a complimentary address to Elizabeth of Bohemia, who held court at the Hague, and this was very kindly received. He continued his journey by sea to Antwerp, arriving about the middle of March; and from there he and his party, in ' one coach, one chariot, and two waggons ', made a leisurely journey to Paris, stopping at Brussels, among other places, ' where he received a visit from the Governor, the Marquess of Castel Rodrigo, the Duke of Lorraine, and Count Piccolomini.'[2] He arrived at Paris towards the end of April, and at once went to wait on Henrietta Maria at St. Germain-en-Laye, presenting her with seven of his Holsatian horses.

Henrietta Maria's retreat abroad had been almost as precipitate as Newcastle's. Immediately after her return to Charles at Oxford, when Margaret Lucas had joined her court, her spirits had been high, but as reports arrived across the winter of great parliamentary preparations, followed by the news of the Scots' disastrous intervention, her courage began to fail. Her nerves were also badly affected by her pregnancy. Frightened of what her fate might be should she fall into the hands of Parliament, she determined to leave Oxford for a safer place, and in April set out for Exeter, in the face of Charles's natural protests. Her child, the Princess Henrietta, was born there in June. But no sooner did Essex threaten the city with a siege in July than she fled to Falmouth and took ship for France, landing at Brest after a very rough crossing. Her maids were all horribly seasick and terrified by the storm, but she herself showed her usual courage,

[1] *H M C, 13 Rep., Pt. ii*, 1893, ii. 134.
[2] *Life*, p. 54.

70

in spite of her serious ill-health, and tried to hearten them. Once she had landed, her condition became so alarming that instead of proceeding immediately to Paris, she went to Bourbon L'Archambault to drink the medicinal waters. When she had recovered sufficiently, she proceeded to the capital, where she was welcomed royally and assigned apartments in the Louvre and given the use of the palace of St. Germain-en-Laye.

The escape to France was Margaret Lucas's first experience of complete separation from her family; and the voyage itself made so deep an impression upon her imagination that the flight of a princess from coast to coast of vague locality, pursued by misfortune in one shape or another, became a favourite theme of her fiction. The heroine of ' Assaulted and Pursued Chastity ', for example, makes three extraordinary voyages and becomes so travelled that she adopts the name of Travelia. And when Margaret described her own fate in verse she chose to liken herself to a ship:

> A ship of youth in the world's sea was sent,
> Balanced with self-conceit and pride it went,
> And large sails of ambition set thereon,
> Hung to a tall mast of good opinion.

The voyage that followed this auspicious launching was at first attended by fair weather, and the ship sailed through a ' calm of peace ' towards the ' land of riches ' in search of a ' golden fame ':

> But when that she had past nineteen degrees,
> The land of happiness she no longer sees:
> For then rebellious clouds foul black did grow,
> And showers of blood into those seas did throw.[1]

Driven off course by these storms, the ship reached with difficulty the haven of ' great France ', but sailing up the Loire to fair Paris, was repaired and found a purchaser.

Henrietta Maria's court immediately became the centre for the numerous English exiles. They were daily increasing in number, and comforted themselves in their present misery with hopes of

[1] *Poems*, pp. 155–6.

an imminent return home, whiling away the time in intrigue and gossip. The atmosphere at court was heavy with anxiety, and the monotony was broken only by the false expectation of success from yet another negotiation for foreign help, or by news from England. Margaret herself had her family to worry about, and hampered by her bashfulness and her ignorance of the language, she can hardly have played a part other than that of a mute in the exchange of civilities with the French court, or otherwise mixed in society, which might have distracted her from her troubles.

When Newcastle arrived to pay court to the Queen at St. Germain and present her with the seven horses, Margaret was in attendance. She was naturally interested in seeing her brother's late commander, and as her romantic imagination had been already awakened to him by her brother's reports and by his own reputation, which was enhanced rather than diminished in her eyes by his misfortunes, she was deeply and immediately impressed by his handsome appearance and self-assured bearing. Later she was to describe her impression of his person: 'His shape is neat, and exactly proportioned,' she wrote; 'his stature of a middle size, and his complexion sanguine.' And as for his behaviour, it was such 'that it might be a pattern for all gentlemen; for it is courtly, civil, easy and free, without formality or constraint; and yet hath something in it of grandeur, that causes an awful respect towards him.'[1] Standing behind the Queen, Margaret watched him closely and admiringly, and listened carefully to his unaffected witty conversation. She was already prepared to fall in love with him, so exactly did he fit both her ideal and her need.

Newcastle talked with her about her brother and gave her some account of his share in Marston Moor, praising his gallantry; and though her lack of confidence may have prevented her from making more than ordinary replies—unless her intense devotion to her brother encouraged her to unusual loquaciousness—or from revealing anything of her true character, Newcastle was at once attracted by her beauty, shown off to advantage

[1] *Life*, p. 150.

by her careful attention to dress. She wore her brown hair fashionably, in ringlets down her neck, and the crisp curls about her brow set off her smooth oval face. Her eyes were widely set apart, her nose was long and shapely and her mouth full, particularly the lower lip, 'as though some bee had stung it newly.' Such, at least, is her appearance in her portraits, which reveal sufficient character to suggest that the artists did not lazily deck her in conventional beauty. Her figure was admirable, and full enough to stir Newcastle's sensuality: 'your plump flesh' is a recurrent note in his praise of her person.

On his later visits to St. Germain, he singled her out for attention and quickly succeeded in winning her confidence. He was very attractive to women and knew exactly how to pay court, neatly adapting his addresses to appeal to their different natures. The evidence of his own daughter, Lady Jane, is naturally biased in his favour, but her verses on him, ragged though they are, do not read simply as a fond daughter's praise:

> Maid, wife, or widow, which bears the grave style,
> Newcastle but name him, I know then she'll smile;
> From thence you may follow this track in her face,
> So read by their eyes, they will run Cupid's race;
> But if once you come nigh them to speak, they cry, fye!
> Looks pretty, what saith he? faith! I'll not deny.[1]

The affection which runs clearly through the many otherwise dull verses which Lady Jane addressed to him shows how deeply she herself admired him as a man, not just as a father requiring a token of filial compliments. And Margaret, too, testified to his attraction for other women: 'I know him not addicted to any manner of vice,' she wrote, 'except that he has been a great lover and admirer of the female sex; which whether it be so great a crime as to condemn him for it, I'll leave to the judgement of young gallants and beautiful ladies.' [2]

Margaret was fated to fall in love with Newcastle. He approxi-

[1] *Poems, Songs, a Pastoral and a Play by the Rt. Honble the Lady Jane Cavendish and Lady Elizabeth Brackley*, f. 13; Bodleian, MS. Rawl. poet. 16.
[2] *Life*, pp. 149–50.

mated so closely to the hero of her 'contemplations', and arrived in Paris so opportunely, when her own situation uncomfortably resembled the predicament in which she had often imagined herself as heroine—an orphaned princess lost in a foreign land, bravely maintaining her integrity in the face of temptations and dangers—that he seemed to be their fulfilment. All her 'contemplations' on her future success in love had not been as wildly extravagant as her vision of the exiled and pursued princess, but even the more ordinary had been equally impossible. She reminded a correspondent many years later that when they were both girls they had used to confess to each other whom they loved; and, as we have seen, she owned to loving only three dead men: Cæsar, Ovid and Shakespeare. Newcastle seemed in her romantic eyes to combine the virtues of all three, though she was not confirmed in her judgement until later.

But he also satisfied one of the deepest emotional needs of her nature—her need for reassurance. She had been brought up so completely under the supervision of her family that, as she herself acknowledged, once out of their company, she was painfully embarrassed, hardly knowing how to control her body, much less retain her presence of mind. Newcastle's self-confidence and long experience equipped him to take the place of her family; to protect and comfort her as they had done. He was able to assume the rôles of both father and lover. He was fifty-two at the time of their first meeting and she was thirty years younger, but his age, which might have seemed a disadvantage to another woman, was an attraction to her as a guarantee of his dependability. And he was also, in fact, as amorous a lover as any mistress could require.

The courtship had to be conducted secretly behind the formalities of the court. The results of transgressing the conventions would have been disastrous: the Queen would have been deeply offended, and it was essential to retain her good opinion; and, more important, Margaret's reputation would have been irretrievably ruined. She might receive his compliments—uttered hurriedly as they moved aside for a moment from the group

74

idling in the state apartments, or sauntering along the terraces—with a shy look of pleasure, or let him take her hand, or, at last, when she was confident of him, allow him a kiss; but she had firmly to forbid him to proceed beyond such subtle play. The difficulty of the game, however, enhanced the value of the prize. Governed by strict rules, the affair proceeded slowly—though it may have been quickened by the uncertainty of Newcastle's stay in Paris: Sir Charles Cavendish wrote to his friend, John Pell, on 27 July, ' it is so long since I heard from you, and our stay here is not likely to be long, that I now write, lest hereafter I find not so fit an opportunity '[1]—and it was not until the beginning of September that the matter was settled between them. By then Newcastle would have had time to write to Elizabeth Lucas and to have received her consent to her daughter's marriage.

Once the marriage had been arranged, Newcastle courted Margaret passionately, writing her poems at the rate, it would seem, of one a day, and sending them secretly to her from his lodgings in Paris, accompanying them with his picture or other love tokens. He sent to her at all hours; once so early in the morning that she wrote in reply: ' I think you have a plot against my healt[h] in sending so early, for I was forst to reed your leter be a candell light for ther was not day enouf; but I had rather reed your leter than slepe, and it doth me more good.' And in the postscript she added, ' If you cannot reed this leter blam me not, for it was so early I was half a slep.' The miniature he sent her of himself was broken in the carriage but she was still pleased with its resemblance, though she thought that his verses gave a truer impression of him than his ' peckter '.[2]

Newcastle inevitably expressed his love in verse, having been devoted to poetry all his life—' he was amorous in poetry and music,' Clarendon remarked, reflecting on his deficiencies as a commander, ' to which he indulged the greatest part of his

[1] British Museum, Birch Coll. 4278, f. 210.
[2] The quotations from Newcastle's love poems and from Margaret's replies are taken from *The Phanseys of William Cavendish*, ed. Douglas Grant, 1956. The poems were printed there for the first time.

time ' [1]; and the many love poems he had addressed to his first
wife had given him practice in the style.[2] He was sufficiently
pleased with his efforts to ask Margaret if she troubled to keep
his verses and was answered rather smartly: ' My lord, I am
sory you should bed me keepe the ferses you sent,' she wrote,
' for it lookes as tho you thought I had flung thos away you sent
before. Shurly I would keep them wer it with deficulty, and
not to part with your muses so easely; and beleve me, I will
part with nothing that you shall command me to keep.'

When he had returned to his lodgings in Paris, Newcastle
would sit up late and try to catch in verse his impression of
Margaret, seen earlier in the day:

> I Now sit downe with Penne and Inke and Paper,
> Invoake my Muse by my dimme single Taper.

Or he would attempt to quiet his anticipation of the time when
he could at last enjoy her fully by imagining its blisses. His
poems are always excited by the idea of her beauty, and though
his honest sensuality is too undisciplined to make them memor-
able in the way of Donne's, it at least raises them above the dry
level of those which hypocritically pretend that love is only to
be expressed in so far as it is platonic:

> When my Lipps, heated, seekes
> Love's cooler Walkes, your Cheekes;
> Or wandringe loves to Roave
> In thicketts, your hayr's Groave;
> Or on love's Mounts that's fayre,
> Your pantinge brests, gives Ayre;
> Or baythe me in love's poole,
> My heated love to coole;
> Or in love's Grotto shunne
> Your Eys, Each a hot Sunne;
> Freshe fountayns there will please me,
> With sweet fan'd Ayre to Ease mee.

He could say no more and stay decent. His excitement is

[1] Clarendon, iii. 381.
[2] Newcastle's love poems to his first wife are among the Portland Papers
deposited in Nottingham University Library by the Duke of Portland, K.G.

too great on this and on many another occasion when he approached as closely as he dared to a flat statement of the exact goal on which his attention was wholly fixed, to allow him to do more than revolve fascinated round the idea, careless of anything but the pleasurable dizziness of his flight; but once or twice he held himself in check and could then celebrate her beauty more coolly, and turn a line, a phrase, a stanza or two, which show that he had a true sense of style:

> So streight, so slender, and so tall,
> But that's not all:
> A face out of the Common Road,
> With smiles so stroad,
> To grace that feature and that forme
> Without a storme.
> You, Heaven's mould, sent downe so fresh and new;
> None can be handsom that's not thought like you.

> So Bewtiful you are, so fayre,
> Transpayrent Ayre
> Doth sully and doth stayne your skinne;
> It is so thinne,
> The Gentlest blushe no where can hide,
> So soone tis spide;
> And your Each curled hayre those locks doth grace,
> Like pensil'd shadows for your lovely face.

The third and last stanza of this poem crumbles under his usual fault, jumbled and obscure syntax, but these two have the modest felicity which justified Margaret in calling her lover a poet.

Newcastle rarely moved with such sustained confidence as he did in this poem, but he was always able to redeem himself from complete failure by a passage of surprising point or grace:

> It is no theft, for when
> I kisse, you take 't agen;
> And doth your lipps renue
> With your owne hony'd dewe
> And Naturall showers, gott
> From your tongue's water pott.

The lines are pleasantly humorous, and it is his humour that often saves him from becoming ridiculous. He was conscious of the comic figure a middle-aged man wild for love is in danger of cutting, and even when he was most unsteady, or indeed had fallen flat, he retained his dignity by showing a sudden self-possessed awareness of the humour of his predicament. The poem ' Love's Answer ' is one example of this quality:

> When one doth aske, what news, I pray you, Sir?
> I answer yett, I did not heare from her.
> S'ounds, I mean Bristoll, says he, can you tell?
> I answer, I doe hope that shee is well.
> The Peace is made in Ireland they say?
> I tell him, I doe thinke shee'le send to-day.
> Are the Scotts turn'd unto the Kinge? pray speake!
> If she not love me then my harte will breake,
> Say I. Says he, your Answers mad doe make me.
> I sweare I love her, Else the Divell take me.

And the pair continue talking at cross-purposes until Newcastle apologizes to the other's satisfaction for his nonsense by explaining that he is in love.

All the poems are not, however, simply a catalogue of his mistress's beauties—a mustering up of his senses with delight, to use his own military metaphor; some of them are more independent of her presence. ' Hymen's Ancorett ', for example, might well stand as an example of the cavalier love-lyric, had it been refined and the original metaphor pursued rigorously:

> Like an old Soldier in Queen Venus' warres,
> My wounds of love turn'd all to mangl'd Scarrs,
> Love's broaken speere and bowed sworde doe meet
> As offrings att your Sacred Alter's feete.
> My discharg'd Pistoll, Rusty Armes, though stronge,
> Dismounted Cannon, here doth lie alonge;
> And all Love's Magazine, that's thought divine,
> I Sacrifise here att love's flaminge Shrine.

And he could also write a ballad in the true royalist style which, again, could have been turned to admiration:

> Sweet harte, we are beggers; our Comfort 's, tis seene,
> That we are Undunne for the Kinge and the Queene;
> Which doth make Us rejoyce, with Royall braggs,
> That now we doe foote it with Royall raggs.

The poems were written hurriedly, by the single taper's dim light, and their chief literary interest lies in the way they unconsciously use the conventions of the seventeenth-century love-lyric; a naïve illustration of those which came most readily to hand. The general style is an alliance of Jonson and Donne; Jonson's preponderating influence decides the manner of approach, an advance to order by way of chosen particulars, and Donne's the use of imagery. The first can be seen most clearly in the rehearsal of Margaret's qualities, though Newcastle never achieved the cool appreciation of his master, and the second can be collected from most of the poems. But Newcastle's metaphysical wit is seldom articulated properly to be effective and lies everywhere in pieces, lacking an intelligence to assemble it.

> To say wee'r like one Snake, not us disgrases,
> That winds, delights it selfe, with selfe Imbrases.

This conceit could have been developed, but the verse's screw slackens and the conclusion is commonplace:

> Love hath no Venum, Poyson, in 't att all,
> But is all sweetnes and Balsamicall.

The boldest of the poems, 'Love's Preparation', a celebration of love in terms of the Christian mysteries, is at the same time the most unusual and the most unpleasant of them:

> Thus be your living Arke, and to mee drawe
> Your Virgin rodd, blest Manna, and your lawe,
> And keepe them sacred; and with nothing fedd
> But with pure Marriage, your shew holy bredd.
> In me your Consecrated Arke shall lie,
> No sinful hand shall touch Us but shall die.
> So Cristall pure I'le be; for you I'l boast,
> Fitt to preserve you, my love's holy Ghost.

79

Newcastle had earlier written devotional verse of merit in the style of Donne, and one poem, 'A Divine Meditation upon receaving the Blessed Sacrament on Christmas day 1637',[1] opens finely:

> Thy birth-time's wheele to mee turnes quickly round,
> Christmass againe! and find my Soule unsound!
> I left it well, and thought, at the same rate
> To find it soe, but 'tis in worse estate.
> Like those who prying at Sol's beautious Light
> Dazle their Senses, and doe dimme their sight;
> Thinkeing, on what they looke, It still doth stirr,
> When 'tis our Mother Earth, not Hee, but Her.
> So on the Nimble waters, all the Bankes,
> You thinke doe move, and give the Boate no thankes;
> And Sinne insensibly still moveing thus,
> Wee find It not, because 'tis borne with us.

The association of the sexual and the devotional in 'Love's Preparation', however distressing, suggests a force which seldom appears elsewhere in the poems to Margaret; and had he possessed something of Donne's brutal energy, the marriage of the two themes might have been successfully consummated.

The seventy poems which Newcastle addressed to Margaret were never revised for publication and cannot bear a detailed criticism, but they are so typical of his character that their original fault should be stressed. The fault is a lack of seriousness. Newcastle was in poetry as in all else an amateur; as in war a professional had to be attached to him to administer the army, so in poetry a 'professional' should always have been detailed to revise his work and ensure that it was in fit shape to take the field against the reader. In spite of his gifts and his inclinations, he was only a poetaster. Yet the blame for his failure was not entirely his own. At the time the opinion was held that a gentleman who seriously followed any pursuits, except those sanctioned as proper by society, was in danger of moving into the ranks of

[1] Nottingham Univ. Lib., Portland Papers, Newcastle's Poems and Plays Vol II, f. 28.

the professionals and losing caste. All that a gentleman had to do to be praised was to prove that he might have excelled had he been so minded. Why strain to shake the tree when the fruit fell in the wind of spontaneous applause? But when a gentleman was serious in poetry, and disguised it beneath the negligent attitude required by society, his verse achieved the appearance of undeliberated grace which distinguishes the finest cavalier poems.

The effect of this inbred opinion is evident in every aspect of Newcastle's verse: clumsy lines could have been turned neatly, vapouring ideas could have been trimmed to burn steadily, and awkward stanzas could have been disciplined into shape; and such improvements, which could have been made with little time or trouble, would have given his work a very different aspect.

Margaret was being courted to the height of her expectations, but her own position was far from easy. She could not, in the first place, respond as her own enthusiastic nature would have liked. Convention required that she should be passive until summoned into complete life by her lover on her marriage-day; and should she prematurely cast off restraint, she might both disgust him and endanger her reputation. The most she could allow herself was a reassurance of her love: ' I thank you for the toaken of love you sent me, for I must confes I want it, wer it but to returne it on your self againe; for tho I give you all the love I have, yet it tis to lettell for your merety; or could I wish for mor love then ever was or shall be, yet my wish could not be so scopus [copious] but you would be stell as farre beyound it as your worth is above other mens.' But no sooner had she sent this letter than she was ashamed of its frankness, and began her next with an apology: ' I am a lettell ashamed of my last leter mor then of the others; not that my affeetion can be to larg but I fear I discover it to much in that leter, for wemen must love silently; but I hop you will pardon the still [style] becaus the intension was good.'

Other difficulties she had to contend with were the gossip at court and the influence of Newcastle's friends. ' Pardon me if I have wright any thing that is not agreable,' she began one letter, ' but if I be carfull in things that may arise to the scandall of my repeta[t]ion, [it] is for fear of a refleckion becaus I am yours; for though it is imposabll to keep out of the rech of a slandering toung from an enves [envious] parson, yet it tis in my power to hender them from the advantag of a good ground to beld [build] ther descoures [discourses] on. For know, me lord, Saintjarmanes [St. Germain] is a place of much sencour [censure] and thinks I send to often.' Newcastle was a very eligible match, even in his reduced circumstances, and Margaret's good fortune aroused jealousy; as her letters show, she had to behave as cautiously as possible. The Queen herself was annoyed when she learnt that she had not been kept informed of what was happening, but Margaret, though professing not to care for her good opinion, was too wise to lose it, and immediately before the marriage wrote, ' I hop the Qeene and I shall be very good frindes againe, and may be the beter for the deffarances we have had.'

The opposition of Newcastle's friends to his marriage was a greater threat to Margaret's happiness and one more difficult to repel, as the chances of directly combating their influence in conversation were few. ' Me lord, me lord Widdrington in his advies has don as a nobell and a true affectshoinit fri[e]nd would doe,' she wrote on one occasion, ' yet I find I am infinnightly obleged to you whose afectshoins are above so powerfull a parswashon.' Widdrington's advice was probably to the effect that his friend was throwing himself away on an almost penniless girl—her portion was only two thousand pounds, and it was very doubtful if any of that would be forthcoming, given the conditions in England—when he might marry with a view to recouping his fortune. Newcastle's own children may have been against the marriage, too, partly for the same reason and partly out of a natural antipathy to a step-mother of their own age. Margaret reacted to these threats in the only way possible to her: ' if I shall prejudgice you in the affaires of the world, or in your judgment of your bad choyce, consider and le[a]ve me; for I

82

shall desir to life no longer then to see you hapy.' An offer of self-sacrifice, as she knew, simply could not be accepted by a man of Newcastle's honour, and his friends' and family's objections were easily defeated by a few such sentences, their effectiveness in no way spoilt by the spelling.

But the greatest danger Margaret had to face came from New-castle himself. He was so impatient for the consummation that on one occasion she had to call him to order directly. ' Me lord, you are a parson I may very confeedently one [own] unles morell meret be a scandall,' she wrote, continuing with surprising frankness; ' but, me lord, ther is a custtumare law that must be sineed [signed] before I may lawfully call you husban. If you are so passhonit as you say, and as I dar not but belefe, yet it may be feared it cannot last long, for no extrem is parmenttary [permanent].' To submit too soon would be to throw her reputation away beyond recall. But there was another reason for her caution. Elizabeth Lucas must have written to her during this period, but Margaret can hardly have needed her urgent written advice when Elizabeth herself had already provided in her person an example of the folly of yielding to any solicitations, however passionately phrased in verse, before the ceremony had been performed. Newcastle had no chance of tempting her to repeat her mother's mistake.

Margaret's letters show how strong her common sense was in spite of her extravagant nature. She was always able to speak sensibly on practical matters and to give Newcastle the best advice in his dealings with the court: ' For the King and Qeene's favour, my lord, I think you will never be in danger of loosing it, for I never hard that any body perfeetly had it.' The remark is both shrewd and sharp; and when she had her attention fixed on reality, she was always a keen judge of character. Even in her relations with her lover himself she revealed a true appreciation of the nature of the passion which underlay his courtship. She was not misled by being continually similized and deified into thinking that his love was paid to an ideal. Her own description of the motive behind his proposal is moving on

83

account of its innocence and simplicity: 'for he, having but two sons, purposed to marry me, a young woman that might prove fruitful to him and increase his posterity by a masculine offspring. Nay, he was so desirous of male issue that I have heard him say he cared not (so God would be pleased to give him many sons) although they came to be persons of the meanest fortunes.'[1] She was, however, equally certain that her love for him held no element of sexual passion: 'it was not amorous love; I never was infected therewith, it is a disease, or a passion, or both; I only know by relation, not by experience.'[2]

Margaret suffered under the strain of waiting, and at times grew very melancholy. 'But supos me now in a very mallancholy humer,' she wrote drearily, but in the pleasant expectation of being comforted; 'and that most off my contempaltions are fext on nothing but dessolutions; for I look apon this world as on a deth's head for mortefecation, for I see all things subject to allteration and chaing, and our hopes as if they had takin opum [opium].' Her depression was a prelude to sickness, and a day or two later she had taken to her bed: 'Wer I much sicker then I was your kaind car would cuer me,' she wrote gratefully. Newcastle promptly apostrophized her sickness in verse, the receptacle of all his emotions at that time:

> Envious Cold, thus to assault
> A Bewty that 's without a faulte;
> To Close shut Up her porous Skinne,
> That is so white, so soft, so thinne:
> To stop those holes it is a Sinne.

Happily Apollo dissipated the cold, to use the poet's expression.

On 8 November a great marriage was celebrated at Paris in the chapel of the Palais-Royal. Marie-Louise de Gonsague-Nevers was wedded to Vladislav VII of Poland. Henrietta Maria and her ladies attended the ceremony, and Newcastle was so struck by the contrast between the Princess of Nevers's fortune in

[1] *Life*, p. 55.
[2] *Natures Pictures*, p. 375.

84

my lord

i think you have a plot against
my health in sending so early
for i was forst to reed your
letter be a candell light for
ther was not dos excuse but i had
rather reed your letter then
sleep and it doth me more good
i my lord i hop you are not
ingare for my aduise of St
ermenes i gaue it semple for the
best as for mrs porter he was
a stranger to me before
i cam in to france i did neuer
see hem or at lest knew hem
not to be mrs porter or my lord
of newcastls frind and
my lord it is a custtom i
obsarue that i neuer speek to
any man before thee adres
them selues to me nor to look
so much in ther face as to
inuit ther descours and i hop i
neuer was instuell to ane
garson of what degree so euer but
to morrow the quene comes to
ueares ther say then i
hop to instifie my selfe to
be 182 my lord

3. Letter of Margaret Lucas to William Cavendish, 1645.

marriage and Margaret's prospects that he at once wrote a melancholy poem on the theme:

> The Princes Mary marrys Kinge of Poland,
> And you, my Deer, do marry Prince of Noland.
> Shee hath a Portion, I hope you have non;
> She hath a Dower, but your Dower's gone.
> Theirs are but rich Externall shews, that move
> Like love, not it; ours pure Internall love.
> She doth imbrase all this world's full delight,
> And you take mee to bid the world good Night.

But the arrangements for his own marriage were at the same time being hurried on. ' I have sent my mayd about som busnes,' Margaret wrote, ' and she and my lady Broune shall agre about the other things you spak of. I understand the parswashon of some againest your marreg,' she continued, turning the key in the lock, ' [su]er [sure] they would not p[ers]wad you but for your good; but if you think you have don unadvisedly in promesis your self to me, send me word and I will resing [resign] up all the intrist I have in you, though unwillingly; but what would I not doe for any thing that may condues [conduce] to your content; for heerafter if you should repent, how unfortunat a woman should I be.'

Lady ' Broune ' was the wife of Sir Richard Browne, the English Resident at the French Court, and she had agreed to help Margaret to make arrangements for the marriage, which was to take place in the Resident's private chapel. John Evelyn, her son-in-law, wrote on her death in 1652 that she was ' universally lamented, having been so obliging on all occasions to those who continually frequented her house in Paris, which was not only an hospital, but an asylum to all our persecuted and afflicted countrymen.' [1] The last arrangement to be made was to engage a priest. ' I find to sattesfy the opinion we are not marred allredy we must be marred by on[e] of the prestes heer,'

[1] Evelyn, ii. 63.

Margaret wrote, 'which I think Cousens to be the fettes [fittest].' 'Cousens' was John Cosin, later Bishop of Durham, who served as chaplain to the royalist exiles at Paris. He was already well known to Newcastle, having been appointed by him in 1642 to view all the sermons preached in the bishopric of Durham.

The marriage took place at the end of November or the beginning of December 1645: 'be ashured I will bring non to our wedding but those you ples,' Margaret had written, so it must have been a quiet ceremony. After the news had reached Elizabeth Lucas in England, she wrote to thank Newcastle for honouring her daughter by marriage: 'And thereby made her extremely happy; for oftentimes these come not together, but by yourself she hath attained to both; the state of the kingdom is such yet that I confess her brother cannot give unto her that which is hers, neither can I show my love and affection towards my daughter as I would, in respect of the great burdens we groan under. God deliver us, and send us a happy end of these troubles which we ought with patience to bear till Almighty God in his due time shall be pleased to deliver us.'[1] The accents are those of a woman who matched her daughter's description of her character.

Elizabeth Lucas's sombre letter served to remind Newcastle and his young wife in their immediate happiness of how much their future turned on events in England. The King's cause was staggering to defeat, a return home was becoming a more distant prospect, and their own fate might be no better than a life of impoverished exile, dependent upon the charity and tolerance of their hosts. But at least Margaret had completed safely the first stage in her career. She had married as well as she could have wished, and if life had so far agreed to conform to the imaginary pattern she had dreamed of imposing on it, surely she might expect to end, like her own Princess Travelia, as well as she had begun, however great her intermediate difficulties might be. Newcastle, too, having been successful in love could now put

[1] Brit. Mus., Portland MSS. List 1B; Cavendish Papers 1604–59, f. 216.

to the proof the argument of one of the poems he had addressed
to her:

> There is no happy life
> But in a wife;
> The Comforts are so sweete
> When they doe meet;
> Tis plenty, Peace, a Calme
> Like Droping Balme;
> Love's wether is so fayre,
> Perfumed Aire;
> Each word such pleasure brings,
> Like soft toucht strings;
> Love's Passion moves the harte
> On Eyther parte;
> Such Harmony together,
> So pleas'd in Eyther;
> No discords, Concords still,
> Seal'd with one will.

5 Sheba and Solomon

I have observed, that those that meddle least in wars, whether civil or foreign, are not only most safe and free from danger, but most secure from losses.

ONCE they were married, Newcastle took Margaret home to his lodgings in Paris, which they were to occupy for nearly two years. Their immediate difficulty was lack of funds. Conditions in England were so uncertain that people were either unable to remit money to their relations abroad, or were reluctant to do so for fear of compromising themselves with Parliament; and their timidity increased as the first Civil War came to an end with Charles's surrender to the Scots. The only way to survive was to find credit among the Parisians, and as they were naturally loath to make advances without security, they charged a high rate of interest when they could be persuaded to be kind. Endymion Porter was so reduced that to avoid starving in Paris itself, he retired to a suburb and wrote that he consequently knew nothing of the intrigues at the Louvre: 'and I want clothes for a Court,' he added, 'having but that poor riding suit I came out of England in.'[1] Lady Fanshawe, who accompanied her husband into exile, proudly claimed that neither of them borrowed money or owed 'for clothes, or diet, or lodgings' while they were abroad, and contemptuously referred to 'the bad custom which our countrymen had that way, which did redound much to the King's dishonour and their own discredit.'[2] The charge is hardly fair. Lady Fanshawe was luckier than most in being able to arrange for the regular remission of funds from home; and for the rest, who can blame them if out of a loyal confidence in the King's ultimate triumph, which would allow

[1] Porter to Nicholas, 19 Jan. 1647; quoted by Dorothea Townshend, *Life and Letters of Endymion Porter*, 1897, p. 230.
[2] Fanshawe, p. 74.

them to repay their debts, they tried to relieve the tedium of exile with greater luxury than they could strictly afford? But many were so unfortunate that, like Endymion Porter, they shifted as best they could from day to day and trusted in God to survive.

At the time of his marriage Newcastle was living on credit, and the uncertainty of his means is shown by Margaret's story of how his steward came to him one day and told him that as his creditors flatly refused to make further advances there could be no dinner. Hiding his irritation, Newcastle turned to Margaret, whom he had taken to calling 'Peg', and told her 'in a pleasant humour' that if she wanted them to eat, she had better pawn her clothes.[1] No doubt alarmed at the idea of her original fashions going on the market, Margaret pointed out that little could be raised on clothes, and turning to her waiting-maid, Mistress Elizabeth Chaplain, she asked her to pawn some 'small toys' she had formerly given her. Mistress Chaplain obliged and dinner was served. The same day in the afternoon Newcastle called his creditors to him and spoke to them so civilly and persuasively that they not only agreed to resume his credit but to advance the money to redeem Mistress Chaplain's 'toys'. Newcastle's fluency in French—which he owed to his travels abroad as a young man in the suite of Sir Henry Wotton—had served him in good stead. The situation, however, was so serious that Margaret sent to her brother begging him to forward the little that was left of her portion, and Newcastle despatched his sons' governor, Mr. Benoist, to England to raise every penny he could. Benoist met with small success.

What was Newcastle doing with a steward in his necessity? The steward and the other domestics seem at first to have been an unnecessary expense, but they were in fact a financial asset. By keeping up his style, which his dignity was quite unable to dispense with anyway, Newcastle was far more likely to be trusted than if he had practised economy. His appearance suggested such self-confidence in his own prospects that he could not but

[1] *Life*, p. 56.

be accepted as a good risk, and once credit had been advanced, the only hope of its return seemed to be by the advance of more. When the creditors' patience was finally exhausted, as it was on the occasion of the dinner, he fell back on persuasion to show them the folly of cutting off their nose to spite their face, and dazzled them with the prospect of the return they might expect once his wealth had been restored. They always found his charm and his arguments irresistible. A second device which he used was to spend lavishly any money which came to hand; a display of extravagance, he found, was a wonderful restorative to creditors' nerves. But his position was always precarious, and until his last years of exile he was never free from anxiety.

His two sons, Charles and Henry, were sent back to England shortly after the episode of the dinner, in the hope that they would agree to make the rich matches which had been proffered to them, thereby relieving both their own and their father's want; but once in England, they both stated that they were unwilling to marry as yet and stayed on in the country, living as best they could. They were probably both glad to leave Paris, upset by the spectacle of their father doting on an independent young wife. Margaret herself always wrote in the most affectionate terms of her husband's children but her true attitude towards them, and her experience as a second wife, is betrayed in an opinion of hers on second marriages. 'It is to be observed,' she wrote, 'that when a second wife comes into a family, all the former children, or old servants, are apt to be factious, and do foment suspicions against her, making ill constructions of all her actions; were they never so well and innocently meant, yet they shall be ill taken; and all that they hinder her of, although it do them no good, but what is gotten from her, they think themselves enriched, not so much by what they get, but by what she loseth, or hath not.' [1]

The only member of Newcastle's family for whom she felt any deep sympathy—and her affection for him certainly bordered on love—was Newcastle's devoted brother, Sir Charles Cavendish.

[1] *Worlds Olio*, p. 81.

Sir Charles had the misfortune to be born so deformed and dwarfish in shape 'that it drew the eyes of men upon him', and so ugly in face that he was 'apter to raise contempt than application': 'but in this unhandsome or homely habitation,'—to transcribe Clarendon's fine phrase—'there was a mind and a soul lodged, that was very lovely and beautiful.' He had proved his courage and his loyalty to his handsome brother by fighting gallantly by his side in all his battles. After mentioning his bravery, Clarendon, who delighted in his conversation more than in that of any other man, continued his admirable character study in this style: 'But then the gentleness of his disposition, the humility and meekness of his nature, and the vivacity of his wit was admirable. He was so modest that he could hardly be prevailed with to enlarge himself on subjects he understood better than other men, except he were pressed by his very familiar friends, as if he thought it presumptuous to know more than handsomer men use to do. Above all, his virtue and piety was such that no temptation could work upon him to consent to anything that swerved in the least degree from the precise rules of honour, or the most severe rules of conscience.'[1] After such praise Margaret's own summary of his character will not read as exaggeration, though her love hurries her spontaneously forward without the grace of Clarendon, writing as always with a cautious eye to his sentences' shape. 'He was nobly generous, wisely valiant, naturally civil,' she began quickly, and maintained the pace; 'honestly kind, truly loving, virtuously temperate; his promise was like a fixed decree; his words were destiny, his life was holy, his disposition mild, his behaviour courteous, his discourse pleasing; he had a ready wit and a spacious knowledge, a settled judgement, a clear understanding, a rational insight.'[2]

Sir Charles's interests lay in science, particularly in mathematics, a field in which he himself showed ability, and he kept abreast of all the latest developments by corresponding with

[1] *Life of Edward Earl of Clarendon, written by himself,* 1857, i. 250.
[2] *Natures Pictures,* p. 378.

many of the leaders of the new philosophy on the Continent. As soon as he arrived in Paris he renewed his friendship with Thomas Hobbes, who had been resident in the city since 1641, and was able to send news of him to John Pell: 'I doubt it will be long ere Mr. Hobbes publish any thing,' he wrote on 1 May 1645; 'so far as I have read I like very well; he proceeds every day somewhat but he hath a great deal to do.' He was upset by Hobbes's antipathy to Descartes, with whom he was also on very friendly terms—' Mr. Hobbes is so averse from a friendship with Mr. de Cartes', he wrote in the same letter, ' that he would not see him when he was here '—but he at last forced him to confess the Frenchman ' to be a good geometrician '. Later he had the satisfaction of reporting that the two philosophers had met and talked, but he had also to admit that ' as they agree in some opinions so they extremely differ in others, as in the nature of hardness.' Among the other philosophers with whom he frequented in Paris were the astonishingly versatile Gassendi and Mersenne, one of the greatest of contemporary mathematicians. Sir Charles told Pell that he was ' much beholding ' to Gassendi ' for his visits and freedom of discourse '; and Mersenne, on his return from Italy, showed him the great rarities he had brought back, ' and doubtless he was a diligent inquisitor.'[1]

Newcastle was as interested in science as his brother but while Sir Charles's concern was that of a professional, skilled in its terminology and aware of its philosophical importance, Newcastle's was that of a virtuoso, attracted by its entertaining effects. The difference is clearly to be seen in their approach to the subject. Sir Charles set himself to study mathematics, seeking instruction from his famous friends, and won enough reputation for Hilarion de Coste, Mersenne's first biographer, to think it worth while mentioning that after Mersenne's death there were found in his study letters from ' le Chevalier Candysh '.[2] Newcastle occupied himself with purchasing perspective glasses with an extravagance little short of that which

[1] Brit. Mus., Birch Coll., 4278, ff. 205, 241, 273, 213.
[2] *La Vie du R. P. Marin Mersenne*, 1649, p. 96.

he showed in the matter of horses. While he lived in Paris, on the verge of bankruptcy, he owned no less than seven: four had been made by Eustacio Divino, the longest of which was ' 37 palms at least ' ; two by the famous Torricelli; one by Fontanus—presented to Newcastle by Sir Kenelm Digby; and at the time when Sir Charles described this observatory, the seventh was on the point of being dispatched by the maker, P. Reieta.[1]

As well as gazing at the stars through his battery of telescopes, Newcastle dabbled in chemistry, and he himself delightfully described one of his experiments, made at Bolsover before his exile with the help of his chaplain, Dr. Payn. Locking themselves up in a room, they set themselves to make *Lapis Prunellæ*, and as the mixture of saltpetre and brimstone flared in the crucible, Newcastle turned to his assistant and said excitedly: ' Mark it, Mr. Payn, the flame is pale, like the sun, and hath a violent motion in it like the sun.' Payn was struck by the comparison. ' It hath so,' he replied, ' and more to confirm you . . . look what abundance of little suns, round like a globe, appear to us everywhere, just the same motion as the sun makes in every- one's eyes! ' They concluded without any difficulty that ' the sun could be nothing else but a very solid body of salt and sulphur, inflamed by his own violent motion upon his own axis.' But as Newcastle held that all were ' but guessers ' in natural philosophy, why should he hesitate to be à-la-mode and set up for himself? The general conclusion he drew from his experi- ments and observations was that ' Salt is the life that giveth the motion to all things in the world.' [2]

Newcastle's interest in science appears highly comical in such experiments, but it was in fact sincere; and by the support of virtuosi like himself the real scientists were encouraged to persist in their remarkable discoveries. He was deeply respectful to all men of science—as indeed he was to all scholars and artists—

[1] Cavendish to Pell, 4/14 Feb. 1648; Brit. Mus., Birch Coll., 4278, f. 271.
[2] *Philosophical Opinions*, 1663, pp. 463, 460.

and entertained them at his table in Paris to discuss with them and his brother the latest opinions. Descartes dined with him at least twice, but as the philosopher could not speak English, Margaret learnt nothing from his conversation—and apart from the handicap of language, he seems to have said little; Margaret remarked that he appeared to her ' a man of the fewest words ' she had ever heard. [1] Hobbes often dined with her husband and though he usually did not talk philosophy at table, she heard him discuss two problems: whether man could ever be made to fly like birds, and whether there was any truth in witches. Newcastle took the lead in both these arguments. He proved in the first to his own satisfaction, and apparently to Hobbes's, that the human anatomy made flight impossible, and showed in the second with considerable shrewdness that witches were self-deluded into believing that they possessed diabolic power. Margaret said nothing on either of these occasions; bashfulness prevented her from joining in the conversation. She also listened silently to a discussion between Hobbes and Bishop Bramhall on free-will, the seed of a later public controversy on the subject between the two men.

She was not silent with her husband or with Sir Charles, however, and she gladly acknowledged that all she knew of science had been learnt from them, or from her own brother, John. They would explain things to her, the anatomy of some animal, for example, and as they told her how the various parts were composed, she would picture them in her mind and at once begin to speculate upon the ideas which the description called up. But the process, so typical of her character, is better given in her own words: ' Likewise if they should tell me all the parts of an animal body . . . I conceive it as perfectly to my understanding as if I had seen it dissected . . . for truly I have gathered more by piece-meals than from a full relation, or a methodical education for knowledge; but my fancy will build thereupon and make discourse therefrom, and so of everything they discourse of (I say they, that is my husband and brothers); for

[1] *Philosophical Opinions,* 1655, p. B3ᵛ.

the singularity of my affections are such, that though I have an ill memory [for] . . . anything long that I shall hear from strangers . . . when from my near friends (especially my Lord), whose discourses are lively descriptions, I cannot forget anything they say, such deep impressions their words print in my brain.' [1]

Newcastle treated Margaret's curiosity with affectionate tolerance, explaining problems to her to the best of his ability and seriously discussing her wildest speculations with her. Sir Charles was equally anxious to help her and found her ideas a constant source of amusement; but the sympathy between the two was so deep that she was content to entertain him. The verses she once wrote to him when he broke in upon her studies show their intimate understanding of each other:

> Sir Charles into my chamber coming in,
> When I was writing of my Fairy Queen:
> ' I pray,' said he, ' when Queen Mab you do see,
> Present my service to her Majesty;
> And tell her I have heard fame's loud report,
> Both of her beauty and her stately court.'
> When I Queen Mab within my fancy viewed,
> My thoughts bowed low, fearing I should be rude;
> Kissing her garment thin, which fancy made,
> Kneeling upon a thought, like one that prayed;
> In whispers soft I did present
> His humble service, which in mirth was sent.[2]

The years spent in Paris under the informal tuition of Newcastle and Sir Charles saw the real awakening of her intelligence, and when one considers her temperament, which could so easily have been crushed by neglect or contempt, and the general prejudice of the time against women showing an interest in anything other than the home, one can only conclude how singularly fortunate she was in her marriage.

Newcastle had not married her, however, to train her in

[1] *Ib.*, p. B1.
[2] *Poems*, pp. 213–4.

95

science but to be the mother of the sons he so eagerly anticipated, and when after two years she still showed no signs of pregnancy, he decided to try remedies and wrote to his old friend, Sir Theodore Mayerne, the greatest physician of the time, for advice. Mayerne had earlier treated Margaret and was familiar with her condition, and in his reply, after touching on her general ill-health, he discussed her barrenness wisely and humanely. 'Touching conception,' he wrote on 24 May 1648, 'I know not if in the estate she's in, you ought earnestly to desire it. It is hard to get children with good courage when one is melancholy, and after they are got and come into the world, they bring a great deal of pain with them; and after that very often one loses them, as I have tried to my great grief and am sorry to have had them. Be in good health and then you may till your ground, otherwise it will be time lost if you enter that race frowningly.' [1] After this sad opening, inspired by the recent death of his own son, Mayerne declined giving any specific advice for lack of detailed information on Margaret's present condition, but he thought that spa waters, those of Bourbon, for instance, might be taken to advantage. Disappointed by Mayerne, Newcastle consulted by letter with another English physician, Richard Farrer, but his 'Receipt for the Sterillitie in women', though a very witch's-brew of ingredients, was ineffectual.

Margaret herself was not openly distressed by her barrenness, though she would naturally have liked children for her husband's sake. Her practical attitude is shown by the comparison she once drew, for the benefit of a correspondent, between two barren women, both of whom wanted children. She felt sincerely sorry for the one, as her husband was the last of his line, but for the other, whose husband had already sons by a first wife, she would not be troubled. A woman has no reason, she wrote, ' to desire children for her own sake, for first her name is lost as to her particular in her marrying, for she quits her own, and is named

[1] A Booke, Wherein is Contained Rare Minerall Receipts; Nottingham Univ. Lib., Portland Papers.

as her husband; also her family, for neither name nor estate goes to her family . . . Also she hazards her life by bringing them into the world, and hath the greatest share of trouble in bringing them up.'[1] She was also highly contemptuous of the fuss raised by 'breeding women', and satirically averred that they were prouder of being big with child than of the child itself, witness the expense they went to in buying fine childbed-linen, swaddling-clothes, mantles, beds, cradles, baskets, hangings, cabinets, plates, artificial flowers, looking-glasses and screens—' besides their banquets of sweetmeats and other junkets, as cakes, wafers, biscuits, jellies and the like; as also such strong drinks as methinks the very smell should put a childbed-wife into a fever, as hippocras and burnt-wine, with hot spices, mulled sack, strong and high coloured ale, well spiced and stuffed with toasts of cake, and the like; all which is more chargeable than to bring up a child when it is born.'[2] How excellently she calls up the ostentatious and oppressive ceremony of the childbed, the only time in a seventeenth-century woman's life when she could taste the powers of privilege. As for Margaret herself, she was glad to be freed from the trouble of children and able to devote herself to her 'contemplations' and to the writing of her books, which, as she said, were her true offspring.

The first two years of the stay in Paris were the most precarious financially, but after Newcastle had skilfully dispensed £2,000, a gift from Henrietta Maria, among his creditors and had once more addressed them so persuasively that they felt honoured to renew his credit, his condition improved so much that he moved out of lodgings and took a furnished house. He was able once again to practise *haute école* and bought a Barbary horse for two hundred pistoles and a second for £100 from Lord Crofts, promising to pay him when he returned to England. He found his horses an excellent exercise and diversion.

But horsemanship and scientific discussion, and even the greater excitement of managing creditors, could not take his

[1] *Sociable Letters*, pp. 183–4.
[2] *Ib.*, p. 96.

M.F.

G

mind off the disastrous course of events in England. Margaret, too, was deeply distressed by the news from home. After Charles's surrender to the Scots in May 1646, which brought to an end the first Civil War, and during the period of negotiations between Parliament, the Army and the King, her family, along with the rest of the Royalists, was compelled to come to terms with the Government. All her brothers and brothers-in-law had to pay heavy compositions in order to save what they could of their estates. The reports of their losses, however, were far outweighed by the news of the death in 1647 of her eldest sister, Mary Killigrew, who died for grief of the loss of her daughter. Six months or so later, Margaret learnt that her mother, too, had died: 'and by her dying, one might think death was enamoured with her, for he embraced her in a sleep, and so gently as if he were afraid to hurt her.' [1] Worse was to follow.

Charles's policy after the Scots had surrendered him to Parliament in February 1647 was to attempt to play off Parliament against the Army and to secure the support of the faction of Scottish presbyterians led by the Duke of Hamilton. At the time a royalist reaction was sweeping the country and plans were laid for a rising in England, under the command of the Earl of Holland, to correspond with an invasion by Hamilton's army. The rising was at first successful. Berwick and Carlisle were seized for the King; and the royalists were greatly encouraged by the revolt of part of the parliamentarian fleet, which sailed for Holland to put itself under the command of the young Duke of York, titular Lord High Admiral of England, who had recently escaped abroad from imprisonment in St. James's Palace.

As soon as the news of the fleet's arrival at Helvoetsluys reached Paris, Prince Charles set out to join it on 25 June, accompanied by many of the royalist exiles. Newcastle himself was particularly desired by Henrietta Maria to accompany her son but was unable to move for his debts. The difficulty was solved by the Queen's engaging herself for them, even though she herself was almost reduced to beggary at the time—pointing

[1] *Natures Pictures*, p. 377.

to a gold cup, she told a friend that that was all the gold she had. But Newcastle was still unable to move for want of ready money, and not until he had borrowed a further £300 or £400, which included a loan of a hundred pistoles from Thomas Hobbes, was he ready to set out. His train was made up of a coach, which held Lord Widdrington, Sir Charles and a few others, three waggons, and 'an indifferent number of servants on horseback.' Newcastle and Margaret travelled by themselves in a little chariot. The coach was a new one, which Newcastle had just had specially made. His creditors may have been encouraged by the sight of it when they gathered on the day of his departure to express their great 'love and kindness for him, accompanied with so many hearty prayers and wishes, that he could not but prosper on his journey.' [1] There can never have been a more popular and respected debtor.

His journey to Holland was attended with almost as much ceremony as his progress south three years earlier. He arrived at Cambrai in the dark, but the Spanish governor had him met by torches to light him to his lodgings, offered him the keys of the city and requested him to give the password for the night. He had also prepared a banquet for him, and when Newcastle declined it on grounds of fatigue and the late hour, he sent the provisions to Newcastle's lodgings and even ordered the landlord not to charge. Newcastle was treated with equal civility at every town he passed through, and arriving at Antwerp he took a boat to Rotterdam, where lodgings had been made ready for him in the house of Mrs. Beynham, the widow of a royalist merchant.

At Rotterdam, where he arrived about 1 August, Newcastle learnt that Prince Charles had already sailed on 22 July with the fleet for the Downs, and he at once made preparations to follow him. 'Coming so near you', Sir Charles wrote on 2 August to John Pell at Breda,[2] 'I cannot but trouble you with this letter, since I doubt I shall not have the happiness to see you at this

[1] *Life*, p. 59.
[2] Brit. Mus., Birch Coll., 4278, f. 273.

99

time, our stay here being, as I suppose, but very short; hastening all we may after our noble Prince.' The only way to follow the Prince was to hire a boat, which Newcastle did and proceeded to victual it; but Margaret was so distressed by the uncertainty of such a voyage that, protesting it would be as hopeless as looking for a needle in a 'bottle of hay', she persuaded him against it. Lord Widdrington and Sir William Throckmorton, however, set out to sea in the vessel, but after being driven by a storm towards Scotland, returned without having found the Prince.

Newcastle continued to make all the preparations he could in readiness against the expected summons to England. He lived at very great expense and kept an open table for all comers, especially 'such as were excellent soldiers, and noted commanders of war', hoping by his hospitality to attract them into offering their services to the King once the royalists in England had succeeded in establishing a bridgehead. It was a time of excitement and optimism; at last fortune seemed to have changed and home lay immediately ahead.

The Prince and his fleet sailed into Helvoetsluys on 1 September, narrowly beating Warwick and the parliamentarian fleet in a race for the port; and slowly the whole disastrous news became known. Everywhere the unco-ordinated royalist risings had failed—in Wales and in Kent; and the Earl of Holland's attempt to secure London had proved equally ineffectual. He had taken the field unprepared at the beginning of July and had been completely routed at Kingston-on-Thames. Worst of all, Hamilton's invasion had ended horribly at Preston on 17 August, and the survivors of the untrained Scottish army were being sold as slaves to the planters of Virginia and Barbados. Later news bore heavily on Margaret. After the Kentish royalists had been crushed by Fairfax, the remnant fled into Essex, where they were joined by others under the command of Sir Charles Lucas and Sir George Lisle. The combined forces threw themselves into Colchester and defended it against Fairfax's army from 12 June until its surrender on 27 August.

Lucas and Lisle conducted the defence with extraordinary severity: the lack of supplies, the want of means to treat the wounded, the utter starvation of the mutinous civilians; nothing could weaken their determination to hold the town, daily more ruined by the enemy's fire. Fanaticism and heroism contended equally in them. St. John's Abbey itself was taken by the besiegers and, finding nothing in it to loot, they ' exercised their brutal rage upon the bare walls, for there was nothing else that remained, this being one of the first houses in England which suffered by that fatal liberty of the subject.' Their next action shows how the ferocities and brutalities of the siege had destroyed all decency and piety: both officers and men broke open the tombs of the Lucas family in St. Giles's Church, and finding the undecomposed bodies of both Elizabeth Lucas and her daughter, Mary Killigrew, they cut off their hair and wore it in their hats, scattering the other corpses' bones about ' with profane jests.'[1] When all means of defence, and of life itself, were exhausted, Lucas and Lisle surrendered the city, and after being tried by court martial, they were both summarily shot, dying with the utmost grace and gallantry. Their deaths were a stain on Fairfax's good name which has never been completely removed.

The shock of her brother's death, heightened as it was by the collapse of all the hopes built up in the previous months, deeply affected Margaret and helped to undermine her health. She wrote several poems to her brother's memory.

> Dear blessed soul, though thou art gone, yet lives
> Thy fame on earth, and men thee praises give.
> But all 's too small, for thy heroic mind
> Was above all the praises of mankind.[2]

These conventional lines make the conclusion of one poem; another refers to the legend that no grass would ever grow where the blood of Lucas and Lisle was spilt.

[1] *H M C, 12 Rep., Pt. ix*, 1891, pp. 27–8.
[2] *Poems*, p. 196.

But the full brunt of these personal sorrows was prevented by the difficulties in which Newcastle now found himself. As soon as he had arrived in Rotterdam he had begun living in the expectation of a reversion of good fortune, and by keeping open table, hiring the vessel and engaging in other extravagances, he had spent all the £2,000 advanced by the Marquis of Hertford and the Earl of Devonshire between them, and a further £1,000 borrowed in Rotterdam itself. The only immediate hope of relief was the bounty of Prince Charles, who had returned from his voyage with some prizes taken from merchant shipping in the mouth of the Thames. On 23 September Newcastle wrote to Robert Long asking for £1,000 promised him by the Prince that he might not starve;[1] but the Prince had many other demands to meet, and as the sale of the prizes fetched much less than their value, it is doubtful whether Newcastle was paid.

Realizing at last that no return to England could now be hoped for, Newcastle decided to remove elsewhere, and after travelling to the Hague to say farewell to the Prince and to assure him of his unfaltering loyalty, he quitted Rotterdam for Antwerp: a fine city comparatively unfrequented by royalist exiles, where he might hope to find credit and live decently and cheaply. On his arrival in Antwerp he had to put up at an inn, but Endymion Porter, who had also taken refuge in the city, 'being not willing that a person of such quality . . . should lie in a public house,'[2] insisted that he should move into his own lodgings. After searching the city for a suitable house, Newcastle at length came upon Rubens's unoccupied mansion and was able to rent it from the painter's widow. At the same time an opportune loan of £200 from William Aylesbury, out of a sum held by him on account with the Duke of Buckingham, whose tutor he had been, allowed Newcastle to establish his credit in the city, and he was able to move his household, now very much reduced in numbers, from Rotterdam. 'I also thought it not amiss to let you know', Sir Charles wrote to Pell on 24 October, 'we are now at Antwerp.

[1] *H M C, Pepys MSS.*, 1911, p. 228.
[2] *Life*, p. 63.

and likely to remain here till it shall please God to reduce the affairs of England to such a condition of peace or war as may become honest men to return home.'[1] Sir Charles had returned to England and died long before these conditions obtained, but Newcastle made his home in Antwerp until the Restoration.

Charles I was executed on 30 January 1649, and when the news reached the Continent, spreading horror among the royalist exiles, it helped to strengthen Newcastle's determination to reside permanently in Antwerp. A return to Paris was out of the question in view of conditions in France, on the eve of the war of the Fronde. Apart from his loyalty, which would never have allowed him to compromise with the King's enemies, he was too notorious ever to be permitted to return to England by Parliament. Later in the year he learnt that he had been proscribed and banished on 14 March, that he was to incur the death penalty should he return, and that his estates had been confiscated. Even his optimism and cheerfulness began to falter under this constant ill-fortune.

The strain of the previous year now began to tell seriously on Margaret's health, adding to Newcastle's worries, and once again Sir Theodore Mayerne's advice had to be sought. The century saw great advances in medicine, and interest in it was widespread. Each family had its book of recipes and its favourite panacea, and the course of a sickness and the remedies taken were one of the staples of every correspondence. Margaret's own interest in medicine, and the various theories which she had formed on the subject, led her to disregard her doctors' advice whenever it ran contrary to her own opinions and to prescribe freely for herself, much to Mayerne's irritation. 'But I believe that to cure my lady Marquesse, your wife, will be yet harder,' Mayerne wrote on 22 May 1649, 'not so much for the nature of the disease, which is rebellious, as for the disposition of the patient, who will not willingly submit to the counsel of her physicians, be they never so good and so skilful.' He particularly criticized her habit of purging and bleeding herself, 'and without

[1] Brit. Mus., Birch Coll., 4278, f. 278.

doubt too much, since it hath been done by her own directions, as often at least as by the advice of her physicians, a thing to be noted but not imitated.' She herself was proud of her ability to prescribe effectively and has a long story to tell of how one of her servants, sick of a fever, was let blood three times under her directions, the colour of the blood each time confirming her diagnosis of the course of the illness. The servant recovered.

Mayerne was writing from Chelsea, but he seldom visited his patients to examine them even when they were close at hand; as Slingsby said, he was fat and rich and a knight, and his patients came to him and were received in his study, which was lined with books and hung with pictures. Once he had accepted a patient, he used to note the disease and the remedies prescribed, and if his services were needed later, he simply looked up the record and recommended a prescription. As he had already treated Margaret, he felt able to recommend a course of physic, knowing well enough, as he said, her indisposition.

Mayerne's method at first seems arbitrary and dangerous, but his wisdom and knowledge were so great that his prescriptions could be more safely and effectively followed than those of many physicians who attended their patients in person. His ability is shown in the sensible course which he recommended Margaret to take. She could, if she chose, use one of her favourite cures, a laxative, but it must be a mild one: ' senna, rhubarb, agaric, syrop of roses compounded, fumitory and the like '—' for by too often scouring a kettle it is at last worn out to holes ', he commented. As for the letting of blood, her other favourite remedy, he would not allow it, thinking that she had already let herself too much; but he permitted her to use leeches if she was set upon phlebotomy. He advised her strongly to drink, with due care and under the direction of a physician, the Spanish waters—liquorice—and, when the autumn came, steel—a popular chalybeate medicine. These were all tried medicines and not to be compared to one recommended by Richard Farrer, who was also consulted on Margaret's health. His dose, he admitted, might not be ' so pleasing to fair ladies as being of excrements of a ram, which she needs not know and then she will not be troubled.' Mayerne ended his letter by remarking shrewdly, ' But I am afraid that my Lady will do nothing at all, or shall do it by piecemeals according to her custom.' [1]

Margaret's illness was melancholy, a superfluity of black bile; and Mayerne accurately diagnosed its cause when he wrote in another letter, ' a sedentary life is absolutely bad for her health, and if she will be a philosopher, I could wish her to be a peripatetic.' [2] She was incorrigibly lazy in body and stirred out of the house with the greatest reluctance; but in order to counter the lack of exercise, which at the most amounted to walking slowly up and down her chamber ' whilst her thoughts ran apace in her brain ', she was sparing in her diet, usually drinking only water and eating boiled chicken or other light foods. But the precariousness of her life fretted her and many of her ailments were imaginary, being suggested by worry; and Newcastle, as shrewd in his way as Mayerne, said as much in his explanation of how she came to be so familiar with medical terms: ' But would you know how we know the great mystery of these physical terms, I am almost ashamed to tell you; not that we have been ever sickly, but by melancholy often supposed ourselves to have such diseases as we had not, and learned physicians were too wise to put us out of that humour, and so these terms cost us much more than they are worth.' [3]

Residence in Antwerp, however pleasant, brought no immediate relief from the most pressing need, want of money; and at the end of 1649 Newcastle was writing despairingly to a foreign nobleman who had befriended him to complain of the meanness of his English friends, who, he had found, were ' friends only to prosperity but not to misery.' [4] The position of all the royalist exiles at this time was desperate; the young King

[1] A Booke, Wherein is Contained Rare Minerall Receipts, Nottingham Univ. Lib., Portland Papers.
[2] Quoted by R. W. Goulding, *Margaret Duchess of Newcastle*, 1925, p. 16.
[3] *Philosophical Opinions*, 1655, p. A2.
[4] Newcastle to an unnamed correspondent, 30 Oct. 1649; Nottingham Univ. Lib., Portland Papers, Cavendish Misc. 67.

was isolated on Jersey for want of any other place to live, and the Queen Mother was enduring great hardship and poverty in Paris, cut off from the help of the French court by the war of the Fronde. The only hope seemed to lie in the Scots, who had again opened negotiations with the King.

The better to discuss the terms they offered, Charles removed from Jersey to Breda, arriving there on 26 March 1650. Newcastle at once left Antwerp to join him and was sworn into the Privy Council. He was one of the councillors who urged Charles to accept the Scots' harsh terms, with the intention that he should break his word as soon as he was in power. ' You have a very precious junta to determine concerning three kingdoms; ' Hyde wrote contemptuously to Secretary Nicholas; ' you will find the Marquis of Newcastle a very lamentable man, and as fit to be a general as a bishop.' [1] Hyde was, with excellent reason, staunchly anti-Scottish, and this policy, which seemed to him to sacrifice both religion and honour for uncertain help, filled him with scorn for all those who advised it. Newcastle tried to persuade the Scots to make concessions, but when he visited the Earl of Cassilis, the principal Scottish negotiator, he was only rebuked by the presbyterian Earl for his habitual swearing, ' and sent home with this good counsel for his conscience.' [2]

Charles at last conceded all the Scots' demands as the only way of returning to his kingdoms and set sail for Scotland on 2 June. Newcastle was not allowed to accompany him as the Scots held him to be, along with many others of Charles's most devoted subjects, a notorious malignant. His part in the sordid intrigues which followed Charles's landing was consequently limited to correspondence, but in the following year when Charles prepared to march into England, he tried his best to raise foreign help, and nearly succeeded in securing the service of troops raised by the Elector of Brandenburg and the Duke of Neuberg, which were to be transported in Danish ships. But this scheme was brought to nothing by events in England; the royalist plot for an

[1] *Clarendon State Papers*, iii. 20.
[2] Quoted by Eva Scott, *The King in Exile*, 1905, p. 136.

English rising was betrayed, and Charles's Scottish army, after a dispiriting march south, was utterly defeated at Worcester on 3 September.

After famous adventures Charles escaped to France, and when the news of his safe arrival reached Newcastle, 'never any subject rejoiced more than he did.' These rejoicings might as well have been the merriment at a wake. Newcastle could not even cheat his misery now with the prospect of a miracle; 'as I am a good protestant,' he had written two years earlier, 'I believe miracles are ceased';[1] and the events of 1651 confirmed him in his belief. His condition was indeed so desperate that as early as May 1649 Charles had advised him to preserve what he could of his estates in England; and writing from Scotland on 5 December 1650 the Duke of Buckingham had advised him in answer to his request for help to make his peace in England, 'for certainly your Lordship's suffering for the King has been great enough to excuse you if you look a little after yourself now, when neither he is able to assist you, nor you in a possibility of doing him service.'[2] Buckingham's advice, so typical of his character, was unthinkable, but if Newcastle was to survive, he knew that he must temporize to some extent with his conscience. The extreme poverty of Newcastle and his household at this time is shown by Clarendon's remark that upon meeting Sir Charles Cavendish in Antwerp he noticed that he was 'in very visible want of ordinary conveniences.'[3] After receiving the news of the King's arrival in France in October, Newcastle decided to send Margaret to England to raise funds and to salvage what she could from his estates.

[1] See above, p. 105, n. 4.
[2] *H M C, 13 Rep., Pt. ii*, 1893, ii. 138.
[3] Clarendon, *Life*, i. 251.

6 The Poet and Her Fancies

Surely those that delight not in poetry or music have no divine souls.

Sir Charles Cavendish had compounded for his estates as early as 1649, but after it had been represented that he was beyond seas at the time of his composition and a 'very dangerous person', they were again sequestered in March 1651. If anything was to be saved, it was essential that he should return to England with Margaret, a course which ran so counter to his loyalty that he was persuaded to adopt it by Edward Hyde only after many arguments. At last Hyde's advice and his brother's plight, and no doubt his reluctance to let Margaret travel by herself, prevailed, and they set sail together for England in the first week of November 1651.

They had so little money between them for the journey that once they had landed they were forced to break their journey at Southwark. Sir Charles sent into London for a man who had formerly been his steward and, after explaining his predicament, asked him to try his credit; but the man pretended that his credit was too small to be useful, and Sir Charles was forced to pawn his watch. The incident was an omen of the difficulties and neglect they were to experience. As soon as the score at Southwark was settled, they proceeded into London, where lodgings had been prepared for them in Covent Garden, and Margaret was at last reunited with her family after an absence of eight years.

The first business was to try immediately to secure a portion of her husband's estates for her maintenance. She asked her brother, Lord Lucas, to claim on her behalf and together they appeared before the Committee for Compounding at Goldsmith's Hall on 10 December.[1] The Committee's answer to their

[1] *C S P D, Calendar of the Proceedings of the Committee for Compounding,* pp. 1733-4.

petition was that Margaret was not entitled to any part of her husband's estate, as she had married him since he became a delinquent and consequently possessed no estate at the time. The Commissioners added unmannerly that she should have no allowance anyway, as Newcastle was 'the greatest traitor to the state'. She was so upset by their hostility that she was unable to say a word and whispered to her brother to take her away. This was the only occasion when she appeared as a petitioner, but rumours were put about that she was haunting Parliament and various committees in the hope of relief; rumours which she later angrily denounced as lies.

Sir Charles was more fortunate. He was able to compound for his estates, though only with difficulty: in order to prevent his composition his enemies reported, for example, that he had kissed the King's hands at Breda. As the brother of a notorious royalist he could not hope to escape lightly, and while the investigations were continuing he had to live on credit; but credit was hard to find, even among friends, until his estates were discharged—'so much is misery and poverty shunned!' as Margaret remarked.[1] The composition was at last fixed at £4,500 but an additional fine of £500 was later imposed, 'which was more than many others had paid for much greater estates'[2]; and to pay the fines Sir Charles was compelled to sell land at less than its value.

These worries were augmented by the news from Antwerp that Newcastle's credit had been stopped and that he was in danger of starvation and imprisonment unless quickly relieved. Sir Charles managed to raise £200 and forward it to him, but before it arrived Newcastle had fallen back on the stratagem which had served him so well in Paris. Calling his creditors to him, he laid his condition before them so frankly and spoke so persuasively that they swore he should not want if they could help it, and promptly arranged for his further subsistence while he lived among them. His position was now more comfortable abroad than his wife's and brother's at home.

[1] *Life*, p. 72.
[2] *Ib.*, p. 73.

While she lived in London Margaret seldom went out of her lodgings. She paid few visits and entertained only occasionally: Hobbes, whom she once met in the street, was invited to dinner but civilly declined. Her principal diversions were to listen to music at Henry Lawes's house, where she went attended by Sir Charles, and to take the air in Hyde Park in company with her sisters. Her few appearances abroad, however, were the beginning of her reputation for eccentricity, especially for eccentricity in dress, rumour dressing her ' in a hundred several fashions '. She later indignantly denied that she had spent her time in exhibiting her fashions, though she admitted that when she visited or entertained, she endeavoured to dress to her ' best becoming '.[1] However few her appearances were, they were more effective than she imagined, and Dorothy Osborne learnt in the seclusion of Chicksands of the extravagance of her dress.

To divert herself in her loneliness she began to write—a greater eccentricity in the opinion of her contemporaries than any originality in dress. She had always spent much of her time in writing—there were the dozen or so ' baby-books ' of her childhood to prove her early devotion to letters, and after her marriage she had written many short essays or opinions, which she was later to collect and publish; but for the first time she now began to write with the object of publication. She chose poetry, and once started she composed rapidly and found in composition some relief from worry and sleepless nights, broken by melancholy speculations on her husband's condition. She strove to turn the stream of her sad thoughts by going to the well of Helicon, she wrote, rather than by following ' the muddy and foul ways of vice.' [2]

Her guide to the well of Helicon was her instinctive love of poetry. ' Poetry is so powerful, and hath such an attractive beauty,' she wrote, ' that those that can but view her perfectly could not but be enamoured, her charms do so force affection. But surely those that delight not in poetry or music have no

[1] *Natures Pictures*, p. 382.
[2] *Poems*, p. A7ᵛ.

divine souls, nor harmonious thoughts.' [1] Whenever she considered the idea of poetry she was enraptured by it; and attributing to it a power to compose chaos, she held that poets and philosophers—for the two were one in her mind—were not only the wisest of men, 'having so deep an insight as to pierce even into the secrets of nature', but the happiest, 'having all the delights of the mind.' [2] But to give an impression of her reverence for poetry in words other than her own would be to obscure her touching simplicity. Poetry 'is the finest work that Nature hath made'—and once the statement was uttered her eloquence began to mount in an attempt to match the loftiness of the subject—'for it animates the spirits to devotion, it fires the spirits to action, it begets love, it abates hate, it tempers anger, it assuageth grief, it easeth pain, increaseth joy, allays fear, and sweetens the whole life of man, by playing so well upon the brain as it strikes the strings of the heart with delight, which makes the heart to dance and keeps the mind in tune, whereby the thoughts move equally in a round circle where Love sits in the midst as mistress, and judges. [3] 'Sure the poor woman is a little distracted,' wrote Dorothy Osborne when she heard that Margaret had published her poems; 'she could never be so ridiculous else as to venture at writing books and in verse too.' [4] How starched her sober words appear beside the unguarded eloquence of Margaret's enthusiasm. Distracted she was, certainly, but distracted as the fire is by the wind that fans it from an ember into a trembling blaze; and without its flames how chill the world would be, warmed by no more than its natural heat.

Inspired by this conception of poetry, Margaret spent the whole of 1652 writing verse. She wrote under every disadvantage, and the heaviest were those of education and temperament. She was simply uneducated. The 'ancient

[1] *Natures Pictures*, p. 365.
[2] *Sociable Letters*, pp. 21–2.
[3] *Worlds Olio*, p. 65.
[4] *Letters of Dorothy Osborne*, ed. G. C. Moore Smith, 1928, p. 37.

decayed gentlewoman ', her childhood's teacher, had given her some elementary instruction but had been quite incapable of training her to spell or to write grammatically. And if her schooling had not reached as far as those rudiments, it had stopped well short of the art of poetry. She could have made up these deficiencies by paying attention to what she read, but she read for the spirit only and entirely neglected the form. She wrote in the same manner as she read. She was always in such hot pursuit of the idea that to pause was unbearable, and rather than correct what she had composed, she let it pass in the hope that errors had been avoided by instinct. Her excuse for this habit was at least honest: 'for besides that I want also the skill of scholarship and true writing, I did many times not peruse the copies that were transcribed, lest they should disturb my following conceptions; by which neglect . . . many errors are slipped into my works.'[1]

Once they were unkindly pointed out, she excused herself for her many errors by generally asserting that it was rather by the spirit than by the form that any work should be judged; or she offered separate excuses for particular faults. As for spelling, she admitted that she could not spell and thought it was 'against nature for a woman to spell right'; and as for grammar, she confessed that she was unable to understand it, but that the little she did know was enough to make her 'renounce it': 'I do perceive no strong reason to contradict but that everyone may be his own grammarian,' she continued wildly in her annoyance at the last charge, 'if by his natural grammar he can make his hearers understand his sense; for though there must be rules in a language to make it sociable, yet those rules may be stricter than need to be, and to be too strict makes them to be too unpleasant and uneasy. But language should be like garments, for though every particular garment hath a general cut, yet their trimmings may be different, and not go out of the fashion.' And as for the charge that she disregarded the rules of poetry, she could only attempt to dismiss it by retaliating on her critics: 'it were worse

[1] *Life*, p. (b).

112

to be a pedantic woman than a pedantic man; yet so ill it is in a man that it doth as it were degrade him from being magnanimous and heroic.'[1] Her vigorous defence, however, cannot hide her pain at the criticisms of a ' carping age ', and as she grew older she took more care over such details, even to the extent of thoroughly revising her poetry to meet the objections. The revisions were technically an improvement but, as they were insufficient in themselves to raise her poetry higher, they hindered the sincerity and spontaneity of her expression by their superficial polish. Rough and ragged though they are, her poems are to be preferred in their earlier shape.

She wrote at all hours of the day and night in her lodgings in Covent Garden, and her habit of starting from bed to note a thought gave rise to the story that she would summon her secretary on such occasions with the cry of ' John, I conceive '— John can only have been her husband's secretary John Rolleston: a fact which makes the story apocryphal. As she paced the room in time to her ' contemplations' and spoke her lines aloud, especially those that were ' sad, serious and melancholy ', before writing them down—finding that words first spoken marched more regularly from her pen on to 'the ground of white paper'[2] —Margaret relied primarily on her own genius. Her knowledge of earlier poetry was narrow. She mentions only five poets by name: Ovid—whom she knew only in Sandys's translation— Shakespeare, Jonson, Donne and Davenant. We can assume that she had also read Spenser, Daniel and Drayton; and her own writings show on every page that she had fallen, like the young Dryden, under the soporific influence of Sylvester's Du Bartas—a kind of poetry that Dryden was later to make fun of; a kind that viewed nature through the distorting glass of the unnatural conceit.

Of the poets whom she names, Ovid and Donne are praised only in passing for their wit, but Shakespeare and Davenant are criticized at some length. Davenant's *Gondibert* was not

[1] *Worlds Olio*, pp. 93–4.
[2] *Natures Pictures*, p. 384.

113

published until 1651, but as early as March 1650 the poet, who had served as Lieutenant-General of the Ordnance in Newcastle's army, sent Newcastle a printed copy of the famous preface, bound together with Hobbes's equally famous reply [1]; and the arguments of the two critics must have been thoroughly discussed by Newcastle and his brother. Margaret's criticism of *Gondibert* may partly repeat what she had heard them say, but it is sufficiently well expressed to suggest that she at least made their ideas her own. She praised the characters and the action of the poem for their imitation of nature, containing as they did neither 'impossibilities nor improbabilities', but she thought the diction and descriptions too laboured, 'for the language is like so curious and finely engraven a seal as one cannot readily see the figure engraven therein without a magnifying glass; or like as many several figures so curiously cut as to be all in the compass of a cherry stone, wherein they cannot be distinguished without often perusal.' [2] This fault alone, in her opinion, prevented *Gondibert* from being a precedent for all heroic poems.

Her criticism of Shakespeare is more important. It is one of the earliest of Shakespeare critiques, and is also an excellent piece of shrewd and enthusiastic writing. She began by scornfully refuting the opinion of someone who had ventured to dispraise Shakespeare's plays as being made up only of 'clowns, fools, watchmen, and the like.' To describe such persons well, she wrote, is as hard as to describe people of higher rank; but Shakespeare is not confined to those low types; he can describe anyone, and does it so well that one might imagine he had temporarily become that person, even to the extent of metamorphosing himself into a woman. [3] And his tragic spirit at least equals his comic: 'he presents passions so naturally, and mis-

---

[1] I 'haue [not] heard from Mr: Hobbes a longe time but Sr: William Dauenant latelie sent my Brother a Preface, to an intended poem of his not yet printed; but the preface printed & directed to Mr: Hobbes, with Mr: Hobbs his answear to it, likewise printed & bound together' (Cavendish to John Pell, 1 March 1650; Brit. Mus., Birch Coll., 4278, f. 295).

[2] *Sociable Letters*, p. 258.

[3] *Ib.*, pp. 244-7.

fortunes so probably, as he pierces the souls of his readers with such a true sense and feeling thereof, that it forces tears through their eyes, and almost persuades them they are really actors, or at least present at those tragedies.' Once begun, she could hardly restrain her enthusiasm for the poet who had such a 'clear judgement, a quick wit, a spreading fancy, a subtle observation, a deep apprehension, and a most eloquent elocution.' Considering his critics, she could only conclude passionately that they were moved by envy.

As these remarks on Davenant and Shakespeare show, she was not without critical discrimination, and had she only taken the time to consider closely the form of the poetry to whose spirit she responded so keenly, she might have been able to give her own verse the shape and elegance which its genuine inspiration deserved. Her poems are too chaotic as they stand to illustrate clearly any particular influence of other poets, but the shadows of those whom she had read fall vaguely across her lines everywhere.

Her theory of poetry—if the one or two direct remarks she made on the nature of poetry can be dignified as a theory—stressed, as one would expect, the poet's originality. The ground of poetry, she wrote, is 'distinguishment and similizing', that is to say, 'judgement and fancy; as for numbers, rhyme and rhetoric, they are but the several accoutrements, but no part of the body of poetry.' Fancy was all important: 'descriptions are to imitate, and fancy to create; for fancy is not an imitation of nature but a natural creation, which I take to be the true poetry.'[1] But these remarks were not really arrived at by reasoning on poetry; they were an attempt to justify her instinctive attitude to poetry by employing the terms current at the time, learnt in her case from the discussions at home centering on the preface to *Gondibert*.

As she wrote her poems, she had them transcribed—her handwriting and spelling made this essential: one can only sympathize deeply with her succession of secretaries, one of whom died at his post—and tried to arrange them into a sort of order.

[1] *Natures Pictures*, p. 349.

The collection as it was published begins with a number of verses devoted to natural philosophy, but it very soon wanders from this world into others of her own imagining; and as she ascends on fancy, her poetry gains in strength as it is freed from the tyranny of inexorable facts.

The first group sets out an atomic theory of matter. As she was soon to dispense with atoms as the basis of her scientific thought, it is hardly necessary to labour the details of the theory. The principle is simple enough to be quickly summarized. Atoms are of four several shapes, flat, round, long, and pointed, which correspond to the four elements they constitute, earth, water, air, and fire. Everything can be explained by a little ingenious adaptation of this idea—but an illustration will make the method clear. The atoms of air are long and hollow and pliant, and interweave 'like to a spider's web'; but the atoms of earth are flat, solid and sluggish. The consequence to the earth is set out in these verses:

> Why earth's not apt to move, but slow and dull,
> Is atoms flat no vacuum hath, but full.
> That form admits no empty place to bide;
> All parts are fill'd, having no hollow side;
> And where no vacuum is, motion is slow,
> Having no empty places for to go.

Her application of the theory resembles nothing so much as a child playing with a meccano set, certain basic pieces being used to construct all manner of things. Why do some bodies last longer than others?—because the atoms are more closely compacted and therefore less easily dispersed. What is a dropsy? for diseases, too, have an atomic explanation—a conglomeration of the round atoms of water, which drowns other atoms of different shapes. How does water quench fire?—the round atoms riddle the sharp atoms' ranks like cannon-balls. How does fire act?—the sharp atoms work through the flat ones like mice nibbling into a cheese. What makes the sea roar? The answer is charming: the watery atoms are spherical and hollow, and as they are stirred by the tides or the winds, they clash together like cymbals.

Set out in this manner the theory seems ridiculous, however engaging; but given the climate of scientific thought at the time, it is not as absurd as it may at first appear. Reading through the works of the seventeenth-century natural philosophers who founded our knowledge, we can find speculations which superficially resemble those advanced by Margaret; and in the writings of the lesser men, who had the advantage of education and the opportunities for discussion denied to her, worlds are disclosed which approximate no closer to reality than hers. She thought, for example, that the earth's magnetic force could be explained by the emission of sharp atoms which transfixed the duller ones and returned home with them like laden bees making for the hive; but her friend, Dr. Walter Charleton, a most intelligent man, explained the properties of the magnet on a similar system of hooked atoms, and postulated as well atoms of divers shapes to account for other phenomena. She explained the sparks which can be struck from a flint by supposing that the sharp atoms were imprisoned by the sluggish ones until released by friction, and her explanation was at least plausible until Robert Hooke published twenty years later his microscopical observations on the particles dropped by a flint when fire is struck from it.

The smallness of atoms caused her to wonder if there might not be other worlds within this world, arranged in size like a nest of Chinese boxes and inhabited by creatures as diminutive as atoms. Once the speculation was broached, she immediately began to imagine a world in a ear-ring, worn by some lady quite unconscious of her responsibility. Within this suspended world the seasons might take their course, the minute inhabitants conduct their affairs and even be overtaken by calamities, without a murmur being overheard by the wearer:

> There meadows be and pastures fresh and green,
> And cattle feed and yet be never seen;
> And gardens fresh, and birds which sweetly sing,
> Although we hear them not in an ear-ring.

Such a world would be horribly exposed to chance, for ' when the ring is broke, the world is done.'

These poems approach very close to faerie, and a later group is devoted to celebrating the kingdom directly. Margaret belonged to the people whom Drayton described in his induction to *Nymphidia*:

> Another sort there be, that will
> Be talking of the fairies still,
> Nor never can they have their fill,
>   As they were wedded to them;
> No tales of them their thirst can slake,
> So much delight therein they take,
> And some strange thing they fain would make,
>   Knew they the way to do them.

She knew how to feign some strange thing about the fairies, and after a prose introduction to justify the plausibility of their existence, she turned to a description of the Fairy Queen. Drayton hung the palace of his Fairy Queen in mid-air between the earth and the moon, and briefly attributed its suspension to the powers of necromancy; but Margaret situated the kingdom of her Queen in the centre of the earth and gave a long pseudo-scientific description of its wonders:

> The axle-tree whereon the earth turns round
> Is one great diamond, by opinion found,
> And the two ends, which called are the Poles,
> Are pointed diamonds.

There are other more conventional marvels:

> 'Tis true there are no birds to sing sweet notes,
> But there are winds that whistle like birds' throats;
> Whose sounds and notes, by variation, oft
> Make better music than the spheres aloft.

But the insistence upon the scientific illustrates remarkably how far the age had travelled in an imaginative absorption of the new discoveries since Shakespeare, Drayton and Herrick—Margaret's principal precursors in fairy poetry—had written.

After describing the geography of the kingdom, Margaret rehearsed the pastimes of the Queen when she is at home:

> . . . she doth sit under a flower
> To shade her from the moonshine bright,
> Where gnats do sing for her delight;
> Some high, some low, some tenor strain,
> Making a consort very plain . . .
> Then to her dinner she goes straight,
> Where everyone in order wait;
> And on a mushroom there is spread
> A cover fine of spider's web . . .
> When dined, she calls to take the air
> In coach, which is a nutshell fair;
> Lin'd soft it is, and rich within,
> Made of a glistening adder's skin.

The pleasure of such poetry lies in the ingenuity shown in adapting the prettiest and most curious of nature's diminutives to accoutre and serve the fairies. The weakness of Margaret's poems is not lack of ingenuity but clumsiness of expression. She lined the Queen's coach with an adder's skin, which is a device as felicitous as the ' wing of a pied butterflee ' which Drayton used as a cover for his Queen; but he described her complete equipage with a clarity and discrimination which make Margaret's lines appear opaque and artless:

> Her chariot of a snail's fine shell,
> Which for the colours did excell:
> The fair Queen Mab becoming well,
>   So lively was the limning.
> The seat the soft wool of the bee;
> The cover (gallantly to see)
> The wing of a pied butterflee,
>   I trow t' was simple trimming.

This much had to be said to avoid exaggerating the worth of her fairy poems; but they show that, however shallowly and obscurely her poetry ran, it nevertheless sprang from the same source as Drayton's flood. And the fairy poems included in her collection of verse are not her highest achievement in the style. Many years later, in 1668, she printed in a volume of plays some lines which are usually chosen to represent her in anthologies, and these, which are probably of early composition—the volume is a collection of fragments—give a fairer idea of her measure:

> My cabinets are oyster shells,
> In which I keep my orient pearls;
> To open them I use the tide,
> As keys to locks, which opens wide;
> The oyster shells then out I take;
> Those, orient pearls and crowns do make;
> And modest coral I do wear,
> Which blushes when it touches air.
> On silver waves I sit and sing,
> And then the fish lie listening;
> Then sitting on a rocky stone,
> I comb my hair with fish's bone;
> The whil'st Apollo with his beams
> Doth dry my hair from wat'ry streams.
> His light doth glaze the water's face,
> Make the large sea my looking glass;
> So when I swim on waters high,
> I see myself as I glide by;
> But when the sun begins to burn,
> I back into my waters turn,
> And dive unto the bottom low:
> Then on my head the waters flow
> In curled waves and circles round;
> And thus with waters am I crown'd.

It was after reading such passages that Virginia Woolf wished that Margaret had kept to the narrow valleys of her poetry rather than shift her bivouac to the high arid plains of natural philosophy.

Atoms and fairies do not, however, make up the greater part of her collection; and there are among the many other miscellaneous verses several moral discourses and dialogues which strike beyond the reach of mere fancy. When her dialogue between Melancholy and Mirth was reprinted a hundred years later, 'Mr. Town' praised it extremely in the *Connoisseur*, No. 69. He saw Margaret as in a vision leap upon Pegasus, her old-fashioned fantastic habit fluttering in the wind, and gallop off helter-skelter. 'However, it was acknowledged, that she kept a firm seat, even when the horse went at his deepest rate; and that she wanted nothing but to ride with a curb-bridle.' He watched Shakespeare and Milton step forward to hand her down and suggested darkly, and wildly, that Milton had collected some hints for *L'Allegro* and *Il Penseroso* from the dialogue between Melancholy and Mirth. The passage which 'Mr. Town' chose to print illustrates excellently the unexpected qualities Margaret can show:

> She [Melancholy] hates the light, in darkness only found:
> Or set with blinking lamps or tapers small,
> Which various shadows make against a wall.
> She loves naught else but noise which discords make;
> As croaking frogs which do dwell in the lake;
> The ravens hoarse, and so the mandrakes' groan;
> And shrieking owls, which in night fly alone;
> The tolling bell, which for the dead rings out;
> A mill where rushing waters run about;
> The roaring winds, which shake the cedars tall,
> Plough up the seas, and beat the rocks withall.
> She loves to walk in the still moonshine night,
> Where in a thick dark grove she takes delight.
> In hollow caves, house thatched, or lowly cell,
> She loves to live, and there alone to dwell . . .
> Then leave her to herself, alone to dwell,
> Let you and I in mirth and pleasure swell.

The poet rejects Mirth's invitation and chooses instead to accompany lonely Melancholy. Retirement and solitude were always Margaret's instinctive choice.

But 'A Dialogue of Birds' is even more remarkable than the dialogue of Melancholy and Mirth. As the poet walks abroad in the fields and woods, she hears the birds talking among themselves:

> I, said the lark, before the sun do rise,
> And take my flight up to the highest skies;
> There sing some notes to raise Apollo's head,
> For fear that he might lie too long abed.
> And as I mount, or if descend down low,
> Still do I sing, which way soere I go;
> Winding my body up, just like a screw,
> So doth my voice wind up a trillo too.

After the Nightingale has praised its own voice, the Robin boasts of its position as a household pet in winter—a direct anticipation of Thomson's famous scene in *The Seasons*—and its remark sets the other birds complaining of their cruel fate at the hands of man. The Sparrow tells how his tribe is massacred for the theft of a cherry:

> And if a child do chance to cry or brawl,
> They strive to catch us to please that child withall:
> With threads they tie our legs almost to crack,
> That when we hop away they pull us back;
> And when they cry 'Fip, Fip,' straight we must come,
> And for our pains they'll give us one small crumb.

The Magpie complains of having his tongue slit in order to aid him to talk, and the Linnet and the Finch of being confined in dark cages to encourage their song; but the game-birds consider these sufferers to be fortunate: are not they themselves killed to satisfy the perverted taste of the glutton? The Swallow is especially bitter as he relates how his people are beaten alive to make a culinary oil. 'Oh, man!' they all cry, 'how can you treat us so?' Is not love 'Nature's chiefest law'? They are hurriedly recalled to the duty of feeding their young, and as night closes in they sing a hymn to God:

> At last they drowsy grew, and heavy were to sleep,
> And then instead of singing, cried, ' Peep, Peep.'
> Just as the eye, when sense is locking up,
> Is neither open wide, nor yet quite shut:
> So doth a voice still by degrees fall down;
> And as a shadow wastes so doth a sound.
> Thus went to rest each head under each wing,
> For sleep brings peace to every living thing.

The humanitarian feeling of ' A Dialogue of Birds ' is expressed more finely in ' The Hunting of the Hare ', certainly her best attempt at narrative verse. Poor Wat, the hare, is pictured at the beginning lying squat between two ridges of ploughed land:

> His nose upon his two forefeet close lies,
> Glaring obliquely with his great grey eyes.

Suddenly he hears the huntsman and the baying dogs and scampers for shelter to a sandpit and from the pit into a wood, where he crouches under a broken bough, his heart aching with terror at every flitter of the leaves. Flushed from the covert, he takes to the open fields and by winding about throws the dogs off the scent:

> And while they snuffling were to find his track,
> Poor Wat being weary his swift pace did slack.
> On his two hinder legs for ease did sit,
> His forefeet rubb'd his face from dust and sweat;
> Licking his feet, he wip'd his ears so clean,
> That none could tell that Wat had hunted been.
> But casting round about his fair great eyes,
> The hounds in full career he near him spies:
> To Wat it was so terrible a sight,
> Fear gave him wings and made his body light;
> Though weary was before with running long,
> Yet now his breath he never felt more strong;
> Like those that dying are think health returns,
> When 'tis but a faint blast which life out burns.

Poor Wat is now doomed and the whooping huntsmen and baying dogs close in to kill a 'shiftless creature', which patiently accepts its end. As for man, who hunts all animals to death on the plea of sport, exercise and health, is he not more cruel and wild than any beast of prey?

The tale of poor Wat, and a similar poem on the hunting of a stag, are not merely outpourings of humanitarian sentiment; they movingly portray the creatures' natures and sufferings. However lame Margaret's verse is, it moves with sympathetic agility in pursuit of the tormented flight of the prey.

Another group of poems was entitled 'Fancies'—'the several keys of Nature, which unlock her several cabinets'; and these poems were, she thought, sufficiently important to require a separate introduction in both prose and verse, justifying originality at the expense of correctness:

> As birds to hatch their young do sit in spring,
> Some ages several broods of poets bring,
> Which to the world in verse do sweetly sing.

> Their notes great Nature set, not art so taught:
> So fancies, in the brain that Nature wrought,
> Are best; what imitation makes are naught.

And changing the form, she continued to affirm the central tenet of her creed:

> Most of our modern writers nowadays,
> Consider not the fancy but the phrase;
> As if fine words were wit, or, one should say,
> A woman's handsome if her clothes be gay.

The 'Fancies' depend upon similizing, a natural habit of her mind. The head is likened to a barrel of wine, the tongue to a wheel, and 'the heart to a harp, the head to an organ, the tongue to a lute, to make a consort of music.' The method often leads to the ridiculous, especially in the verses where life or Nature is similized to a cook:

> Life scums the cream of beauty with time's spoon,
> And draws the claret wine of blushes soon.

But occasionally the effects are charming. A young girl is likened in these verses to a bisk—a soup—for Nature's table:

A forehead high, broad, smooth, and very sleek;
A large great eye, black, and very quick;
A brow that's arch'ed, or like a bow that's bent;
A rosy cheek, and in the midst a dent;
Two cherry lips whereon the dew lies wet;
A nose between the eyes that's even set;
A chin that's neither short, nor very long;
A sharp and quick and ready pleasing tongue.
A breath of musk and amber in do strew,
Two soft round breasts, that are as white as snow . . .
A stomach strong, and easy to digest;
A swan-like neck, and an out-bearing chest:
These mixing all with pleasure and delight,
And strew upon them eyes that's quick of sight;
Putting them in a dish of admiration,
And serves them up with praises of a nation.

How close she often comes to true poetry in these displays of fancy can be shown by glancing aside at Andrew Marvell's poem 'Upon Appleton House.' In one of the poem's loveliest passages Marvell compares the meadows to a sea:

To see men through this meadow dive,
We wonder how they rise alive;
As, under water, none does know
Whether he fall through it or go;
But as the mariners that sound,
And show upon their lead the ground,
They bring up flowers so to be seen,
And prove they've at the bottom been.

The same simile but in reverse had also occurred to Margaret; she compares the sea to meadows and the sailors to shepherds:

Then mariners, as shepherds, sing and talk.
Some whistle, and some on their pipes do play,
Thus merrily will pass their time away;

And every mast is like a maypole high,
Round which they dance, though not so merrily
As shepherds do, when they their lasses bring . . .
Instead of lasses they do dance with death,
And for their music they have Boreas' breath.
Instead of wine and wassails, drink salt tears,
And for their meat they feed on nought but fears . . .
The porpoise, like their watchful dog, espies,
And gives them warning when great winds will rise.

Her poem will not stand comparison with Marvell's, but the simile itself and the sensibility are not so remote from his that she cannot be brought into association with him in order to try the quality of her inspiration.

When her collection was published under the title of *Poems, and Fancies* in March 1653 it caused a sensation. 'And first let me ask you if you have seen a book of Poems newly come out, made by my Lady Newcastle,' Dorothy Osborne wrote to William Temple on 14 April; 'for God sake if you meet with it send it me, they say 'tis ten times more extravagant than her dress.' Three weeks later she wrote again to Temple to say that he need not trouble to send her the book: 'You need not send me my Lady Newcastle's book at all for I have seen it, and am satisfied that there are many soberer people in Bedlam; I'll swear her friends are much to blame to let her go abroad.'[1] What possible justification is there in the poems for such an extravagant denunciation? Margaret's speculations on atoms are certainly odd enough but they do not comprise the greater part of the collection, and elsewhere she writes with sensibility and occasionally with grace. Her real fault in Dorothy Osborne's eyes was an offence against taste. Disregarding for the moment the settled opinion that women, and especially women of rank, had no right to trespass upon literature, a masculine preserve, Margaret's whole attitude to poetry flouted decorum. Her own description of her style sums up the grounds of her offence:

[1] Osborne, pp. 37, 41.

126

Give me the free and noble style,
Which seems uncurbed, though it be wild;
Though it runs wild about, it cares not where,
It shows more courage than it doth of fear.
Give me a style that Nature frames, not art,
For art doth seem to take the pedant's part;
And that seems noble, which is easy, free,
Not to be bound with o'er-nice pedantry.

Affirmations of this kind, and the collection abounds with them, could not but rouse the innate propriety of women like Dorothy Osborne, whose one idea was to govern their behaviour by the conventions, however repressive.

Margaret's 'free and noble style' that ran 'wildly about', to Dorothy Osborne's concern, is matched by the general impression of wildness given by the book itself. Margaret's faults of grammar, spelling, metre and rhyme alone were sufficient to disturb any reader, but they were exaggerated by the extreme untidiness and carelessness of the printer, baffled by the state of the manuscript and hurried on by Margaret to finish setting it up as soon as possible. Later she tried to shuffle some of the blame for her faults on to the printer: 'and as for the rhymes and numbers,' she wrote, 'although it is like I have erred in many, yet not so much as by the negligence of those that were to oversee it; for by the false printing, they have not only done my book wrong in that, but in many places the very sense is altered.'[1] The most amusing of the printer's unwitting emendations occurs in some verses similizing Spring to the weaving of a carpet. Margaret wrote:

The ground was wrought like threads drawn from the sun,
Which shin'd so blazing like flaming fire to burn.

The printer proved himself a metaphysical by emending the second line to read, 'Which shin'd so blazing like to a fir'd gun.' It is the printer, however, who wins our sympathy, though he was certainly not expert.

[1] *Worlds Olio*, p. 93.

Far more disturbing than such errors were the preliminaries. Once her book was finished, Margaret viewed its entry into the world with such trepidation that she scribbled one preface after another in an attempt to justify it and to anticipate criticism. As her bashfulness distracted her behaviour in society, so it forced her to adopt similar mannerisms in print. The collection opens with a loving dedication to Sir Charles Cavendish: 'And since your charity is of that length,' she wrote, 'and generosity of that height, that no times nor fortunes can cut shorter or pull down lower, I am very confident the sweetness of your disposition, which I have always found in the delightful conversation of your company, will never change, but be so humble as to accept of this book.' An epistle to 'all noble and worthy ladies' follows, in which she asks for their sympathy in her literary venture, and this theme is enlarged upon in an epistle to Mistress Topp—her waiting-woman, the former Elizabeth Chaplain, recently married to a prosperous merchant. Mrs. Topp's reply, praising her mistress as the first English poet of her sex, precedes Margaret's epistle to natural philosophers, in which she explains that she has chosen to give her atomic theories in verse because she thinks 'errors might better pass there than in prose, since poets write most fiction, and fiction is not given for truth but pastime.' The plain 'Reader' is entreated in the next epistle not to censure her too harshly, for she has not had 'so many years of experience as will make me a garland to crown my head; only I have had so much time as to gather a little posy to stick upon my breast.' Three sets of apologetic verses end this remarkable fanfare. The intention was to predispose opinion in her favour but it had the opposite effect; her readers were invited to laugh at her extravagance and naïvety.

But her repeated appeals for sympathy and her reiterated claim for recognition as a poet were never marred by arrogance. If she was inordinately ambitious in poetry it was because her vision of a poet's felicity was so powerful: in the garden of the mind, she wrote, there 'grow tall trees of contemplations, whereon the birds of poetry sit and sing, and peck at the fruit of fame with their bills of glory; from whence they fly over the groves of eternity with their wings of presumption.' [1] She did not presume that she would ever take such a flight; the shrewdest judgement on her poetry is her own: ' though I am a poetess, yet I am but a poetastress, or a petty poetess; but howsoever, I am a legitimate poetical child of nature, and though my poems, which are the body of the poetical soul, are not so beautiful and pleasing as the rest of her poetical children's bodies are, yet I am nevertheless her child, although but a brownet [brunette].' [2] Would it not be churlish in the face of such modesty, however disguised elsewhere by nervousness, to disallow her at least a perch on one of her tall trees of contemplation and an uncertain flight over eternity's grove?

Many readers of Margaret's poems were of Dorothy Osborne's opinion. Edmund Waller, who had dined at Newcastle's table in Paris, is reported to have said that he would have given all his own works to have written ' The Hunting of the Stag ', but when charged with excessive adulation, added that ' nothing was too much to be given, that a Lady might be saved from the disgrace of such a vile performance.' [3] But her critics by no means carried the day, and there were many sympathetic readers to appreciate and praise her originality and sensibility. Mildmay Fane, Earl of Westmoreland, wrote a poem in her honour on the fly-leaf of his copy of *Poems, and Fancies* [4]:

> No wonder 'twere though Schools went down,
> Now learning shifts from Gown to gown;
> Whilst petticoat and kirtle may
> The banners of the Nine display,
> And atomize whate'er the quill
> Recorded from the twin-like Hill;
> Make wit and fancy so combine
> In numbers true, and feet to join,

[1] *Ib.*, p. 107.
[2] *Sociable Letters*, p. 301.
[3] Perry, p. 179.
[4] Westmoreland's copy of *Poems, and Fancies* is in the Huntington Library.

M.F.   I

As if all dance and music's art
Were here brought in to bear their part.
For the contrivement, I'd aver,
'Twould puzzle a philosopher;
The style, the methods and the phrase
Do heighten so the authoress' praise,
That I should too injurious be
To cast into such treasury:
For all the Graces here are met
To make a pearl of Margaret.

Margaret had no sooner sent her poems to be printed than her fancy, still under the excitement of the past eight or nine months of composition, restlessly set to work on another collection of verses. She wrote it very quickly, within three weeks, hoping to add it as a supplement to the volume already in the press, but she was too late and it had to appear separately. This duo-decimo volume, *Philosophicall Fancies*, which was published at the beginning of May 1653, is a pigmy among her extensive folios.

Its particular theme is a brief statement and illustration of the new theory of nature which she had evolved in the course of her year's cogitations. Atoms were dethroned and matter and motion elevated in their stead; but as the elaboration of this theory was to preoccupy her for the next fifteen years, its discussion belongs to a later chapter. The theory is stated in prose but the illustrations are in verse, and the verses show her imagination working fantastically. It is impossible to separate the strands of her thought, but the idea behind the following verses is the possibility of the rational spirits compelling vegetable and mineral matter to assume animal shapes. Were this miracle ever to happen what a bizarre world there would be!

Then coral trouts may through the water glide,
And pearled minnows swim on either side;
And mermaids, which in the sea delight,
Might all be made of wat'ry lillies white . . .

Large deer of oak might through the forest run,
Leaves on their heads might keep them from the sun;
Instead of shedding horns, their leaves might fall,
And acorns, to increase a wood of fawns withall . . .
Then silver grass may in the meadows grow,
Which nothing but a scythe of fire can mow;
The wind, which from the north a journey takes,
May strike those silver strings and music make.
Thus may another world, though matter still the same,
By changing shapes, change humours, properties and
    name.

As these pretty and ridiculous verses show, *Philosophicall Fancies*
only reinforces the impression already made by her earlier collection, and amply confirmed her reputation for extravagance
and eccentricity.

Without the diversion of poetry the eighteen months Margaret
spent alone in England would have seemed unbearably tedious.
She stayed on in the lingering hope of the Government's relenting
towards her husband and also in the capacity of an observer on
the disposal of his property. Sir Charles Cavendish, once his
composition had been settled, acted with characteristic generosity
and bought back Bolsover Castle, Newcastle's favourite house,
from its purchaser. The purchaser was proposing to pull down
the buildings, already partially destroyed in the wars, and to
sell the materials. Sir Charles was luckily able to prevent this
vandalism but only at great cost. Margaret celebrated the incident
by writing a dialogue between Sir Charles and the Castle and
included it among her poems. ' Alas, poor Castle,' Sir Charles
exclaims,

That wealth I have for to release thy woe,
Will offer for a ransom to thy foe.

' Most noble sir,' the Castle replies,

        you that me freedom give,
May your great name in after ages live . . .
And may great fame your praises sound aloud:
Gods give me life to show my gratitude.

At last Margaret could bear the separation from Newcastle no longer and, learning that he was ill, she hurriedly applied to the Council of State for a pass to enable her to proceed to Flanders. The Council insisted at first that she should take the engagement not to support its enemies but she resolutely refused to bind herself. After a delay of a fortnight, on 2 March 1653, a pass was granted to her and to her four men-servants and four maids to leave the country.[1] Without even waiting to see her poems in print she joyfully embarked for the reunion with her husband.

Her only regret at leaving England was the thought of being separated from Sir Charles, who was sick of an ague; but as he had appeared to be in no immediate danger she had pressed ahead with her arrangements. His illness was fatal, and he died on 4 February and was buried on 25 February 1654 at Bolsover, within a stone's throw of the castle he had saved.

[1] *C S P D, 1652-3*, 1878, pp. 467, 469.

7 The Diversions of Exile

Most cities of note in Europe, for all I can hear, hath such like recreations for the effeminate sex, although for my part I had rather sit at home and write, or walk in my chamber and contemplate.

ANTWERP ' is one of the sweetest places in Europe '. The opinion is Evelyn's and his reason was the quietness, cleanliness, elegance and civility of ' this magnificent and famous city ', which he never found surpassed elsewhere on his travels. William Temple was equally enthusiastic and praised it in similar terms; and the judgement of the two, both men of the most refined taste and intelligence, may be taken as recording the impression which the city made on all its visitors. Its noble and lavishly decorated churches, its splendid public buildings, and the ' delicious shades and walks of stately trees ', which ran along the fortifications, helped to make a fit setting for its intellectual and commercial life. A stroll from the Jesuits' Church, where Rubens's great pictures hung in their original splendour, to the Vrijdagmarkt, where the offices of the Plantin press stood, linked together two of the greatest figures of western civilization.

The walk from the Jesuits' Church to the Plantin press might lead down a narrow lane, the Vaart, and on the left, hardly to be appreciated for lack of space to view it properly, stretched the long irregular façade of Rubens's house. The outside was solid and decent enough to conform to a mercantile society's conception of wealth and respectability, and witnessed to one side of Rubens's character, to the prosperous conformable man of property, trusted by the state and his fellow-citizens as completely as if he had been a broker on the bourse; but the inside might have belonged to another world, to Italy, renaissance Italy, and to another man; to the artist whose sensuous imagination was

133

revealed as strongly in the privacy of his own house as in his public art.

The doorway led into a cobbled courtyard, and facing the entrance and joining the two flanking wings of the house was a stone screen of three rusticated arches, each surmounted by a bust set in a niche. The elaborate pediment of the central arch supported standing figures of Mercury and Minerva; the side arches were more modestly crowned with vases and balustrades. Through the middle archway a pavilion in the classical style could be seen at the far end of the gardens, whose formal symmetry was pointed by urns placed at each corner of the intersecting paths. Immediately to the right of the entrance rose the great staircase and beyond it a colonnade, leading to the wing used by the painter as a studio. This building was the tallest and most impressive part of the house and, well lit by tall windows, contained rooms spacious enough for master and pupils to work at their ease. The outside was decorated with busts and painted in fresco after the Italian fashion—an optimistic gesture in such a climate. The other more modest wing contained an art gallery, a semi-circular museum and the living quarters. Rubens had designed the greater part of the house himself, and though it was hardly palatial, it had style and flamboyance, and illustrated his flair for architecture and his Italian sympathies.

On the painter's death in 1640 the house had passed to his widow, Helena Fourment, and when she married again in 1645 she ceased to live in it. She rented it to Newcastle. The only change he made was to turn a round building in the garden—sometimes known as the 'Pantheon', which the painter had used as an auxiliary studio for his largest canvases—into a riding-school, where he spent the greater part of his time.

The house was symbolic of Newcastle's extraordinary triumph over adversity. Judging by his circumstances, he should have been living uncomfortably in lodgings rather than luxuriously in a mansion; but his address was as adroit at Antwerp as it had been in Paris, and he was able to persuade his creditors that it was their duty to see he was kept in the style to which he was accustomed. He required all his resources of persuasion once Margaret had rejoined him in March 1653. His creditors wrongly assumed that she had returned with money and clamoured for payment, but he was able to show them their error and persuade them to extend their credit. As Margaret piously remarked, ' certainly it was a work of Divine Providence that they showed so much love, respect and honour to . . . a stranger to their nation.'[1] The city also granted him the extraordinary favour of exempting him from the payment of all excise and taxes. His position slowly began to improve after Margaret's return. He inherited the little that remained from Sir Charles's estate and his sons were able to remit some money to him from England; the total amounted to about £2,400 a year. He used this ready money to pay off the smaller tradesmen and to buy in the market for cash, ' by which means there was in a short time so much saved, as it could not have been imagined.'[2]

Newcastle was so well pleased with the treatment he received at Antwerp that he decided to stay there all the time of his exile. Margaret was just as taken with the city; the inhabitants, she wrote, ' are the civilest and best behaved people that ever I saw.'[3] At their first coming there were very few royalist exiles but the number quickly increased as the difficulties of living in France became greater; and their arrival added to society. The change could be seen in the number of coaches making the ' tour '. This was a daily procession made by society through the principal thoroughfares ' to see and to be seen ', and everyone who could afford a coach followed the custom. When Newcastle first arrived only four coaches went the ' tour ' but by the time he left there were more than a hundred, many of them belonging to royalists. Margaret enjoyed this diversion so much that Newcastle had another expensive coach built for her.

[1] *Life*, p. 75.
[2] *Ib.*, p. 83.
[3] *Ib.*, p. 65.

Margaret found her closest friends, however, not among the exiles but in local society. One of the most prosperous merchants was a Portuguese, Signor Duarte. Evelyn visited his palace, which was 'furnished like a prince's', in 1641 and was entertained by his three daughters 'with rare music, vocal and instrumental.'[1] The three accomplished daughters, Eleonora, Katherine and Frances, and the son, Gaspar, often entertained Margaret with music, and Gaspar set some of Newcastle's songs. Margaret sang, too, but only ballads. She refused to attempt anything more ambitious, pleading as an excuse when she was pressed that her untrained voice would make discord and nonsense of the songs the three sisters rendered so well. But their voices, she told Eleonora, would equally spoil a ballad: 'a sweet voice, with quavers, and trilloes, and the like, would be as improper for an old ballad as golden laces on a thrum suit of cloth.' Old ballads, she continued, should not be sung 'so much in a tune as in a tone, which tone is betwixt speaking and singing, for the sound is more than plain speaking, and less than clear singing, and the rumming or humming of a [spinning] wheel should be the music to that tone.' 'For my part,' remarks Lady Solitary in one of Margaret's plays, *The Comical Hash*, 'I had rather hear a plain old song than any Italian or French love songs stuffed with trilloes'; and the sentiment is Margaret's, however often she might tell the sisters that their voices invited the soul 'to sit in the hollow cavern of the ear.' Her liking for ballads—and if the incident in one of her plays of a maid of honour winning ten shillings by singing a ballad is autobiographical, which it appears to be, she must have sung them well—is shown by the number that occur in her plays:

'O that I were so happy once to be a wedded wife,
I would fulfil my husband's will all the days of my life.'

'O pity take upon me now some gentle body,
And give me the willow branch, for no man will have me.'

'O the lovely brown, as 'tis, how it shames the lilies.'

[1] Evelyn, i. 53.

These are a few of the lines which she quotes; and her fondness for the ballad illustrates once again the natural and vigorous taste which underlay her insubstantial affectations.

Apart from listening to music at Duarte's, and making the 'tour', which provided her with an excellent opportunity for showing off her original fashions, she preferred to keep to her room and her contemplations; but occasionally she joined in Antwerp's other diversions, observing them with remarkable shrewdness for one whose eye was more accustomed to a parade of fancies.[1] One winter it was so cold that the ink froze in her standish, and her very thoughts moved as slowly as if they had been benumbed. She likened the weather to an assaulting army, which attacked the city with ammunition of snow, hail and wind, supported by men-of-war, the ice-floes on the river. The attack was resisted by the beleaguered with all their might—with coals and logs, brush-faggots and bellows; and also with 'great pieces of beef . . . for men-of-war, with cabbage for sails, sausages for tacklings, carrots for guns, and marrow-bones for masts, ballasted with pepper, and pitched or tarred with mustard.' But the weather was irresistible and back the company were driven to sit and shiver in the chimney-corner. As long as the snow lay, the young men of the city, got up 'antickly' as coachmen, led their mistresses on horse-drawn sleds at a gallop through the thoroughfares. The ladies were dressed in 'feathers and rich clothes', and at night footmen ran ahead with torches to light them on their way. Though she admired this spectacle from her window, Margaret was loath to go out into the cold and join the fun, but Newcastle made her dress up warmly in a mantle and drive with him in their coach to watch the people sliding on the frozen river. She was so delighted by the gaiety and sweetness of the sliding motion that she wanted to slide too, but as she could not face doing so without assurance that she would outshine all other performers, and that the ice was wholly to be trusted, she

[1] These anecdotes of Margaret's life in Antwerp are taken from *Sociable Letters*, nos. CCII, CXC, CXCIV, CXCV, CLXXII, CXXIV and CL.

returned home without venturing herself but 'very well pleased with the sight.'

Shrovetide was carnival time: 'the most pleasant and merry time in all the year in this city for feasting, sporting, and masquerading.' The people wandered about the streets in vizards. The women dressed themselves up as men and the younger men as women, but the men looked more uncomfortable in their costume, Margaret noticed, as if they counted it a disgrace to their manhood. Others habited themselves as devils. One year it was clear sunshiny weather and though she had a touch of ague, Margaret braved the chill air to watch the celebrations which ushered in Lent. The next day was Ash Wednesday and the revellers marked their foreheads with a black mourning cross: 'I know not whether it be to cross out their former sins,' she remarked sceptically, 'or a barricado to keep out following sins.'

Another diversion she enjoyed especially was the fairs. Some of the wonders on display were brought to her for her personal inspection; a man wearing a white beard down to his waist and claiming to be a hundred, a woman as hairy as a 'shagg-dog'. She was impressed by neither of these oddities, nor by the tumblers, jugglers, dromedaries, apes and 'many the like'; but she was completely enthralled by an Italian mountebank, his fool, 'Jean Potage', and their dancing wives. She even took the trouble to hire a room in a house overlooking the stage and went every day to see them. She could not understand a word of the mountebank's harangue but she delighted in the fool's antics and particularly in his wife's dancing. The show was closed down, to her disappointment, by order of the magistrates for fear of the plague, and to console herself Margaret acted out the performance in her fancy until judgement, reason, discretion and consideration, the magistrates of her brain, closed down the imaginary sideshow and would not suffer the phantasmal actors 'to cheat or fool any longer.'

Once or twice there were civil disturbances to frighten her. The common people rioted against the magistrates, threatening to plunder their houses and fire the churches; and as the trumpets and drums of the soldiery sounded and the tocsin rang out dolefully across the city, Margaret's maids ran to her with white faces to tell her they had heard that the soldiers would 'have liberty to abuse all the women' and that the citizens would be put to the sword. Margaret ran in her turn to her husband at every noise, and he tried to quiet her fears. But nothing worse happened and the city was soon pacified.

A more amusing disturbance was caused by a neighbour. The neighbour's wife, a 'proper, handsome woman' who had been married for two years, suspected her husband, of whom she was insanely jealous, of making love to one of Margaret's maids, a very pretty, honest girl. There was an 'unfortunate' door and window—at least, they were 'unfortunate' to the wife, Margaret remarked slyly—to facilitate the affair. The window belonged to the man and overlooked Newcastle's garden, but the door was owned by Newcastle and opened into his neighbour's garden. As soon as the man from his window saw Margaret's maid walking in the garden, for it was summer-time, he would run downstairs to the door and push flowers through a hole in it to the girl. His wife sent a message to Newcastle by her confessor asking him to close up the hole. Newcastle chivalrously offered in reply to wall up the door. Six weeks later the wife charged her husband with giving the girl presents of linen and sweetmeats, and again complained to Newcastle. He refused to interrogate the girl but Margaret questioned her and learnt that one night the husband had tossed into her chamber through an open window, while she was undressing for bed, 'a lawn buttoned handkerchief, tied up in two or three knots, with sweetmeats in them.' Newcastle thereupon sent for the lady's confessor, and after explaining to him that she had nothing to fear from the girl, asked him to make peace between her and her husband.

Margaret's maids caused her other trouble. She heard her neighbours say that the girls were spoiled with idleness and had nothing better to do than to sun themselves in the garden and to ' dress, curl and adorn ' themselves. Upset by this gossip, she charged the girls with being lazy, but she had to own the force of their defence: though they were willing, they said, she never set them to work. ' The truth was,' she admitted, ' they oftener heard of their lady than heard or saw her themselves; I living so studious a life, as they did not see me above once a week, nay, many times not once in a fortnight.' She sent at once for her housekeeper and suggested that she herself and her maids should sit and spin together; but when she learnt what a difficult and noisy task spinning was, she dropped the idea in favour of making silk flowers. The silk flowers that were to be bought in the shops, the housekeeper explained, were both better and cheaper than any that could ever be made at home. Preserving fruit? Margaret suggested. The housekeeper helped her out of her dilemma. She recommended that her mistress should return to her writing and contemplating and that the maids should be set to read, for ' by reading they will enrich their understandings, and increase their knowledges, and quicken their wit, all which may make their life happy, in being content with any fortune that is not in their power to better.' Margaret was relieved to follow her advice.

On her return to Antwerp, Margaret had taken up again the book which she had begun before setting out for England, and which she had promised to publish in a postscript to *Philoso-phicall Fancies*. The work was a collection of essays and observations on every idea and subject which had ever fallen under her attention, and when it appeared in 1655 it was appropriately entitled *The Worlds Olio*. An olio is a highly spiced hotchpotch; and, spiced with her personality, the contents of the book are as various as the ingredients of the most catholic stew. ' What Romancy is,' ' Of the Labyrinth of Fancy ', ' A man that is mad is not out of his wits ', ' Of Tyrannical Government ', ' Of Partiality of the World ', ' Memory is Atoms in the Brain set on Fire ', ' Of Gentlewomen that are sent to board Schools ', ' On Swimming ': these are a sample of the titles of the essays, which vary in length from two or three lines to as many pages.

The disorder of the arrangement is extreme. A rough group-
ing of subjects is discernible, but the reader is usually whisked
from one idea to another with surprising suddenness. She herself was conscious of the confusion and offered a typical excuse
in a preliminary epistle to the reader: 'I being of a lazy disposition, did choose to let it go into the world with its defects rather
than take the pains to refine it'; rather than refine it, she preferred to hurry on to her next book, taking 'more pleasure and
delight in making than in mending.' Her erratic procedure,
however, is hardly a disadvantage. The delight of the book
lies in its kaleidoscopic revelation of character, in its artless
juxtaposing of common sense and fantasy, of originality and
banality, of wisdom and folly. One merit she always has: she
never lapses from eloquence.

The variety makes the choice of an example very difficult, but
her defence of cosmetics will show her at her best. She defends
women's painting in theory as a device to hide nature's defects,
as proper as a wig to cover a bald head, or a surgical boot to
raise a short leg; and as its use keeps or increases 'lawful affection', it deserves the praise that cannot be accorded to the arts
of war. 'But, say some, it is a bawd to entice, in begetting evil
desires. It is answered, no more a bawd than nature is in making
a handsome creature; but if they must do nothing for fear of
enticing, then mankind must neither cut their hair, nor pare
their nails, nor shave their beards, nor wash their selves, which
would be very slovenly.' But she strongly disapproved of cosmetics in practice. As cosmetics contained mercury, they led
to consumptions and caused swellings about the neck and throat,
and eventually brought about the decay of the 'life and youth
of a face, which is the greatest beauty'. Also they were slut-
tish; 'especially in the preparatives, as masks of cerecloths,
which are not only horrid to look upon, in that they seem as
dead bodies embowelled or embalmed, but the stink is offensive.'
She thoroughly approved of all other aids to beauty: 'But for
other adornments in women, they are to be commended, as
curling, powdering, pouncing, clothing, and all the varieties of

accoutrement, in that they have none of the said former qualities, but give a graceful advantage to the person. Besides, dressing is the poetry of women, in showing the fancies, and is the cause of employing the greater part of a commonwealth.'

The collection was introduced by several preliminaries. A dedication to Fortune—' Wherefore if Fortune please, with her helping hand, she may place my book in Fame's high tower, where every word, like a cymbal, shall make a tinkling noise '— precedes an epistle to her husband, in which she explains that she had not yet dedicated any particular work to him since it was her intention to dedicate to him the ' whole sum ' of her writings. She also gratefully acknowledges her indebtedness to his conversation for much of her knowledge; and his influence is indeed evident throughout the collection, particularly in those essays dealing with war and statecraft. She includes an epistle to Sir Charles Cavendish, written before his death, and addresses three epistles to the reader, one of which, a splendid defence of women, will come under discussion later.

There were two innovations in the prefatory matter: a portrait frontispiece and some commendatory verses by Newcastle. Newcastle acted as crier to the book:

> The world, to the *World's Olio*, we invite you,
> And hope these several cates they may delight you . . .
> An olio of confections not refrain;
> For here 's a sumptuous banquet for your brain:
> And this imaginary feast pray try;
> Censure your worst, so you the book will buy.

Once having begun, Newcastle made a habit of introducing Margaret's books in halting but pleasantly urbane verse. The frontispiece was by the Antwerp artist, Abraham van Diepenbeke, who was to be closely associated with the Newcastles' literary ventures all the time they stayed in the city. The portrait shows Margaret in a toga standing in a niche supported by Apollo and Minerva. The coronet set at a rakish angle on her long curling hair adds a touch of insouciance to the proud pose.

Diepenbeke was called upon again to provide the frontispiece to Margaret's fourth book, also published in 1655, which she had been engaged upon since her return to Antwerp. This was an enlarged and radically revised version of her second book, *Philosophicall Fancies*, entitled *The Philosophical and Physical Opinions*—the change from 'fancies' to 'opinions' indicating the greater seriousness of her intentions. The portrait shows her seated in her study beside a table on which are a clock, a bell, a writing pad and a standish; a pen is in the inkwell ready for use. She is dressed in a tightly-bodiced, loose-sleeved dress of dark stuff, cut low enough to show her pretty throat and bosom, to which attention is also called by a single necklace of large pearls. The oddity of the room in which she sits, considered as a study, is the absence of books; but the want is explained in the verses, probably of Newcastle's composition, engraved at the foot of the portrait:

> Studious she is, and all alone,
> Most visitants when she has none;
> Her library on which she looks,
> It is her head; her thoughts her books:
> Scorning dead ashes without fire,
> For her own flames do her inspire.

The lack of books in her study was presumed to be complete proof of her originality, and Richard Flecknoe, Dryden's ' King of Nonsense ', who frequently be-rhymed the Newcastles, commented in verse upon the fact:

> What place is this! looks like some sacred cell
> Where ancient hermits formerly did dwell . . .
> Is this a lady's closet? 't cannot be;
> For nothing here of vanity we see,
> Nothing of curiosity or pride,
> As most of ladies' closets have beside . . .
> Nor is 't a library, but only as she
> Makes each place where she comes a library.[1]

[1] Flecknoe, *Epigrams*, 1670, p. 26.

The Philosophical and Physical Opinions opens with the usual absurd number of prefatory epistles to the reader, in which Margaret vigorously defended herself against the charges levelled against her earlier works. The most serious was that her writings were none of her own but someone else's, to which she had lent her name. She had already denied the accusation in the postscript to *Philosophicall Fancies*: 'And truly I am so honest,' she wrote, 'as not to steal another's work and give it my own name; nor so vainglorious as to strain to build up a fame upon the ground of another man's wit.' As she was a woman and uneducated, her critics had argued, she could not possibly be familiar with all the scientific and philosophical ideas and terms mentioned in her works, and must have plagiarized them at the best. Her poetry had also been severely blamed for carelessnesses in rhyme, metre and spelling; a charge for which there was every justification. Margaret felt herself unable to reply adequately to these criticisms and called upon Newcastle to supply not only a set of commendatory verses but an epistle justifying her against 'false and malicious aspersions.'

Newcastle's epistle is a delightful example of his manner at its best. Urbane and self-assured, he humorously rallies her critics and tries to awaken their chivalry as well as to convince them of their mistakes. He takes up the matter in hand immediately without any preliminary compliments: 'I would willingly begin with the common and Dunstable road of epistles, gentle readers, but finding you much otherwise, I will fall to our discourse in hand.' He first rebuts the charge that she must have learnt all she knew from professional scholars; had she not had the advantage of the conversation of her own brother, Sir Charles Cavendish and himself? 'and for myself I have lived in the great world a great while, and have thought of what has been brought to me by the senses, more than was put into me by learned discourse; for I do not love to be led by the nose by authority and old authors; *ipse dixit* will not serve my turn.' Her knowledge of medical terms, for example, choler and phlegm, nerves and ventricles and the like, was no greater than

Maison Hilverue a Anvers.   Dit I'hostel Rubens. 1684.

4. View of the Courtyard, Rubens's House, Antwerp, 1684.

that of 'a good farmer's wife' who has seen one of her sheep opened. And as for the slips in rhythm and metre, many were printer's errors, and those of her own were surely insufficient to damn the book: have you 'no mercy, gentlemen, when for the numbers every schoolboy can make them on his fingers, and for rhymes Fenner would have put down Ben Jonson?' He ends by stressing her originality, while admitting that many of the opinions in *The Worlds Olio* are his own newly phrased. His behaviour is exactly that of a knight-errant riding to the rescue of a distressed lady and is calculated to set an example to others: 'Truly I cannot believe so unworthily of any scholar, honouring them so much as we both do, that they should envy this lady, or should have so much malice or emulation to cast such false aspersions on her, that she did not write those books that go forth in her name . . . . But there's the crime, a lady writes them, and to intrench so much upon the male prerogative is not to be forgiven; but I know gown-men will be more civil to her, because she is of the gown too.'

Margaret's confidence in the 'gown-men' was so great that she dedicated her book to the universities of Oxford and Cambridge, and the dedication is one of her most eloquent and spirited defences of the rights of women. She, too, wrote at length in other prefatory epistles against her detractors, but her irritation was less effective in refuting them than Newcastle's good-natured banter.

The theories set out in the book can be more conveniently held over for later discussion, but as her attention was so preoccupied by scientific speculation during these years, her epistle to the reader on natural philosophy, which poetically states her devotion to the subject, must be quoted to illustrate the depth of her feeling. Of all the branches of philosophy, she wrote, natural philosophy rewards the student with the greatest delight; moral philosophy is an 'excellent study' and theology a 'glorious study', but the doctrines of the first are too strict for practice and those of the second—and her opinion was formed by the horrors of the Civil War—instead of 'uniting mankind with love' lead to factions and bloodshed. Only natural

145

philosophy pleases men's curiosity and harmlessly satisfies their imagination: 'it carries their thoughts above vulgar and common objects, it elevates their spirits to an aspiring pitch; it gives room for the untired appetites of man to walk or run in, for so spacious it is that it is beyond the compass of time; besides it gives pleasure in varieties, for infinite ways are strewed with infinite varieties.' Her opinions may often exasperate by their silliness or tedium, but much can be excused anyone who was illuminated by such ardour and capable of expressing it with such instinctive grace.

While Margaret lived retired in her study contemplating, stirring out only when she was compelled to take air and exercise for her health's sake, Newcastle spent his time in his riding-school. The two Barbary horses he had bought in Paris both died in Antwerp, but he quickly replaced them and bought other horses until he eventually had eight altogether. Of all the breeds he preferred the Spanish and the Barbary; the Spanish horses, he used to say, were like princes, and the Barbs like gentlemen. In his opinion a good horse was so rare that it could not be valued in money, and he would say 'that he who would buy him out of his pleasure (meaning his horses) must pay dear for it.' When a chapman once tried to buy a fine Spanish horse from him, he told him that the price to-day was £1,000, to-morrow £2,000, the next day £3,000, and so on; and the Duke of Guise displeased him greatly by offering through a gentleman 600 pistoles for another horse. 'So great a love hath my lord for good horses!' Margaret remarked after reporting these offers, and the love was apparently reciprocal: 'And certainly I have observed,' she continued, 'and do verily believe, that some of them had also a particular love to my lord; for they seemed to rejoice whensoever he came into the stables by their trampling action and the noise they made; nay, they would go much better in the manage when my lord was by than when he was absent; and when he rid them himself, they seemed to take much pride and pleasure in it.' [1]

[1] *Life*, pp. 65-7.

146

His school quickly became one of the sights of Antwerp and all notable visitors to the city were taken to it. The Duke of Oldenburg and the Prince of East Friesland came and presented Newcastle with horses of their own local breeds in token of their appreciation. When Don John of Austria, the Governor of the Spanish Netherlands, visited Antwerp for two days, almost all his court resorted to the school; there were no less than seventeen coaches drawn up at once, Margaret reckoned, all belonging to persons of quality. Don John was unable to attend in person, being overwhelmed with business, but he sent for Newcastle and received him with extraordinary civility. Some of the Spaniards in the Governor's entourage pressed him to go to Spain, assuring him of their King's kindness; but Newcastle was too wise to remove from where he was so comfortably settled. The Marquis of Caracena, Don John's successor in the governorship, also visited the school and begged Newcastle to ride himself, though he was only just recovering from a two months' sickness. Newcastle reluctantly obeyed his command and rode first ' a Spanish horse called Le Superbe, of a light bay, a beautiful horse, and though hard to be rid, yet when he was hit right, he was the readiest horse in the world. He went in curvets, forward, backward, side-ways, on both hands; made the cross perfectly upon his voltoes; and did change upon his voltoes so just, without breaking time, that no musician could keep time better; and went terra-à-terra perfectly.' He then rode a second Spanish horse, ' Le Genty ' and lastly a Barb ' that went a metz-ayre very high, both forward and upon his voltoes and terra-à-terra.' ' And when I had done riding,' Newcastle remarked disingenuously in his description of the scene, ' the Marquess of Caracena seemed to be very well satisfied; and some Spaniards that were with him, crossed themselves, and cried Miraculo! ' [1]

Newcastle's love of horsemanship was his most enduring passion. ' I have loved, practised and studied the art from my

[1] William Cavendish, *A New Method and Extraordinary Invention*, 1667, pp. 2 (b)^v–(c).

youth,' he wrote, ' and have spent much time on it, with as much pleasure; for there is no other exercise which is so worthy a man, and no art which is so useful, noble and graceful as that of horsemanship.' He decided to write a book on the art and to publish it in a form worthy of its great theme.

The chief difficulty in publishing lay in the cost. Newcastle wrote to Secretary Nicholas on 15 February 1657 to complain of being ' tormented ' by the book; only a loan from two of his friends had allowed him to raise the £1,300 necessary to print it.[1] When *La Methode Nouvelle et Invention Extraordinaire de dresser les Chevaux* appeared at last in folio in 1658 from the press of the Antwerp printer, Jacques van Meurs, it proved to be worth every penny of the high cost; the plates alone, engraved after Abraham van Diepenbeke, made it one of the most handsome books of the century, and the type and paper were of fine quality. [2]

The book is, however, much more than a memorial to New-castle's devotion to horsemanship; it is a moving expression of his loyalty to the crown and of his love for England. He dedicated the work to the King, his pupil in horsemanship. His devotion to the royal person and his confidence in an eventual restoration were unshaken by his sufferings and exile. When Margaret was depressed and said that she could see little chance of the King's return, ' my husband would gently reprove me,' she wrote, ' saying, I believed least what I desired most, and could never be happy if I endeavoured to exclude all hopes and entertained nothing but doubts and fears.' [3] This spirit is reflected in the style of the book; its concern with the most gentlemanlike of the arts, its distance from all controversies, and

---

[1] *C S P D, 1656–7*, 1883, p. 279.

[2] The text of Newcastle's book on horsemanship is in French, translated from the English. The full title, omitting only the catalogue of the author's dignities, reads: *La Methode Nouvelle & Invention extraordinaire de dresser les Chevaux les travailler selon la nature, et parfaire la nature par la subtilité de l'art; la quelle n'a jamais été treuvée que par Le tres-noble, haut et tres-puissant Prince Guillaume Marquis et Comte de Newcastle.*

[3] *Life*, p. 76.

its sumptuous appearance were an assertion of the old cavalier spirit.

But however staunchly Newcastle faced exile and adroitly adapted himself to its difficulties, he could not exorcise nostalgia. The idea of England—of its calm, its people, its customs, its countryside—haunted every exile, and was touchingly expressed by Sir Kenelm Digby, writing from Calais to Lord Conway in 1647. 'Those innocent recreations which your lordship mentioneth,' he wrote, 'of tabours and pipes, and more innocent dancing ladies, and most innocent convenient country houses, shady walks and close arbours, made me sigh to be again a spectator of them, and to be again in little England, where time slideth more gently away than in any part of the world.' [1]

Newcastle heard the same music and remembered the same diversions. While at Antwerp he wrote 'a little book, or rather a letter' to the King, in which he advised him on the policy to be adopted once he returned to England. Newcastle stressed with Hobbesian shrewdness the necessity of authority and justice in both church and state, but he particularly emphasized popular amusements as essential to the people's contentment. The poorer folk of London must have playhouses, he wrote, and spectacles, music and dancing, and 'all the old holidays, with their mirth and rites set up again; feasting daily will be in merry England, for England is so plentiful of all provisions, that if we do not eat them, they will eat us, so we feast in our defence.' And the country folk, too, must be satisfied by the restoration of all their old pleasures: 'May games, morris dances, the Lord of the May, the Lady of the May, the Fool and the Hobby Horse must not be forgotten; also the Whitsun Lord and Lady; thrashing of hens at Shrovetide; carols and wassails at Christmas, with good plum porridge and pies, which now are forbidden as prophane ungodly things . . . after evening prayer every Sunday and holiday, the country people, with their fresher lasses, to trip on the town green about the maypole to the louder bagpipe, there to be refreshed with their

[1] *Conway Letters*, ed. Marjorie Hope Nicholson, 1930, p. 27.

ale and cakes. . . . Then there should be players to go up and down the country.'[1]   But he is not forecasting the future, he is reporting on the past.   Unfamiliar with contemporary England, he could not yet know how hopeless any attempt to restore the past must always be.

The book on horsemanship and the little book or letter to the King were both written out of a desire to assuage his longing to return to the life and places which he so dearly loved, and for which even Rubens's Italianate mansion and Antwerp's great churches, shady walks and civil inhabitants were a poor compensation.

[1] S. Arthur Strong, *A Catalogue of Letters and other Historical Documents . . . at Welbeck,* 1903, pp. 226–7.

8 The Voyage of Fancy

I desire all my readers and acquaintance to believe, though my words run stumbling out of my mouth, and my pen draws roughly on my paper, yet my thoughts move regular in my brain.

ONE of the illustrations made by Abraham van Diepenbeke for the book on horsemanship was a group portrait of Newcastle and his family. Newcastle and Margaret are shown seated under the middle arch of a portico of five arches. Newcastle's three daughters and their husbands, the Earl of Bridgewater, the Earl of Bolingbroke and Charles Cheyne, are arranged in wedded pairs, each pair to an arch. His two sons, Charles and Henry, exhibit their horsemanship in front of the portico, and their wives are placed together under the fifth arch. A dog scampers excitedly about the horses; a vain attempt on the artist's part to enliven the stiff formality of the scene.

Diepenbeke had earlier drawn a conversation piece of Newcastle and his family, which had appeared as the frontispiece to Margaret's large collection of tales published in 1656. The title-page to the collection deserves to be transcribed in full, so typical is it of the author's style: *Natures Pictures drawn by Fancies Pencil to the Life. Written by the thrice Noble, Illustrious, and Excellent Princess, The Lady Marchioness of Newcastle. In this Volume there are several feigned Stories of Natural Descriptions, as Comical, Tragical, and Tragi-Comical, Poetical, Romancical, Philosophical, and Historical, both in Prose and Verse, some all Verse, some all Prose, some mixt, partly Prose, and partly Verse. Also, there are some Morals, and some Dialogues, but they are as the Advantage Loaves of Bread to a Bakers dozen; and a true Story at the latter end, wherein there is no Feignings.* A more specific and inclusive title could hardly have been devised.

Diepenbeke's conversation piece shows the family seated

151

round a table in a room warmed by a winter fire; the blaze is so
hot that one of the servants is seen in the act of opening a window
to let in air. Newcastle and Margaret, their heads crowned with
laurel, are seated at the head of the table, and as Newcastle
addresses his children, stressing his words with a gesture of the
hand, they lean forward or loll back comfortably in their chairs.
The principal difference between the artist's preliminary study
for the engraving and the engraving itself is in the narrator.[1] In
the study it is Margaret herself who holds up her hand for
attention, and her relinquishment of the rôle of narrator to her
husband in the engraving was probably made to avoid further
offending those who would have thought that she was entrench-
ing again on ' the male prerogative '. Margaret withdrew the
concession, however, in her verses describing the frontispiece:

> My lord and I here in two chairs are set,
> And all his children, wives and husbands, met,
> To hear me tell them tales as I think fit,
> And hope they're full of fancy and of wit.
> Ladies, I ask your pardons, mercies, I,
> Since I talk all, and many ladies by.

Newcastle did contribute one or two tales in verse to the collection to justify his prominence in the frontispiece, but his
chief contributions were two commendatory poems, one on
the tales themselves and the other on all Margaret's published
works, which is largely his earlier preface to *The Philosophical and
Physical Opinions* set in rhyme. His verses in praise of the tales
are in the style of a pedlar's crying of his wares:

> Gallants and ladies, what do ye lack? pray buy.
> Tales *à la mode*, new fashioned here do lie,
> So do romancies, your grave studies too;
> Academies of Love, teaching to woo
> And to be wooed, corrupts more virgins than
> Hot satires turned to amorous courtly men:
> But these are innocent; then be not nice;
> Will you not buy because they teach not vice?

[1] The study is in the Print Room of the British Museum.

Nature will teach you that; then do not look
To do 't by art and learning by the book:
A vestal nun may read this and avow it,
And a Carthusian confessor allow it.

The tales in verse which open the collection are supposed to
be told in turn by a group of men and women as they sit round
a winter's fire. The greater number are hardly more than
anecdotes phrased in poor rhyme: a young widow is found
weeping at her husband's grave and, rejecting consolation, dies;
or, a man swears to his dying wife to be constant to her memory
and when he marries again, he marries a shrew and quickly dies.
A few of the tales are more ambitious. In 'A Description of
Constancy' a young girl is sent by her widowed father to the
Queen's court as a maid of honour. She falls in love with a
handsome and martial prince, who is unfortunately intended as
a match for the Queen's niece. She writes to him protesting her
love and, luckily for her modesty, he writes to her simultane-
ously in the same strain. They conceal their affection out of
policy but once they are discovered, the prince is despatched to
the army and the girl is abducted and given out for dead. When
the prince learns of her supposed death, he adopts the life of a
hermit, and the girl, persuaded in turn of his death, spends her
days weeping and mourning. But disasters overtake the army
and the prince, under threat of execution, is ordered by the
Queen to resume his command; this he refuses to do and is
told to prepare for death. The girl, too, is warned of her
execution. But when the lovers are reunited on the scaffold, the
Queen has a change of heart and forgives them, and the tale ends
with their marriage.

As we read through one story after another of this kind, we
may remember that the list of contents given on the title-page
concludes with a promise of 'a true story at the latter end
wherein there is no feignings.' The true story is 'A true Relation of my Birth, Breeding, and Life', one of the most charming
autobiographical sketches of the century, in which Margaret

simply and hastily sets out the main facts of her life. Believing later that it lessened her dignity, she omitted it in 1671 from the second edition of the book. What relation does it bear to all the preceding stories? It serves in effect, though not in intention, to show that all her tales were essentially autobiographical. They were the daydreams prompted by her own experience and are variations, more or less fantastic, upon it. Each story has its heroine and each heroine is Margaret in disguise; in the disguise of the learned lady or of the lovely innocent. The two are occasionally kept apart but generally they alternate in a single character. And as the scenes of a daydream succeed each other imperceptibly and have neither a beginning nor an end, so her tales are the contiguous scenes of a single story, loosely and uncertainly narrative. They move idly forward, repeating one another, stagnating for whole pages; and were only concluded, one imagines, when some outside interruption forced her to break off hastily her endless unravellings.

One of the longer stories, ' Assaulted and Pursued Chastity ', can serve as an example of all the rest. The ostensible moral is ' to show young women the danger of travelling without their parents, husbands or particular friends to guard them.' A well-bred orphan, the Lady Affectionata—Margaret's heroines are always short of at least one parent—returning to her native country at the end of a civil war, is shipwrecked upon the coast of the Kingdom of Sensuality and falls into the hands of a bawd. This infamous creature tries to procure her for a young Prince, ' a grand monopolizer of young virgins ', who is already married to a woman much older than himself. On the plea that a wizard once advised her to fire off a shot on her birthday to ensure good luck, Affectionata persuades a maid in the establishment to lend her a pistol, and promptly shoots the Prince with it when he refuses to desist from his advances. The wound only strengthens the Prince's love and he manages to have Affectionata removed from the bawd's to his aunt's house, and by his assiduous attentions and presents he makes Affectionata fall in love with him. One day when he is heated with wine he assaults

Here on this Figure Cast a Glance,
But so as if it were by Chance,
Your eyes not fixt, they must not stay,
Since this like Shadowes to the Day
It only represent's; for Still
Her Beuty's found beyond the Skill
Of the best Paynter, to Imbrace,
These louely Lines within her face,
View her Soul's Picture, Iudgment wit,
Then read those Lines which Shee hath writt,
By Phancy's Pencill drawne alone
Which Peice but Shee, Can iustly owne.

5. Margaret Cavendish, Marchioness of Newcastle. Frontispiece to *The Worlds Olio*, 1655. By Abraham van Diepenbeke. Engraved by Peter van Schuppen.

her, but she frustrates him by quickly breaking a convenient phial of poison in her mouth and falling into a coma. Revived by the aunt, she determines to escape, and cutting off her hair, donning a page's suit and adopting the name of Travelia, she makes her way to the coast in the hope of boarding a ship bound for her own country. By mistake she boards a vessel bound 'for new discoveries towards the south.'

In spite of its obvious absurdities, the tale so far retains touch with reality and moves at a much quicker pace than Margaret usually shows; but Affectionata-Travelia's escape towards the south is the opportunity for fantasy to board as pilot. The cruise ends in shipwreck and the captain of the vessel and Affectionata-Travelia, whom the captain has adopted as his 'son', make for the shore in the ship's boat only to be astonished by the natives lined up to greet them as they step ashore: 'they in the boat never saw such complexioned men, for they were not black like negroes, nor tawny, nor olive, nor ash-coloured, as many are, but of a deep purple; their hair as white as milk, and like wool; their lips thin, their ears long, their noses flat, yet sharp, their teeth and nails as black as jet and as shining; their stature tall and their proportion big; their bodies were all naked.' These strange creatures mount them on beasts yet stranger—half calf and half fish, with a horn like a unicorn's—and carry them to the governor of the kingdom. The wonders of the country unfold as they ride along: houses made of fish-bones and tiled with fish-scales, trees without either branches or leaves, having their flowers inlaid in the smooth wood, and all manner of fabulous beasts—especially one: 'There was one kind of beast in the shape of a camel, and the neck as white as a swan, and all the head and face white, only a lock of hair on the top of his crown of all manner of colours; the hair of his body was of a perfect gold yellow, his tail like his fore-top, but it would often turn up like a peacock's tail, and spread it as broad, and the hairs being of several colours made a glorious show; the legs and feet of the colour of the body, but the hoofs as black as jet.'

The metropolis to which they are carried is crammed with wonders, the most remarkable being the persons of royal blood: they ' were of a perfect orange colour, their hair coal-black, their teeth and nails as white as milk, of a very great height, yet well shaped.' The dew might fall in flakes like snow on this kingdom and taste of double-refined sugar but the inhabitants are anthropophagi; and after a year in captivity, Affectionata-Travelia and the captain understand that they are to be sacrificed. The heroine copes with the danger in an original manner. Having learnt the country's language and made the captain devise two pistols, she shoots the high priest dead as she is about to be sacrificed publicly to the sun, and pretending to be a messenger from the gods, she harangues the people on the nature of the soul and of God to such effect that she breaks them of cannibalism, civilizes them and becomes their beloved legislator.

We are now returned to the libidinous Prince. He sets out in search of Affectionata-Travelia and after being taken by pirates, adopts their profession. Among his first prizes are Affectionata-Travelia and the captain, who are on their way home. The pirate ship sinks, but all the crew and their goods are safely landed on a fertile uninhabited island. The Prince recognizing Affectionata-Travelia through her male disguise, proposes that they should pass their lives together on the island as man and wife. This proposal is sufficient to inspire Affectionata-Travelia's escape to the Kingdom of Amity; and still in disguise, she becomes confidante to the Queen of that country. The Prince, after several adventures, lands in the neighbouring Kingdom of Amour, and on the orders of its King leads an army against Amity. He succeeds in defeating the Queen but after Affectionata-Travelia has assumed command, he loses the day to her superior military genius and is taken prisoner. A plausible ending is at last within sight. The King and Queen marry and live in Amour, and Affectionata-Travelia and the Prince, whose elderly wife has died in his absence, follow suit and reign in Amity as joint-viceroys. And they all live happily ever after.

After reading this tale, and the many others in a similar style,

it is with some surprise that we come upon Margaret's protestations that she did not, could not read romances, the leisured
class's favourite literary diversion. She had tried to read them
but having once sampled them, whenever she picked one up later
by mistake she promptly threw it aside as 'an unprofitable
study.' Romances, she affirmed, contained little 'which ought
to be practised, but rather shunned as foolish amorosities and
desperate follies.' Her own tales, on the contrary, excited to
virtue and quenched 'amorous passions.' Her moral objections
to the form were sincere—had they not been she would never
have risked alienating her readers' attention with the unbearable
tedium of pages of moral discourse—but in improbabilities and
wonders she far outdid any romancer. How could the heroic
and languorous worlds of even the most polished French
romancers compete with her kingdom of purple savages and
plumed camels? The truth is that there was a marked affinity
between her imagination and theirs, and she was as instinctively
conforming to the spirit of the age in the composition of her
tales as she was in her natural philosophy.

Her weaknesses as a writer of fiction—though they are
so apparent that it seems redundant to set them down—lie
in narrative and characterization. 'Assaulted and Pursued
Chastity' has a livelier opening than most of her tales but becomes
intolerably confused and disjointed by the end, a failing which
may not be obvious in the résumé; and many of the others
hardly progress at all, settling immediately into a pool of stagnant
speculation. The heroines are always interesting to the extent of
revealing Margaret's own personality, but the other characters
are insubstantial and have even less connection with life than the
abstractions which people the usual contemporary romances.
The only reward her tales generally offer is an occasional passage
of poetic fantasy, like the journey made to the centre of the earth
by the hero of 'The Travelling Spirit': 'So when he came to
the centre of the earth, he saw a light like moonshine: but when
he came near, he saw the circle about the centre was glow-
worms' tails, which gave that light; and in the centre was an

157

old man, who neither stood nor sat, for there was nothing to stand or sit on; but he hung, as it were, in the air, nor never stirred out of his place, and had been there ever since the world was made; for he having never had a woman to tempt him to sin, never died.'

But Margaret's genius is disconcerting. There is one tale in the collection which shames the others with its brilliance. 'The Contract' is the story of the orphaned Lady Delitia, who is brought up by an uncle. The Duke of the province persuades the uncle to betroth his niece while yet a child to his second son. The Duke and his elder son die and the younger son inherits. He promptly forgets his obligation to Delitia and makes love to the young wife of an aged grandee. The uncle is naturally distressed by this conduct but determines to educate Delitia as well as he can; he instructs her in moral philosophy, ' to lay a ground and foundation of virtue ', in history, ' to learn her experience by the second hand ', and in the poets, ' to delight in their fancies and recreate in their wit '. When the Duke has married the pretty widow of the grandee, the uncle brings Delitia, now aged thirteen, to the capital, to live incognita and to continue her education, in music, dancing, natural philosophy, chemistry, etc.

Delitia's beauty grows in proportion to her knowledge and at length her uncle decides to present her to the world, choosing as the occasion a masque-night at court. She arrives attired in black. Both the Duke and his Viceroy fall in love with her at sight, but she slips secretly away like Cinderella without revealing her identity. Determined to see her again, the Viceroy commands a ball and she attends, dressed this time in white satin, embroidered in silver. Her beauty was such that ' she produced the same effects as a burning-glass; for the beams of all eyes were drawn together, as to one point placed in her face, and by reflection she sent a burning heat, and fired every heart.'

The Duke is overcome with grief and shame when he learns her identity but the Viceroy, unimpeded by a wife, proposes to her; a proposal which she is reluctantly persuaded by her uncle to accept. The Duke in despair writes to her protesting his love and she replies admitting her affection. At an interview, he persuades her to go to law over him with his wife, pleading her prior claim; and at the trial she argues her case so well that his marriage is declared null and he is free to marry her. The Viceroy, who really behaves rather badly, is rewarded with the Duke's cast-off wife.

A résumé of 'Assaulted and Pursued Chastity' sets the tale off to advantage by abridging its devious and tiresome length, but as certainly 'The Contract' is spoilt in a résumé by the stress which inevitably falls on the apparently implausible ending. In fact the narrative moves forward so swiftly and directly, the characterization is so consistent and the dialogue so crisp and natural that the ending is satisfactorily integrated into the whole. The material is the same as that of the other stories—once again Margaret is dramatizing herself and her ambitions—but this time she has succeeded in expressing it perfectly. Were all the tales in the collection of this quality, she would have enjoyed a considerable reputation as a writer of fiction.

Why do her other tales fall so far short of 'The Contract'? She was quite incapable of deliberation or revision: 'the brain being quicker in creating,' she wrote, 'than the hand in writing, or the memory in retaining, many fancies are lost, by reason they oftimes out-run the pen.' She was always running a race with her fancy, and, carried far ahead by her speed, she could not face the boredom of turning back to methodize what she had already written. Good, bad or indifferent, everything was sent to the press exactly as it was written, and having cleared her desk of papers she sat down again to take up the next subject, careless of what had gone before.

The second of Newcastle's commendatory verses prefixed to *Natures Pictures* was in praise of all Margaret's works which had appeared so far, 'except her tragedies and comedies, which will shortly come out.' Unfortunately the publication of her plays was delayed. The manuscript was lost when the ship carrying it to England to be printed foundered. Margaret was prudent enough to keep copies of her 'poor labours' until after they had appeared in print, when she burnt the copies, but the loss post-poned publication of her plays until after her return to England. The volume appeared in 1662 and a shorter collection of dramatic fragments in 1668.

Since Margaret owed so much to Newcastle for intellectual stimulus, it was inevitable that she should turn her attention sooner or later to the stage. He was more ambitious to appear as a dramatist than in any other literary rôle, and in 1649 he had had printed two of his comedies, *The Country Captaine* and *The Varietie*. The first was largely the work of James Shirley [1], to which Newcastle gave his name, and was written and acted in 1639 or 1640. The second is almost certainly of Newcastle's own composition. On the evidence of *The Varietie* Newcastle's conception of a play was to associate arbitrarily a few characters, each of them a 'humour' after the style of Ben Jonson, to en-tangle them in matrimony and to keep them justifiably on the stage by a slight pretence to plot. The tediousness and coarse-ness of *The Varietie* are hardly redeemed by the few passages of brisk dialogue. He had one gift which was not well displayed in this comedy—a pleasant sense of humour, which he showed particularly in his depiction of 'low' characters, grooms, servants and country folk; a class which he understood with the instinctive sympathy of the true aristocrat.

Newcastle's dramatic practice, however, cannot give a fair idea of his conception of the worth and dignity of the stage. In one of the many epistles to the reader prefixed to her plays, Margaret argues that a public theatre greatly benefits youths of quality: 'it learns them graceful behaviours and demeanours, it puts spirit and life into them, it teaches them wit, and makes their speech both voluble and tuneable; besides, it gives them confidence, all which ought every man to have, that is of quality . . . to conclude, a poet is the best tutor, and a theatre is the best school that is for youth to be educated by or in.' The argument is unquestionably Newcastle's, and as Margaret heard him expound such themes and listened to him read his own plays, which in her

[1] Shirley's share in *The Country Captaine* is discussed by Perry, pp. 104–12.

Thus in this Semy-Circle, wher they Sitt,
Telling of Tales of pleasure & of witt.
Heer you may read without a Sinn or Crime,
And how more innocently pass your tyme.

6. The Marquis and Marchioness of Newcastle and their family. Frontispiece to *Natures Pictures drawn by Fancies Pencil*, 1656. By Abraham van Diepenbeke. Engraved by Peter Clouwet.

ond opinion were the equal of Shakespeare's in wit, she decided that she, too, must write for the stage.

The disadvantage of writing plays during the interregnum was the impossibility of their being produced. The London theatres were closed and the actors were either dead or dispersed. But the disadvantage was only theoretical in Margaret's case. As she herself readily admitted, her plays could never have been performed. They were far too long to be staged and ' might tire the spectators,' as she wrote so innocently, ' who are forced or bound by the rules of civility to sit out a play, if they be not sick.' A unique epidemic would have unhoused the theatre long before one of Margaret's plays reached half-way. But length is the least of their failings. They are nothing more than a collection of disconnected scenes. ' I would have my plays to be like the natural course of all things in the world,' she wrote, distinguishing this weakness, '. . . some of my scenes have no acquaintance or relation to the rest of the scenes, although in one and the same play, which is the reason many of my plays will not end as other plays do.' They neither end nor proceed in the usual fashion; but even if they had conformed to the rules, they are so utterly undramatic that it is impossible to imagine them upon the boards—the only appropriate stage was, as she herself suggested, her own brain. But she was not at all sorry that they could never have been produced, for she could not have borne to hear them hissed: ' it would have made me a little melancholy to have my harmless and innocent plays go weeping from the stage, and whipped by malicious and hard-hearted censurers.' And the impossibility of their performance could not detract from their high purpose, which was ' to extol virtue, and to honour merit, and to praise the graces.'

Her plays are of the same substance as her tales, and their matter and manner can be most conveniently illustrated by a brief outline of one of the longest and the most coherent, ' Love's Adventures '. The play has a double plot—and several underplots, which must be disregarded—and each has its own heroine, Lady Bashful and Lady Orphan, who are both Margaret in disguise. To begin with the less important, Lady Bashful suffers extremely in company from shyness, which hides her sharp intelligence and good sense. She has several suitors, the most extraordinary being Sir Serious Dumb, a silent man. His silence however, is only assumed and once he has won Lady Bashful's affection and defeated his rivals, he becomes as eloquent as any, revealing himself as a man eminently suitable in character to becoming Lady Bashful's husband.

The adventures of Lady Orphan are more complicated and are reminiscent of Affectionata-Travelia's in 'Assaulted and Pursued Chastity.' Lady Orphan falls in love with Lord Singularity, whom she was intended from childhood to marry, and comes to the bold decision of joining him in Italy, where he is serving as General to the Venetians and winning a golden name. Travelling south in the company of her foster-father, Father Trusty, she presents herself to Lord Singularity in the disguise of a page and is taken into his service, quickly winning his confidence. After several adventures—for example, falling under suspicion of being a spy—she accompanies her master to the wars and acquits herself so gloriously that the Venetians make her Lieutenant-General to their army. She travels home in the company of Lord Singularity and at the Pope's urgent request breaks her journey in Rome, where she defeats the whole College of Cardinals in argument. The Pope is so impressed that he offers to make her a saint or a cardinal as she chooses, but as either of these honours would have interfered with her relation to Lord Singularity, she declines them and continues on her way. She doffs her disguise of a boy only when her foster-parents are accused of murdering her, and Lord Singularity's affection for her immediately becomes love. The play ends with their marriage.

An outline cannot reflect the confusion of the play, which is so long that it had to be broken into two parts, like so many of the others. The three unities, of time, place and action, are completely disregarded; time is indefinite in extent and operation, place is an appendage of character, and action creeps through a delta of tedium. As for the characters, they unaccountably emerge and disappear like figures in a dream and are to be recognized only by their names, indicative of their humours— Lady Wagtail, Sir Roger Exception, Nurse Fondly, Sir Peaceable Studious, Mrs. Reformer, *et al.*

All her other plays fall under the same condemnation; none lives up to the promise of its title: ' Youths Glory and Deaths Banquet ', ' The Publick Wooing ', ' The Comical Hash ', ' Bell in Campo ', etc. There is not an exception to contradict the impression that Margaret's genius was quite unsuited for the stage. The greatest rewards her plays offer are a deeper insight into her own character, an occasional passage of smart dialogue, commenting satirically on the follies, fashions and conventions of the day, and many eloquent speeches expressive of her poetic sensibility.

A few of her scenes have sometimes been complained against as exceptionally coarse for a woman, even allowing for the greater licence of the age; but the charge is not well grounded. She could not help but catch the tone of Newcastle's loose conversation, but when she imitated it she was revealing her longing to speak with the freedom of men rather than an innate coarseness of character. If society tolerated adultery and seduction on the stage when they were drawn by a man, why should she as a woman not expect the same licence? Was the discussion of vice also to be a male prerogative? Her frankness may not be prepossessing but it is introduced rarely, and then so formally that her intention is patent.

In a general prologue to all her plays Margaret explained that their faults were due to the rapidity of their composition; they were, she continues,

> So quickly writ that I did almost cry
> For want of work, my time for to employ:
> Sometime for want of work, I'm forced to play,
> And idly to cast my time away.

And in another place she confessed that as she found pleasure only in writing, she was constantly anxious lest her brain should grow barren, ' or that the root of my fancies should become insipid, withering into a dull stupidity for want of maturing subjects to write on.' [1] During her last years in Antwerp she was running out of subjects; poetry, natural philosophy, fiction and the drama, she had attempted them all, and having exhausted her stock of ideas on them, she was at a loss for new subjects or, more correctly, for further opportunities to relieve her fancy.

Luckily one of her correspondents suggested that she should write a volume of orations. At first she demurred, and not only on account of her ignorance of the rules of rhetoric; even supposing that she possessed the necessary ' wit, eloquence and learning ', how could she speak on matters of war and peace, or on affairs of state, the usual themes of orators, without knowledge of them, which, being a woman, she had been denied? However, she agreed to make a trial of one or two orations and to send them to her correspondent for her approval, and if they were approved, she would attempt others, sufficient to make a book.

The suggestion was fruitful because she admired orators above all others; not formal orators but natural orators, ' that can speak on a sudden upon any subject, whose words are as sweet and melting as manna from Heaven, and their wit as spreading and refreshing as the serene air, whose understanding is as clear as the sun, giving light of truth to all their hearers, who in case of persuasion speak sweetly, in case of reproof, seasonably, and in all cases, effectually.' [2] The greater number of the heroines of both her stories and plays are called upon to speak in public, and a few actually make oratory their profession, revealing Margaret's own longing to have the freedom and opportunities of men to address assemblies. Lady Sanspareille, the demi-heroine of ' Youths Glory and Deaths Banquet ', persuades her doting father to let her preach her opinions. She first addresses an audience of philosophers on nature, and they

[1] *Natures Pictures*, p. 385.
[2] *Sociable Letters*, p. 53.

are so struck with admiration that one of them suggests—need-
less to say, the remark is an interjection by Newcastle—that
they should all shave off their reverend beards ' and stuff boys'
footballs with them.' Other gatherings which she enlightens
in the course of her brief career are composed of moral philosophers, orators, poets, young students and soldiers; and as she
dies prematurely, she is comforted by the thought of the several
monuments to be erected to her memory.

Denied Lady Sanspareille's opportunity, Margaret had to
address ' reading auditors ', and her collection of orations,
Orations of Divers Sorts, Accomodated to Divers Places, which
appeared in 1662, after her return to England, was the closest
she came to shining in public as an orator.

Margaret's *Orations* is one of the most systematic of her works
and yet one of the most disappointing. Alarmed by criticisms
that her plays were without plot, design or catastrophe, which
hurt though she had herself anticipated them in the preliminaries
to the collection, she attempted a methodical arrangement of
her orations and explained it in a well-ordered address to the
reader. Her orations were, in the first place, general orations,
adapted to any kingdom or government. She wished her readers
to imagine themselves in the market-place of a metropolitan city
listening to a debate on peace and war. War is the people's
choice, and a number of orations on the field of battle follow,
succeeded in turn by further orations delivered in the city,
ruined by the war and now rebuilding. The series is so far a
reflection of Margaret's own time. Orations in the king's
council and in the judicature are the necessary sequel and prepare
for orations suitable to domestic occasions. Orations on civic
affairs, on the merits of a country life, on trade and commerce
and on scholarship wind up the cycle, which has touched upon all
the activities, deserving of eloquence, of any community.

The scheme is admirable, but unfortunately Margaret's self-
consciousness under criticism, and her lack of knowledge of
many of the subjects treated, inhibited her fancy, and the delightful irrelevancies, satiric, shrewd, or poetic, which are the reward

of the most tedious pages of her other works, are missing. The style is clear and smooth but flat and monotonous; and the self-imposed restraint, the deliberate avoidance of eccentricities, injects an insipidity into her thought and sentiment which is quite uncharacteristic. On very few occasions does she reveal her true qualities. A peasant's address to prove the happiness of rural life offers her an opportunity to express yet again her deep love of the countryside, a theme which whenever it occurs, as it frequently does, in her stories and plays is as refreshing as a gust of chill evening air through a hot room. 'Can there be more odoriferous perfumes than the sweet vegetables on the earth?' the peasant exclaims, in accents unlike those of any peasant: 'or finer prospects than stately hills, humble valleys, shady groves, clear brooks, green hedges, cornfields, feeding cattle, and flying birds? Can there be more harmonious music than warbling nightingales and singing birds? Can there be more delightful sounds than purling brooks, whispering winds, humming bees and small-voiced grasshoppers? Can there be a more delicious sweet than honey? More wholesome food than warm milk, fresh butter, pressed curds, new-laid eggs, seasoned bacon, savoury bread, cooling salads, and moist fruits? Or more refreshing drink than whey, whig, and butter-milk? Or more strengthening drink than ale, mead, perry and cider? And are we not our own vintage?'

The speeches of the quarter-drunk and half-drunk gentlemen are disappointingly flat, but in 'a sleepy speech to students' and in 'a waking oration', its reply, Margaret enters for the first time in the collection into her own realm of fantasy. The first orator contends that the drowsy world of dreams, provided the dreams be pleasurable, offers more than the contemplative or poetic worlds, for not only the mind but the senses, too, are engaged: 'The truth is, the poetical world, and contemplative life, is rather a world for thoughts, and a life for the mind, than the senses: yet, if the senses were as sensible in contemplation as in dreams, it would be the best life of all; because it might make the life what it would, and the pleasures of that life to

Studious She is and all Alone
Most visitants, when She has none,
Her Library on which She looks
It is her Head her Thoughts her Books.
Scorninge dead Ashes without fire
For her owne Flames doe her Inspire.

7. Margaret Cavendish, Marchioness of Newcastle. Frontispiece to *Philosophical and Physical Opinions*, 1655. By Abraham van Diepenbeke. Engraved by Peter van Schuppen.

continue as long and to vary as oft as it thought good; and for the poetical world, or rather worlds, they would be a delight to view as well as to live in.' This strange opinion is rejected by the second speaker, who condemns the drowsy world as only suitable for ' dull, lazy, unprofitable creatures ', a mad chaotic world. ' And as for dancing balls and French fiddles,' which the first speaker had professed to enjoy to perfection only in dreams, ' when the gallants, in dreams, are dancing in smooth measures and with fair ladies, and the music keeping tune to the dancing-time, on a sudden the courtly dancers, or dancing courtiers, turn topsy-turvy, dancing with their heads downwards and heels upwards; a very unbecoming posture for fair-faced ladies! And as for the music, that is quite out of tune, and the fiddle-strings broken, and the musicians as mad as March hares.' This surprising vision, which occurs at the very end of the collection, is Margaret's typical way of protesting against the unnatural restraint which she had imposed upon herself throughout its course, and is identical with the protests which she lodged at the conclusion of several of her writings on natural philosophy.

The letters in which Margaret discussed the composition of the *Orations*, along with many other letters, were collected by her and published in 1664 under the title of *CCXI Sociable Letters*. *Sociable Letters* is her most delightful work in prose and deserves to be far better known than it is. Who her correspondent was it is impossible to say, perhaps her friend and former maid, Mrs. Topp; but the informality of the letters strongly suggests that though written with the idea of publication in mind, they were actually addressed to someone and were not simply self-communings. The form suited her excellently. Unable to give her attention to any one subject for long without digressing restlessly into fantasy, the flexible length of the letter allowed her to concentrate upon a single topic and to dismiss it once she had made her relevant observations. And as there were no rules to govern their composition, she was not continually set on edge by the suspicion that she was unwittingly transgressing them.

A further advantage was that intimate correspondence with a trusted friend released her from bashfulness. Bashfulness, she once wrote, is a tyrant, whipping the body with 'pains of restraint' and imprisoning thoughts, words and wit; and many of her defects as a writer were caused by her bashfulness at appearing before the public. At ease with her correspondent, she was spared these agonies and could avoid their effect.

The naturalness of the *Sociable Letters* allowed her to give a clearer and fairer impression of her own character than in any of her other works. Neither her comedies nor her comical tales would lead the reader to suppose that she had a genuine sense of humour; the humour there is largely unintentional, as when she adds to a scene of duelling the stage direction, ' Meantime the women squeeks '. But her letters show that she could laugh at a ridiculous situation—at the behaviour of her neighbour's jealous wife—and gently at herself, at her attempts to employ her maids. They also reveal an uncommon shrewdness in observing society; and her opinions were expressed so sharply that had she thought of it, she could have written social satire to effect.

Her comments on the manners of society are many and various, ranging from opinions to descriptions of incidents. The behaviour of Lady D. D. and Lady C. C., for example, is compared in a sketch of what happened at the dinner parties they gave. Though hurt by an unkind remark of her husband's, Lady D. D. suppressed her tears and continued to entertain her guests, excusing her husband to them afterwards by saying that even the dearest and lovingest of friends would on occasion give cause for exception: ' thus her discretion did not suffer her passion to disturb her guests, and her good nature did excuse her husband's folly, and her love did forgive his disrespect to her.' Lady C. C. behaved to the contrary. Being a ' mode ' lady she would have a ' mode ' dinner, and was highly disgusted when the cook sent up a chine of beef, knowing his master loved it. The serving of beef was ' not only an old but a country fashion ' to her refined taste, and she commanded its removal.

Her husband objected, she repeated the order, and very quickly the pair fell from words to blows, and she retreated weeping to her chamber, to her guests' discomfiture: 'the truth is, she showed herself a fool and behaved herself as mad.' Or there is the anecdote of Sir S. P., who was foolish enough to lose £500 at tennis and £2,000 at cards and dice, which led Margaret to consider the evils of tennis and gambling, whoring and drunkenness. She condemned tennis because it wasted a man's vital spirits 'through much sweating', and whoring because it destroyed his health and property and brought his family to misery; and 'so with the pot and the rot, the ball, the card and the dice, men busy the whole time of their life, or rather waste the whole time of their life, together with their life; and not in any one of these actions is honour, nor, as I can perceive, pleasure.' Her social comments are constantly entertaining and surprising.

The variety of the *Sociable Letters* includes speculations in natural philosophy, literary criticism, and anecdotes taken from her own experience; but as many of these letters have been quoted already, or will be used later, it only remains to refer to those in which she generalizes on life with an ease and eloquence superior to many moralists of reputation. Good sense always governed her private life and is equally revealed in her letters. 'Indeed time runs so fast upon youth,' she wrote in reply to her correspondent's desire to anticipate the passage of time, 'as it doth oppress youth, which makes youth desire to cast it by; and though the motion of time is swift, yet the desire of youth is swifter, and the motions of thoughts are as far beyond the motions of time, as the motion of time is beyond the motion of nature's architecture; so as youth through its sharp, greedy hungry appetite devours time, like as a cormorant doth fish, for he never stays to chew but swallows down whole fishes, so youth swallows, as it were, whole days, weeks, months, years, until they surfeit with practice, or are fully satisfied with experience.'

Margaret's writing had swallowed down the years of exile. *CCXI Sociable Letters* was the last of her works composed in

Antwerp. When she had travelled to England in company with Sir Charles Cavendish in 1651, she had been entirely unknown beyond the narrow circle of her family. Between her departure from England in 1653 and her return at the Restoration, she had published four books and was famous, or notorious, as the leading literary woman of the age.

9 Restoration

I observe, that spleen and malice, especially in this age, is grown to that height, that none will endure the praise of anybody besides themselves; nay, they'll rather praise the wicked than the good; the coward rather than the valiant; the miserable than the generous; the traitor than the loyal; which makes wise men meddle as little with the affairs of the world as ever they can.

THE practice of horsemanship and the preparation of his great book on the art served to distract Newcastle's attention from the continual plotting which was, too often, the only and unhappy diversion of the royalist exile. Though Antwerp was, as a major centre of communications, an excellent residence for anyone wishing to keep in touch with the conspiracies and quarrels which were spun or waged between the King's court at Cologne or, later, at Bruges, the Queen Mother's at Paris, and the parties of royalists, presbyterians and sectaries at home, Newcastle himself was no longer in the middle of affairs. His influence and reputation were still sufficiently great to make him indirectly familiar with the complicated machinations which went on; but he had been slowly ousted from the King's inner counsels, which were engrossed by Hyde and Ormonde, the unreliable Digby, and the group of younger men about the King, for the most part a dissipated quarrelsome crew. For example, at the beginning of 1658 when Ormonde passed secretly into England at great danger to himself to attempt a co-ordination of the factions there, whose rising was to coincide with an invasion by Charles from Flanders at the head of troops raised and supported by Spain, Newcastle was not informed of his destination, which had been given out as Germany. He learnt of it from other sources and spoke about it so freely that his conversation came to the attention of Hyde and others in the secret. Thomas Ross, the emissary of one of the royalist factions at home, wondered 'that anyone who knows Newcastle would trust him with so important a secret, for it might as well be proclaimed at the cross.' [1]

Ross's charge need not be taken seriously—the royalists were seldom to be found speaking good of one another; but his explanation that Newcastle's discontent at being kept in ignorance of the negotiations in progress was fanned by Margaret is plausible. According to Ross, Margaret swore 'that the affair can not and shall not be effected without her husband.' [2] Her own conception of Newcastle's wisdom and ability was so high that she was naturally unable to believe that success could possibly attend any plan uninformed by his advice; and his exclusion made her suspect that in the event of a restoration in which he had had no part, he might be cheated of the reward for his sufferings by the self-seeking schemers about the King.

Newcastle himself was shrewdly aware of the dangers of being cheated by the courtiers; as early as 1654 he had written to Secretary Nicholas asking him to remind the King to renew to him the offices which he had once held; [3] and for this reason alone he tried to be familiar with, though he could not control, the various negotiations for the King's return. He preferred, however, to wait patiently on the course of events rather than to engage in any impossible attempts to bring about a restoration. The comforts of Antwerp, uneasily enjoyed though they were under the shadow of uncertainty and debt, had not made him less willing to hazard himself in the cause. When the Marquis of Montrose visited him on his way to Scotland in 1649 and asked him whether he was not also prepared to venture, Newcastle replied that while he was always ready to risk his own life at the King's command, he would not risk the lives of his friends, whom he would certainly draw to follow him by his example, ' in a desperate action, without any probability

[1] Ross to Nicholas, 24 Feb./6 March, 1658; *C S P D*, *1657-8*, 1884, p. 300.

[2] Same to same, 1/11 March 1658; *ib.*, p. 311.

[3] Newcastle to Nicholas, 5/15 August 1654; *ib.*, *1654*, 1880, p. 288.

of doing the least good to his Majesty.'[1] The several risings
planned after Montrose's ill-fated journey were actions even
more desperate, and Newcastle was entirely justified in not
embarking either himself or his companions upon them.

Though Charles's moral degeneration was by this time complete, he still regarded his old governor affectionately, and when
he checked him for spreading reports of Ormonde's where-
abouts, he did so gently, 'having real kindness for him, rather
pitying his weakness than forgetting his inadvertency'[2]—but
the report is Ross's, and he may have chosen to imagine a rebuke
out of dislike for Newcastle.

The occasion of the 'rebuke' was the moment of Charles's
departure on 4 March 1658 from Antwerp where he had been
holding court to confer the Order of the Garter on the French
count, Jean-Gaspard de Marchin, Lieutenant-General of his
army. The conferring of such honours was Charles's only way
of rewarding his servants. On Monday, 25 February, in the
afternoon, Marchin was introduced into the King's presence
between Newcastle and the Earl of Bristol, preceded by Sir
Edward Walker, Garter King of Arms, and after being knighted
was invested with the insignia. The most notable of the celebrations accompanying the investiture was a ball given by Newcastle at his house on the following evening. A splendid company assembled in Rubens's studio: Charles and his brothers,
James and Henry, his sister, Mary, Princess of Orange, the
Comtesse de Cantecroix and her two children, with others of
the nobility, and many of the leading citizens, particularly
Gaspar Duarte and his three sisters. The King was brought
into the room with music and when the company were placed,
Major Michael Mohun, the actor, wearing a black satin robe and
crowned with a garland of gilded bays, stepped forward to
welcome him in hyperbolic verse of Newcastle's composition.
After French dancing, Lady Moore, 'dressed all up in feathers',
sang one of the host's songs, which had been set to music by

[1] *Life*, p. 131.
[2] See above p. 172, n. 2.

Nicholas Lanier, Master of the King's Music. The banquet followed. Eight great chargers were carried in by sixteen gentlemen of the court, and other gentlemen carried in the wine. As soon as the company were refreshed, they fell to country dancing for two hours, and at midnight Major Mohun, in cloak and bays, closed the festivity by speaking an epilogue prophetic of Charles's happy restoration.[1] The entertainment was only a faint reflection of the extravagant celebrations which Newcastle had once offered to Charles I, but he could congratulate himself on making so fine a show in the face of adversity and necessity. The King himself was reduced at this time to such extreme poverty that as he looked round him, he may have remarked, as he did on another occasion after dining with Newcastle, ' that he perceived Newcastle's credit could procure better meat than his own.' [2]

Sir Edward Walker, concluding the report on the ball which he sent to Secretary Nicholas, remarked: ' Thus how melancholy soever you are at Bruges we spend our time merrily here, and it were well if it could still be so, but I fear faction (considering the time of the year) will speedily ensue.' There was never a time when faction was not the order of the royalist exiles, and it worsened in the course of the two years following Newcastle's entertainment. But after the death of Cromwell in September 1658 it became increasingly evident that the King would be returned to England, though upon what terms was most uncertain. As Newcastle viewed the struggle for supremacy between the parties at home, he grew cautiously optimistic. ' I am confident God has many blessings in store for my dear and most gracious master,' he wrote to Secretary Nicholas on 9 March 1660, ' but I cannot conclude what will be the issue of the great distractions and cross interests in England. That the King will be called in is probable, but on what conditions the Lord knows. I am not of the opinion to come in on

[1] Cotterell to Nicholas, 19 Feb./1 March 1657/8; *C S P D, 1657–8,* 1884, p. 311; Walker to same, same date, *ib.,* pp. 296–7.
[2] *Life*, p. 80.

any terms, and be trammelled and made a Duke of Venice of, which is but Lord Mayor during his life.'[1]

Newcastle had prepared for his own return as well as he could by firmly directing the affairs of his family through correspondence with his sons, conducted under the aliases of Joseph Forreste and Robert Deane. The elder boy, Charles, died in May 1659 and was succeeded as Viscount Mansfield by the younger, Henry. Newcastle's letters were chiefly concerned with the best ways to preserve the estates and especially the goods: ' The next is for the goods ', he wrote to Henry on 12 October 1659, ' which troubles me much, that so long gathering by your ancestors should be destroyed in a moment.'[2] His advice was always shrewd and to the point, and as he was tactful enough to see that his sons might suspect Margaret's interest in the preservation of the property, he would add a phrase implicitly exonerating her of any ulterior motive: 'for she is as kind to you,' he remarked in the same letter, ' as she was to your brother, and so good a wife as that she is all for my family, which she expresses is only you.'

Within a month of Newcastle's letter to Nicholas deploring the possibility of the King's return to England in the rôle of Lord Mayor for life, Charles had issued his Declaration from Breda on 14 April. Events now moved quickly. On 8 May Charles was proclaimed King of England, Scotland, France and Ireland, and shortly afterwards he removed to the Hague in readiness to sail for England. Newcastle, leaving Margaret behind, hurried from Antwerp to pay court to the King, ' who used him very graciously '; and the Duke of York offered him the use of one of the ships ordered to transport the royal party to England. But Newcastle's impatience to see his own country again was too great to bear delay and he asked for and received permission to hire a vessel for himself and his company. The person entrusted to hire the ship chose an ' old rotten frigate '— so unsound that Margaret said she ' might better call it a boat than

[1] *C S P D, 1659–60*, 1886, p. 378.
[2] *H M C, 13 Rep., Pt. ii*, 1893, ii. 143.

a ship'—and several of the people who were to have travelled in it refused to set sail.[1] Having trusted to luck for sixteen years, Newcastle could not believe that Fortune would now play him false, and set sail in the 'ship' along with his more faithful friends. The joy of the voyage—a voyage anticipated for so long that it must have seemed the incredible single performance of a scene endlessly rehearsed—must be given in Margaret's own unaffected words, though she herself had to wait until their reunion in England before hearing Newcastle's account. 'My Lord (who was so transported with the joy of returning into his native country, that he regarded not the vessel) having set sail from Rotterdam, was so becalmed that he was six days and six nights upon the water, during which time he pleased himself with mirth, and passed his time away as well as he could. Provisions he wanted not, having them in great store and plenty. At last, being come so far that he was able to discern the smoke of London, which he had not seen in a long time, he merrily was pleased to desire one that was near him to jog and awake him out of his dream, for surely, said he, I have been sixteen years asleep, and am not thoroughly awake yet. My lord lay that night at Greenwich, where his supper seemed more savoury to him, than any meat he had hitherto tasted; and the noise of some scraping fiddlers, he thought the pleasantest harmony that ever he had heard.' [2]

Charles sailed for Dover on 22 May and a huge crowd gathered on the cliffs to pay him homage when he landed two days later, to fall dramatically on his knees in thanksgiving. Among those welcoming him was Newcastle's son, Henry, Lord Mansfield, who fully expected to find his father with the King. When the King told him that his father had sailed from Holland before his own departure, Mansfield became greatly alarmed and his alarm was increased by reports of the condition of the ship in which Newcastle had sailed. The ship deserved its bad name: it foundered and sank on its next voyage. Setting out

---

[1] *Life*, p. 84.
[2] *Ib.*, pp. 84-5.

at once in search of his father, Mansfield found him alive and well at Greenwich; and the joy with which ' they embraced and saluted each other ' was too great to be expressed by Margaret's pen.

Margaret herself had been left ' in pawn ' at Antwerp for Newcastle's debts. He instructed her to stay there until he could raise the money to redeem her, and to apologize to the magistrates for his not taking a civil leave of them or thanking them for their many civilities, so great had been the hurry of his departure. As his estate was still uncertain, he had difficulty in raising money and when the sum necessary to redeem his wife was advanced by Sir Joseph Ash, an Antwerp merchant, it fell short by £400 of the amount Margaret required, taking into account the debts she had acquired since Newcastle's departure and the cost of her transportation into England. Showing the practicality which was to become a marked trait of her character as she grew older, Margaret borrowed the £400 from another English merchant in Antwerp and made arrangements for her journey. Asking Gaspar Duarte to act as her interpreter, she sent for the magistrates and thanked them on her own and her husband's behalf for all their kindness. They replied expressing their sorrow at her departure and wished her ' soon and well to the place where she most desired to be '; and after they had withdrawn they sent officials with the customary present of wine.

After the back-rent of the house had been paid, and the coachmaker's, mercer's and brewers' scores settled, Margaret set out with her servants for Flushing, cutting all her links, except for some later correspondence with the Duarte sisters, with the city that had been her home for ten years. At Flushing she had hoped to find an English man-of-war to carry her into England—' being loath to trust myself with a less vessel '; in her timidity how unlike her husband. There was no English man-of-war in harbour but hearing of a Dutch man-of-war which waited to convoy some merchantmen, Margaret sent for the captain and asked him to carry her to England. He agreed to take her but he had first to ask permission of the Dutch States General. As soon as he had received permission, they set sail; Margaret and her chief servants in the man-of-war and the rest of her company and her goods in 'another good strong vessel, hired for that purpose.'[1]

Several months passed between Margaret's reunion with Newcastle in London and their retirement into the country, but in her *Life* of her husband, Margaret hurriedly passes over this interval in a paragraph, betraying its disappointment only in a phrase or two. When she joined him, she found him living in lodgings too small to house all his family and not 'fit for a person of his rank and quality.' 'Neither did I find my Lord's condition such as I expected,' she added darkly; and she asked him in 'some passion' to retire into the country. He 'gently reproved' her for her precipitancy, and for the remainder of their stay in London they removed to Dorset House, which, though better than the former lodgings, was still not entirely to her satisfaction. At length Newcastle told her that as his business was finished, they must prepare to move, which 'was no unpleasant news' to her, 'who had a great desire for a country life.'

The truth was that Newcastle had found, along with many other returned exiles, that his loyalty and sufferings did not admit him to play any significant part in the new reign. Though he had earlier composed a letter to the King advising him on the policy he ought to pursue at his restoration, his counsel was based upon nostalgic recollections of a world that had long since disappeared under the cataclysm of civil war. The England he had returned to was ordered by new men and new ideas, and as a representative of the past his antiquated wisdom could expect little attention. His age was a further disadvantage. Charles surrounded himself with young men as pleasure-loving and unscrupulous as himself, and though he continued to regard Newcastle affectionately, he did not want him at court, an anachronism, a witness to virtues for which he had lost all respect. The Restoration settlement, too, was a compromise, and Newcastle discovered that however great his desert, his

[1] *Ib.*, pp. 86–8.

reward would not be proportionate. With wisdom if not with entire justice, the King thought fit to satisfy first the claims of those at home, whose help in engineering his return had been more effective, if less honourable, than that of the exiles who had suffered with him abroad.

Newcastle was no fool, and when once he had recognized the hopelessness of expecting to play any part at court, he decided that the best course would be to retire to the country and set about restoring his wasted estates. He delayed in London until the bill restoring to him all ' his honours, manors, lands and tenements ' had been passed; the ' business ' to which Margaret refers. This was not done without a scene in the Lords. The bill was for the joint reparation of Newcastle, the Duke of Buckingham, and the Earl of Bristol, but Bristol having named only Newcastle in his speech proposing it, Buckingham rose and angrily asked why Newcastle rather than himself had been named? Bristol replied that he thought Newcastle ' a man of more merit ' than Buckingham; and the quarrel would have led to a duel had not the King intervened and commanded them to stay in their lodgings.[1] The bill was passed on 7 August and received the royal assent on 13 September.

Before retiring to the country, Newcastle went to the King and begged leave to do so. ' Sir, I am not ignorant that many believe I am discontented,' he said, ' and 'tis probable they'll say I retire through discontent; but I take God to witness that I am in no kind of ways displeased; for I am so joyed at your Majesty's happy Restoration, that I cannot be sad or troubled for any concern to my own particular; but whatsoever your Majesty is pleased to command me, were it to sacrifice my life, I shall most obediently perform it, for I have no other will but your Majesty's pleasure.'[2] All Newcastle's sentiments were of this kind, and of his complete loyalty there can be no question; but the speech clearly reveals how deeply hurt he was by the King's disregard of his services. For the new courtiers he had

[1] *H M C, 5 Rep.*, 1876, pp. 155, 177.
[2] *Life*, p. 89.

179

M 2

only contempt, and he expressed it in a scene which he contributed
to one of Margaret's plays. 'When they use you kindest,' says
Underward of courtiers, having just come to a decision to quit
the court for the country, 'then look to yourself, for then they
have deceived, or mean to deceive you; all is interest and
particular end, that is all the kindness and friendship they
have.' [1]

After his retirement to Welbeck at the end of 1660, Newcastle
set about recovering and ordering his estates, as a preliminary to
repaying his debts. Welbeck itself was much out of repair and
Bolsover was partly destroyed, only Sir Charles Cavendish's
selfless intervention having saved it from complete destruction.
Nottingham Castle came on the market at this time and Newcastle sold land to buy it because it had been a seat beloved of
his father. But of all his houses Bolsover pleased him best.
Dr. Francis Andrewes had written some pleasant verses on the
mansions of the Dukeries before the Civil War.

> Hardwick for hugeness, Worksop for height,
> Welbeck for use, Bols'er for sight.
> Worksop for walks, Hardwick for hall,
> Welbeck for brewhouse, Bols'er for all.
> Welbeck a parish, Hardwick a court,
> Worksop a palace, Bols'er a fort. [2]

And the comparisons are rung like a chime of light bells down to
the concluding peal:

> The rest are jewels of the shire,
> Bols'er the pendant of the ear.

Bolsover's romantic situation, overlooking a landscape as lovely
as any before industrialism came to spoil it, and its even more
romantic appearance, grey, embattled, ornamented and fantastically styled, are not unaptly described in the phrase ' the pendant
of the ear '. Within the keep, the rooms—the Elysium Room,
the Pillared Hall, the Marble Closet—are painted or panelled or

---

[1] ' Scenes ', p. 147; *Plays*, 1668.
[2] Brit. Mus., Harl. MSS. 4955, f. 67[v].

decorated in marble and reflect Newcastle's striking and luxurious taste, modelled on his father's. 'Welbeck for use,' Andrewes had written, and as long as Bolsover was in disrepair Newcastle made Welbeck his home. It, too, was celebrated by one of Newcastle's poets, Richard Flecknoe; but his imagination was, as usual, dulled by his belly when he wrote in its praise. Welbeck, he thrummed,

> Whose cellar and whose larder seem t' have been
> Of ev'ry foreign land the magazine. [1]

When Margaret came to write her husband's life, she set out at length the devastation of his property and faithfully counted up his enormous losses; and though it is unnecessary to follow her into all the details, the more remarkable must be repeated so as to give an idea of his sacrifices in the royal cause. Of his eight parks, only one, Welbeck, had not been completely destroyed. When he saw the shape of Clipstone Park, the pleasantest of them all, he showed distress for the first time, 'though he did little express it, only saying he had been in hopes it would not have been so much defaced as he found it, there being not one timber-tree in it left for shelter.' Among his other property stolen or lost were linen, hangings—out of a hundred and fifty suits only ten or twelve were saved—silver plate to the value of £2,700, furnishings, horses and cattle, etc.; the whole amounting in value to well over £12,000, the sum actually spent on replacing those losses in part. As for his losses in money, they amounted to no less than £941,303, taking into account uncollected interest and rents, lands sold and woods destroyed, loans and debts.

Once in the country, Newcastle carefully began the restoration of his property: houses were repaired, stables rebuilt and parks and farms restocked; but in addition to these practical difficulties there were legal complications to hinder his task. His London house in Clerkenwell, for example, had been sold in 1654 to repay a debt, and when he claimed it back under the

[1] Flecknoe, *Euterpe Revived*, 1675, p. 46.

bill for the restoration of his estate, the purchaser petitioned the Lords to be allowed to go to law to vindicate his right. Newcastle eventually regained possession, but only after many vexations; and the vexations were endlessly multiplied as he tried to reduce all his affairs to order.

Newcastle accepted his losses and anxieties with remarkable philosophy, and in spite of their provocation he showed no sign of wishing to revenge himself on his old enemies. When John Hutchinson's house at Owthorpe was plundered of all his personal weapons and armour by the soldiery in 1660, his son complained to Newcastle as Lord-Lieutenant of the county, and Newcastle immediately ordered their return. Two years later he showed even more extraordinary kindness to Hutchinson. After Hutchinson had been carried before him on suspicion of plotting against the Government, he treated him, in Lucy Hutchinson's words, 'very honourably',[1] and in the belief of his innocence sent him home on parole without a guard, promising to do what he could to prevent further action being taken against him. No incident redounds more to his honour than his kindness to Hutchinson, a representative of all that he hated politically and of the forces which had condemned him to sixteen years of exile.

His rewards from the Crown were comparatively small in the light of his losses. He had been appointed a Gentleman of the Bedchamber on 21 September 1660 with a pension of £1,000 a year, but he received nothing until November 1668, when a warrant was issued for the payment of arrears and the pension itself confirmed.[2] He also had great difficulty in securing the repayment of £3,500, the remainder of a loan of £10,000 made to Charles I in 1639.[3] He had had to pay interest on this sum himself and his claim on the Crown in 1663 amounted to £9,240, but a year later he was told that he could expect at the most repayment of the remainder of the principal. He may have

---

[1] Hutchinson, ii, 291–2.
[2] C S P D, 1668–9, 1894, p. 83.
[3] H M C, 13 Rep., Pt. ii, 1893, ii. 144.

helped by both Newcastle himself and his secretary, John Rolleston. She relied on Rolleston for the account of his master's early life and, especially, of his campaigns in the Civil War; and she was probably indebted to him for the explanation and summary of his losses. She drew much of her information of particular incidents from Newcastle; the details of Marston Moor and of his first glimpse of London on returning from exile are clearly given in almost his own words. But in the main she relied upon her own knowledge, and the style and sentiment are hers alone. It was Newcastle's express command that she should write according to her own lights. When she said she would need 'a learned assistant' to help her, protesting her ignorance of the rules of writing history, he told her that 'truth could not be defective.' But 'rhetoric', she argued, 'did adorn truth.' 'Rhetoric was fitter for falsehoods than truths,' was his reply. Thrown back upon her own resources, she proceeded to write a biography which the ministrations of any 'learned assistant' would certainly have spoiled.

Her method, however, was by no means undeliberated. In the preface to the biography she distinguished between three kinds of history; general, national, and particular or biographical. The first is useful because it teaches 'the known parts and people of the world'; the second is pernicious because it is partial and continues the memory of old quarrels, domestic and foreign, 'that would otherwise have been forgotten'; but the third 'is the most secure, because it goes not out of its own circle but turns on its own axis, and for the most part keeps within the circumference of truth.' Her life of her husband falls into the third category. It is not, however, concerned with the whole of his life but chiefly with his 'heroic and prudent actions . . . as also of his sufferings, losses, and ill-fortunes': in other words, with his life from the outbreak of the Civil War down to the Restoration. She could have collected further details of Newcastle's earlier life from John Rolleston, but as it was her single purpose to perpetuate the memory of the years of war and exile, she did not draw largely upon him. She could also have extended the life by including Newcastle's correspondence and declarations, but omitted them as unnecessary; or by describing the actions of his enemies—but this she was commanded not to do by Newcastle, to avoid reviving old dissensions.

She is so specific in defining her purpose that it is disappointing to come across Donald Stauffer's remark in his history of English biography before 1700 that ' after her fanfare of prefaces, wherein mountains travail, the ensuing life of the Duke of Newcastle seems somewhat unworthy of its heralds.' [1] Margaret is habitually verbose but her preface—there is in fact only one, in addition to the dedication to the King, an epistle to Newcastle himself and a prefatory letter by John Rolleston: a very modest score for Margaret—is greatly to the point, and no one reading it carefully need be under any misconception of her purpose. Her intention was fully grasped by Sir Charles Firth. ' The special interest of the book lies rather in the picture of the exiled royalist,' Firth wrote in his edition of the *Life*, ' cheerfully sacrificing everything for the King's cause, struggling with his debts, talking over his creditors, never losing confidence in the ultimate triumph of the right, and on his return setting to work uncomplainingly to restore his ruined estate.' [2]

Stauffer was at least right when he affirmed that the biography ' is individual and follows no pattern.' The work is divided into four Books. The first two are narrative, dealing with the Civil War and the years of exile respectively; the third is composed of observations on Newcastle's particular achievements and on aspects of his character; and the fourth is a collection of his miscellaneous opinions—' essays and discourses gathered from the mouth of my noble lord and husband.' We are so used to the art of biography as settled by James Boswell that we are conscious of the weakness of the scheme rather than of its boldness and originality. Even the warmest admirers of Izaak Walton will admit that he occasionally borders on ' garrulity and discursiveness ', and it was exactly to avoid such faults, which she

[1] Donald A. Stauffer, *English Biography before 1700*, 1930, p. 153.
[2] *Life of Cavendish*, ed. Firth, pp. viii–ix.

well knew by this time to be the principal defect of her earlier, especially of her philosophical works, that Margaret devised this unusual arrangement. It allowed her to separate narrative and commentary, which haphazardly mingling together ruined the form of even the best of contemporary biographies. In practice the attempt failed because the third and fourth Books read as appendices, containing material which she was incapable of working into the first two, the proper place. Had she attempted the synthesis which Boswell finally achieved, she would probably have succeeded moderately well, for the narrative, written in the ' natural plain style ' of which she boasted in the preface, moves forward easily and swiftly. The only impediment is a lack of dates; a carelessness which she regretted in the preface.

Her greatest achievement is the distinct impression which she gives of Newcastle's character. From first to last the reader is aware of his urbane, tolerant and accomplished presence, and cannot but feel an affection for him. He emerges most clearly in the greater episodes—in the accounts of Marston Moor, of the return from exile and of the conversations with Hobbes; but these are reinforced by many details—' Flemish details ', as Boswell called the similar touches which he used to such effect in his life of Johnson. When Newcastle and one of his cousins were young, she relates, they were both given some money; the cousins purchased land but Newcastle bought a singing boy, a horse and a dog, which pleased his father so well that he remarked that he would disinherit any son whom he found so covetous as to buy land before he was twenty. He had so little regard for rank—' except it be for ceremony '—that ' to the meanest person he'll put off his hat, and suffer every body to speak to him.' He was ' neat and cleanly ' in his person, which made him ' to be somewhat long in dressing ', and he shifted into clean clothes once a day and always after exercise. As for his diet, he ate one good meal a day, contenting himself with a morsel of bread and a glass of sack for breakfast, and an egg and a draught of small beer for supper, and owed his health and his longevity to his temperance. The artless introduction of such

187

details prevented the portrait of Newcastle from hardening into the formality of a ' set piece '.

But the biography was more than an attempt to stave off forgetfulness; it was also a memorial to Margaret's love and gratitude. She had found in his company a happiness which it is highly unlikely she would have found in that of any other man. Not only did he complement her own weaknesses and tolerate her idiosyncrasies but he actively encouraged her writing, which to her was dearer than all else. ' But though your Lordship hath many troubles, great cares, and much business in your particular affairs,' she wrote in a preface to one of her books, 'yet you are pleased to peruse my works, and approve of them so well as to give me leave to publish them, which is a favour few husbands would grant their wives.' [1] The biography was her way of repaying her debt.

The Life of the Thrice Noble, High and Puissant Prince William Cavendishe, Duke, Marquess, and Earl of Newcastle, etc., was published at the end of 1667, and Samuel Pepys read it in the new year. ' Thence home,' he noted on 18 March, ' and there, in favour to my eyes, stayed at home, reading the ridiculous History of my Lord Newcastle, wrote by his wife, which shows her to be a mad, conceited, ridiculous woman, and he an ass to suffer her to write what she writes to him and of him.' [2] ' Where a book is at once both good and rare,'—it is Elia writing a century and a half later, '—where the individual is almost the species, and when that perishes,

> We know not where is that Promethean torch
> That can its light relumine—

such a book, for instance, as The Life of the Duke of Newcastle, by his Duchess,—no casket is rich enough, no casing sufficiently durable, to honour and keep safe such a jewel.' [3] No two opinions could be more opposed than Pepys's and Lamb's. What

[1] Philosophical Opinions, 1663, p. Æ3ᵛ.
[2] Pepys, vii. 343–4.
[3] Lamb, ' On Books and Reading ', Essays of Elia, Everyman ed., 1950, p. 203.

the diarist found offensive—the parading of affection and the details of private life—the essayist enjoyed for its singularity, sincerity and delight. At least the reactions of both men prove that the biography does not lack character.

It is impossible not to compare Margaret's biography with two others of the same kind: Lucy Hutchinson's life of her husband and the autobiography of Anne, Lady Fanshawe, which is also, in effect, a biography of her husband, Sir Richard Fanshawe. Margaret's work appears at a disadvantage, particularly when contrasted with the first; but the fairness of making this usual comparison may be questioned. Lucy Hutchinson wrote her biography under the inspiration of Margaret's to console herself in her grief for her husband's death and to instruct her children in his character. She never intended it for publication and could consequently treat at length of her relations with her husband— of his courtship of her, for example, which is among the most delightful passages in the work—with a frankness which Margaret, for all her boldness, dared not attempt. Margaret dismisses Newcastle's courtship in a paragraph, though she had at hand all his love letters and poems and could have given a delightful account of the Queen's opposition to the marriage. Mrs. Hutchinson was secure in her privacy. Again, the power of Mrs. Hutchinson's biography derives in part from her skilful integration of the events of the Civil War and of her husband's character, and her determination to vindicate his character gives her historical excursions an edge which would be unusual at any time. Margaret, too, wished to vindicate Newcastle but was expressly forbidden by him to deal in history or personalities. Had she not been so shackled, she might—to choose at random —have given information about the relations between New-castle and Prince Rupert before Marston Moor, or of the negotiations which led to the King's journey to Scotland in 1649, or of the quarrels of the royalist exiles, which would have been at least equal in interest to any of Mrs. Hutchinson's information. Certainly she would not have excelled Mrs. Hutchinson in style or analysis, lacking as she did the other's power of forceful reasoning and sharp discrimination, but had she had freedom, she might have written a work more various and curious than the *Memoirs of Colonel Hutchinson*.

The same arguments hold good in considering Lady Fanshawe's *Memoirs*. It, too, was written for the instruction of her children and was not prepared for publication—it was not even completed; and safe in her privacy Lady Fanshawe was able to speak of her great love for her husband, which gives her writing its rare quality, with a particularity she would never have dared to print. 'He was married at 35 years of age, and lived with me but 23 years and 29 days.' What would have been Pepys's comment on that fond calculation? Apart from her love, Lady Fanshawe's book is especially interesting for the account of her adventures during the Civil War. Once read, the anecdote of her clandestine visits at dawn to her husband imprisoned in Whitehall cannot be forgotten: 'He that after the first time expected me never failed to put out his head at first call. Thus we talked together; and sometimes I was so wet with rain that it went in at my neck and out at my heels.' [1] But Margaret, too, had had adventures which could have been plausibly worked into her biography; her flight to France in the Queen's train, or her experiences of poverty, or any of the other curious incidents which must have occurred in her travels. Again, she was prevented from using such material by the enforced propriety of publication.

Without wishing in any way to make a ridiculous attempt to belittle Mrs. Hutchinson or Lady Fanshawe, their works cannot be seriously compared with Margaret's biography; not because they are beneath it in quality but because they were not intended for publication. The only true standard of comparison is with other published biographies, and compared to them Margaret's is an entertaining, interesting and highly original contribution to the art.

When the biography was published in folio in 1667 it was handsomely printed in 'a fair print', as Pepys described it,

[1] Fanshawe, p. 80.

finding it easy on his sore eyes, and it was dedicated, as was proper, to Charles II. The dedication reaffirmed that Newcastle so loved the King that Margaret had often heard him say 'that he would most willingly, upon all occasions, sacrifice his life and posterity' for him. The biography was a memorial to his loyalty, and by writing it Margaret had completed the second of the two tasks she had most at heart. The first had been to prove herself 'an honest and good wife' and the second 'to declare to after-ages' the truth of her husband's 'loyal actions and endeavours' in the service of his King and country.

10 The Pursuit of Nature

Many say that in Natural Philosophy nothing is to be known, not the cause of any one thing; which I cannot persuade myself is truth.

THE spirit of the age, Walter Charleton affirmed in 1657, ' inclines men's minds to some one study or other,' and the spirit of the seventeenth century directed men to natural philosophy, a study above the dissensions caused by theology and law, displayed so disastrously at home and abroad. Margaret was remarkably sensitive to the spirit of the age. By temperament a poet, her longing for fame diverted her interest from poetry to natural philosophy, which commanded increasing attention and seemed to offer greater opportunities for originality—the ground, she believed, of every lasting fame.

Sitting alone in her study, with only her contemplations for company, she surveyed nature without the guide of books; and without verifying her conjectures by experiment, concluded arbitrarily about its order. The habit was dangerous, though common. The importance of experiment was widely recognized by the time that Margaret published her first speculations in 1653, but many natural philosophers, while accepting Francis Bacon's injunction to put everything to the test, failed to apply it rigorously, especially in matters which they believed they could sufficiently demonstrate by argument and analogy. Sir Kenelm Digby, who was close to Margaret in temperament, wrote in 1644 that ' we must narrowly take heed, lest reflecting upon the notions we have in our mind, we afterwards pin those airy superstructures upon the material things themselves, that begot them; or frame a new conception of the nature of anything by the negotiation of our understanding upon those impressions which itself maketh in us; whereas, we should acquiesce and be content with that natural and plain notion which springeth immediately and primarily from the thing itself: which when we do not, the more we seem to excel in subtility, the further we go from reality and truth; like an arrow, which being wrong levelled at hand, falleth widest when shot in the strongest bow.'[1] That is well said, but it did not prevent Digby from trying fourteen years later to prove by analogy the magical efficacy of his powder of sympathy in the cure of wounds; and very wonderful analogies they were, including the common superstition of the effects of a pregnant woman's longings upon her child, and the extraordinary remedy for clearing a bad breath: the sufferer's head was to be held over a privy until the 'greater stink' drew unto it the less.[2] But it is hard to know which to admire more, Digby's credulity or his humour.

Margaret herself was aware of the need for observation and experiment. While she was living in Antwerp her maids brought her a butterfly chrysalis attached to a piece of wood or stone, and she had the curiosity to watch its metamorphosis closely, describing the development in one of her later books. But all her writings show her keen observation of the natural phenomena which fell within her range, though her vision was too often warped by preconceptions for her to distinguish clearly the significance of what she saw. Of greater interest and importance in the illustration of her attitude towards experiment is her correspondence with the great Dutchman, Constantijn Huygens. A staunch anglophile, Huygens had numerous English connections—in fact, he was the principal link connecting the intellectual life of the two countries—and as he was also a friend of the Duarte family, sharing its musical interests, he quickly became intimate with the Newcastles when once they were established in Antwerp. Margaret presented him with a copy of her poems in 1653, and in a letter to Utricia Swann, a relation of Newcastle's, he complained that Margaret's 'extravagant atoms kept me from sleeping a great part of last night in this my little solitude.'[3]

[1] Kenelm Digby, *Two Treatises*, 1644, pp. 4–5.
[2] Digby, *A late Discourse*, 1658, p. 76.
[3] *De Briefwisseling van Constantijn Huygens*, ed. J. A. Worp, 1916, v. 187.

Huygens's correspondence with Margaret turned on the puzzling glass drops, known in England as Rupert's drops, formed by dropping molten glass into water; scratch their tails and they explode, invisibly detonated as a result of the stress set up by their rapid cooling. After spending a whole afternoon in 1657 with her discussing problems in natural philosophy, Huygens, on his return to the Hague, forwarded a few of the drops for her examination and in a covering letter, written on 12 March, asked for her opinion on the cause of their detonation, a phenomenon which had puzzled the wits ' of the best philosophers of Paris.' ' Your Excellence hath no cause to apprehend the cracking blow of these little innoxious guns,' he continued; ' If you did, Madam, a servant may hold them close in his fist, and yourself can break the little end of their tail without the least danger. But, as I was bold to tell your Excellence, I should be loath to believe any female fear should reign amongst so much over-masculine wisdom, as the world doth admire in you.' Margaret rose to the challenge and replied at once offering her opinion on the little ' guns '. Huygens's description of them as ' guns ' had provided her with the essential simile. If the drops were like guns they must contain an explosive, and sure enough she detected the signs of an oily substance, which might be ' oily spirits or essences of sulphur '; the scratching of the tail must then discharge the ' fiery spirits ' after the manner of a firelock discharging the powder in a gun, and as ' dilation is the way to desolation ', the glass was shattered by the explosion, as guns would be shattered were they made of glass. She also thought sceptically that some ' artificer ' must have inserted this liquor into the drops, for to her mind they resembled and were inferior in wonder to the glass ear-rings worn by women, which were often filled with coloured silks or black cotton-wool.[1]

Her ingenious theory could hardly satisfy Huygens, and in his reply he disproved it by recounting how he had heated one of the drops ' to the reddest height of heat ' without an

[1] *Ib.*, pp. 284-6.

194

explosion; had it contained the sulphurous liquor she suspected, it would have burst in the crucible. More wonderful still, the action of heating it had destroyed its explosive virtue. He was bringing these facts to her notice, he wrote, so that if she thought it worth her pains, she might ' bring herself to the true notice of the mystery.' [1] She replied at length on 30 March suggesting that the explosive liquor might have been evaporated by the excessive heat applied to the drop, but she was willing to forego her theory in the face of his superior knowledge. ' Thus, Sir,' she concluded, ' you may perceive by my arguing, I strive to make my former opinion or sense good, although I do not bind myself to opinions but truth; and the truth is that though I cannot find out the truth of the glasses, yet in truth I am, Sir, your humble servant.' [2]

The truth is also that it would have been very extraordinary if Margaret had solved the mystery of the drops. The ' best philosophers of Paris ' having failed to unravel it, Charles II sent five of the drops to the Royal Society in 1661 for its judgement on them, in the hope perhaps that English wits would succeed where those of the Continent had failed. The Royal Society, too, was baffled.

Margaret's failure was no disgrace, but the correspondence illustrates the principal difficulties which hindered her as a natural philosopher. The first was simply her lack of education. She was intelligent enough to speculate on a natural mystery but as she wanted the training to bring her speculations to the test, she never advanced further than fancy. The simile of the guns to explain the action of the drops is ingenious, but as Huygens pointed out, it would not stand up to demonstration. As she was unable to check her conjectures by experiment, she could never proceed to firmer conclusions. But again, had she been fully aware of the importance of experiment, she would have had great difficulty in putting her belief into practice. Opinion was set against women dabbling in such matters, and

[1] *Ib.*, pp. 286–7.
[2] Brit. Mus., Add. MSS. 28,558, f. 65.

however splendidly she rose in her writings above convention, she could not mount higher. She might attend the Royal Society once as a visitor, but to have frequented its meetings would have been unthinkable; and for such intercourse and stimulus, the few experiments she might conduct in Huygens's sympathetic company were a poor substitute. She summarized her difficulty in her apology to doctors for any anatomical errors which might appear in her discussion of diseases. She had never seen 'any man opened, much less dissected,' she wrote, 'which for my better understanding I would have done; but I found that neither the courage of nature, nor the modesty of my sex would permit me. Wherefore it would be a great chance, even to a wonder, I should not err in some.'[1] Her slight anatomical knowledge was learnt in the kitchen or the shambles.

Margaret's earliest theory of nature, as set out in her poems, was atomic. Atoms of various shapes and properties were fitted together in the manner of a mosaic to explain every diverse natural phenomenon. This simple but ingenious theory has already been discussed, but before it is dismissed as merely idiosyncratic it is worth showing the resemblance it bears to Walter Charleton's, a man actively in touch with the most informed opinion of the day. He believed in atoms of different shapes and sizes and in what he termed a 'vacuity disseminate', and used the conception to explain, for example, why water saturated with common salt would still dissolve other salts, alum, sal ammoniac, etc. The atoms of salt are cubical and fit conveniently into the cubical spaces between the atoms of water, but as the 'vacuity disseminate' is not entirely occupied by the cubical atoms, room is left for the 'octohedrical, sexangular and spherical' atoms of the other salts: 'which is no obscure nor contemptible evidence that water doth contain various insensible loculaments, chambers, or receptaries of different figures.'[2] So much for Charleton; but his example shows how far Margaret was in the fashion in 1653.

[1] *Philosophical Opinions*, 1663, p. 250.
[2] *Physiologia Epicuro-Gassendo-Charltoniana*, 1654, p. 31.

Her attachment to atoms was short-lived. A new theory of nature was tentatively set out in *Philosophicall Fancies*, which followed quickly upon the publication of her poems. This theory was developed in *Philosophical and Physical Opinions*, published in 1655, and augmented and finally settled in a second edition of the book, which appeared in 1663, after her return to England. Her reason for her repudiation of atoms is typically candid: 'And as for atoms,' she wrote, 'after I had reasoned with myself, I conceived that it was not probable that the universe and all the creatures therein could be created and disposed by the dancing and wandering and dusty motion of atoms.'[1]

The principal difficulty in summarizing Margaret's philosophy is her terminology. She herself made a virtue of being unread in natural philosophy and there is no certainty that her use of the current terms, picked up in conversation, meant the same to her as to her contemporaries. Worse still, she is inconsistent in their use, and it is often impossible to disentangle her meaning from her jargon. After her return to England, she became aware that her ignorance of her contemporaries' work was a weakness, hampering the reception of her own, and she set herself to read in natural philosophy; but though she consequently became more fluent in terminology, she gave little evidence of having really understood it. A summary of her arguments foists upon them a coherence which they do not in fact possess and yet at the same time fails to do justice to their real subtleties.

The fundamental assumption—one common enough at the time—of her philosophy was that nature itself could be considered under three heads, the general soul, life and body of nature. These three she named rational matter, sensitive matter —and both could be grouped together as animate matter—and inanimate matter. The three made up 'the infinite matter of nature, that is, the soul, life and body of nature; the sensitive and rational being the quintessence, spirit or purity of nature,

[1] *Philosophical Opinions*, 1663, p. c2.

197

but the other part a more gross and senseless matter.'[1] In addition there was motion; but motion is integral to matter and is itself a substance or 'thing'. There are six basic kinds of motion—contraction, attraction, retention, dilation, digestion and expulsion—but countless variations of each kind: attractive motions, for example, to quote her illustration only in part, 'draw as if one should pull in a line, or draw in a net, some slope-ways, some straight-ways, some square-ways, some round-ways; and millions of the like varieties, in this sort of motion, yet all attracting motion.'[2] Such was the ground of her natural philosophy, and having distinguished it at length, she proceeded to apply the theory ingeniously and arbitrarily to all the phenomena which fell under her observation.

The general tendency of her philosophy is much more interesting than its particular application. She emerges as a materialist, insisting that matter itself is both cause and effect and making an absolute and Baconian distinction between the natural and the supernatural. God is recognized, but the consideration of His power and attributes is the proper study of theology and not of natural philosophy, and He is thus respectfully but safely removed from the universe, which is to be considered only under its own terms. Her writings, she explained, 'contain pure natural philosophy, without any mixture of theology'; 'it is folly to dispute,' she wrote, 'since neither study nor disputation can inform him [the reader], for disputations and arguments do rather deform religion than inform the creature; wherefore it is better to pray than to preach, to believe than to dispute; the one will reform men from vices and combine them in unity, the other will bring men into atheism, or cause a confusion and division amongst mankind.'[3] She insisted equally upon the inability of religious persecution to change opinion, and demanded in the name of Christianity itself the right of everyone to freedom of conscience.

[1] *Ib.*, p. b2.
[2] *Ib.*, 1655, p. 34.
[3] *Philosophical Opinions*, 1663, p. b3.

Her outspoken materialism and tolerance brought her into disrepute with those who were still lodged in a past which she, being more sensitive to the spirit of the age, was able to reject. John Stainsby, for instance, a friend of Elias Ashmole, spoke for her critics in an epitaph on her, written in verse as barbarous as its sentiments:

> Here lies wise, chaste, hospitable, humble . . .
> I had gone on but Nick began to grumble:
> ' Write, write,' says he, ' upon her tomb of marble
> These words, which out I and my friends will warble.
> Shame of her sex, Welbeck's illustrious whore,
> The true man's hate and grief, plague of the poor,
> The great atheistical philosophraster,
> That owns no God, no devil, lord nor master;
> Vice's epitome and virtue's foe,
> Here lies her body but her soul's below.' [1]

The attraction of Margaret's philosophical writings does not lie in the exposition but in the occasional illustrations. Her thought and expression are too diffuse and disconnected to be read continuously with either attention or pleasure, but when her subject gave her fancy freer play she could write eloquently and poetically. Walter Charleton finely expressed this quality in her philosophical work when he wrote to her that ' they who read your books with design to be informed in points of philosophy find themselves at the same time introduced also in rhetoric.' [2] There are many examples to choose from, but the description of light and air should be sufficient to illustrate her manner. ' Natural air,' she wrote, ' seems to be made by such kind of motions as spiders make cobwebs, for the animate matter's motions spin from a rare degree of inanimate matter small lines, interweaving those lines into a clear substance, which thin, clear, spreading substance or creature spreads upon and enters into most of the creatures of the whole universe through her porous passages; also this sort of air is the chief

[1] Bodleian, Ashmole MS. 36, f. 186^v.
[2] *Letters and Poems*, p. 93.

substance that the sunbeams spread and dilate upon, or through; I say upon, for the sunbeams do not intermix, for what is intermixed doth nor cannot suddenly separate. . . . But there be as many several lights and airs as of other creatures, as some I will express; for example, as sunlight, which I name natural light, then fixed stars' light, then ordinary firelight, meteor light, glowworm light, rotten wood light, cats' eyes light, fish scales light, and fish bones light, diamond light.' [1] And even her explanation of the needle deviates into poetry. She suggests the experiment of placing a quantity of iron beside the needle to prove whether or not its motion towards the north is voluntary or compulsive: ' So if a quantity of iron can cause the needle to vary, it shows that the loadstone turns to the north by a self-motion, and not the motions of the north that make it turn to it, but if it varies not towards the iron, then the north forces it, unless the loadstone takes more delight to view the north's frowning face than to embrace hard iron, or that the feeding appetite is stronger than the viewing delight.' [2]

After her return to England, Margaret became increasingly conscious of the danger of disregarding contemporary philosophy, and in the seclusion of Welbeck she set herself to study. ' Truly, my Lord,' she wrote in the prefatory epistle to the life of Newcastle, ' I confess that for want of scholarship I could not express myself so well as otherwise I might have done in those philosophical writings I published first; but after I was returned with your lordship into my native country, and led a retired country life, I applied myself to the reading of philosophical authors of purpose to learn those names and words of art that are used in schools.' The thoroughness of her study is indicated by the payment of £39 14s. 0d. for books, made by John Rolleston on her behalf in 1664. [3] Once begun on this study, she found herself in sharp disagreement with the several authors she read and immediately set to work to answer them publicly in a

---

[1] *Philosophical Opinions*, 1663, pp. 182–3.
[2] *Ib.*, p. 193.
[3] Nottingham Univ. Lib., Portland Papers, Cavendish Misc. 77.

volume entitled *Philosophical Letters: or, Modest Reflections upon some Opinions in Natural Philosophy*, published in 1664.

The principal authors to whom she objects are Hobbes, Descartes, Henry More and Van Helmont, and whenever she clearly understands them, and is not befuddled by her own pre-conceptions, she argues surprisingly well, proving herself to have possessed some power of analysis. The epistolary form itself suited her temperament and enforced a discipline. She was incapable of continuous exposition, being continually sidetracked by her fancy into irrelevancies, or lengthily misled by her ignorance, but she could write with point when she was forced to attend to the matter in hand and was limited in space; and these advantages the form entailed on her. She comes off worst in her arguments with Hobbes and Descartes, as their speculations on the physical universe were simply beyond her comprehension, but whenever they descended into an area where she herself could move untrammelled, she could score with a certain degree of skill. She challenges, for example, Hobbes's assertion that man excels all other animals in understanding, particularly in his use of language, which allows him to reduce experience to general rules, called 'theorems or aphorisms'. This opinion offended her deep sympathy with animals, and she replied sharply and feelingly: 'according to my reason I cannot perceive but that all creatures may do as much; but by reason they do it not after the same manner or way as man, man denies they do it at all, which is very hard; for what man knows whether fish do not know more of the nature of water, and ebbing and flowing, and the saltness of the sea? or whether birds do not know more of the nature and degrees of air, or the cause of tempests? . . . and whether they do not make their aphorisms and theorems by their manner of intelligence? For, though they have not the speech of man, yet hence doth not follow that they have no intelligence at all. But the ignorance of men concerning other creatures is the cause of despising other creatures, imagining themselves as petty gods in nature.'

Her disagreements with Descartes turn largely on his theory of vortices, on his placing the mind in the glandula or 'kernel' of the brain, and on his opinion that animals lack reason; but though her objections are not without interest, they are not solidly grounded upon any general understanding of his philosophy. Throughout her discussion of his work and of Hobbes's, she took the opportunity of reaffirming her own philosophy, which is seldom enlightening, though on points of common uncertainty it could be said that her own guesses were only wilder than theirs.

She is seen to greater advantage in her duels with Van Helmont and More, especially More. More's neo-platonism exasperated and irritated her extremely, and though she disclaimed in her preface any wish to stir up controversy, she showed in her approach to him the true spirit of a controversialist, employing sarcasm and contempt and striking swiftly at his more obvious weaknesses. She begins by asking why More thought it worth while to write a book, the *Antidote*, to prove the existence of God when on his own admission ' there is no man under the cope of heaven but believes a God '? and affirms that he would have been better employed in trying to convert pagans to Christianity or in encouraging lapsed Christians to practise piety. She continues by attacking systematically his opinion that man is the ' flower and chief of all the products of nature ', his condemnation of the theory of self-moving matter—the crux of her own philosophy—and his conception of immaterial spirits. She replies to his debate on the seat of common sense with her favourite assertion that sense and reason are in all parts of the body, being integral to rational and sensitive matter: ' Wherefore I am not of the opinion that that which moves the whole body is as a point, or some such thing, in a little kernel or glandula of the brain, as an ostrich egg is hung up to the roof of a chamber; or that it is in the stomach, like a single penny in a great purse; neither is it in the midst of the heart, like a lady in a lobster; nor in the blood, like a minnow or sprat in the sea; nor in the fourth ventricle of the brain, as a lousy soldier in a watch-tower.'

Among the many other opinions which she disputes with More

are his notions of the *tabula rasa*, of the passions and sympathies, and of the animal spirits performing under the command of the soul. She herself divides the soul into two, the material and the divine, and refusing to speak of the divine, a subject proper only to theology, she asks sarcastically how the material soul could progress through space as More envisaged: the material or natural soul 'is not like a traveller, going out of one body into another, neither is air her lodging; for certainly, if the natural human soul should travel through the airy regions, she would at last grow weary, it being so great a journey, except she did meet the soul of a horse, and so ease herself with riding on horseback.' One of the more amusing of the anecdotes connected with Margaret is the reply that John Wilkins, the author of *The Discovery of a World in the Moone*, is supposed to have made to her query as to how she should get up to the world in the moon, which he had discovered. 'Oh, Madam,' he answered, 'your Grace has built so many castles in the air, that you cannot want a place to bait at.' The remark is so suspiciously like Margaret's own gibe at More's travelling soul that perhaps a version of a current jest has become traditionally attached to her. Wilkins would never have had the face to make such a reply to a woman of Margaret's rank.

Margaret completely fails to do justice to More's poetic perceptions but she successfully damages his more insubstantial conjectures. She sent a copy of the work to him and it is little wonder that after reading the well written and lively letters in which he was discussed, he should write to his friend, Lady Conway, half-seriously suggesting that she should answer them. 'I wish your Ladyship were rid of your headache and pains,' he wrote, 'though it were no exchange for those of answering this great Philosopher. She is afraid some man should quit his breeches and put on a petticoat to answer her in that disguise, which your Ladyship need not. She expresses this jealousy in her book, but I believe she may be secure from anyone giving her the trouble of a reply.' [1]

[1] *Conway Letters*, p. 237.

Van Helmont set Margaret much greater difficulties. She was completely ignorant of chemistry and, being unconscious of his greatness in this field, she was forced to concentrate on his esoteric philosophy. But she was no more able to understand his terminology than she was his chemistry and wrote in despair: 'what with his spirits, mere beings, non-beings and neutral beings, he troubles nature, and puzzles the brains of his readers so, that, I think, if all men were of his opinion, or did follow the way of his philosophy, nature would desire God she might be annihilated.' Her bafflement was constant and the only occasions when she could move freely were those which allowed her to display sound common sense. She refuses to believe that a pregnant woman's longing can sympathetically imprint a birth-mark on a child: she rejects witchcraft out of hand, sympathizing with the 'good old honest' women who have been burnt on the suspicion of it; and she insists in opposition to Van Helmont that diseases may be spread by putrefying carcases.

The remaining letters in the volume are hurried and dis-organized. A few opinions by other writers whom she had been studying—by her friend, Walter Charleton, and by the great Robert Boyle, whose style is described as 'a gentleman's style' —are commented upon at random but little of particular interest is said. In a reference to the microscope, she affirmed that the small creatures discovered by its means were the same as the 'fairies' in her poems, which she had figured as 'fairies', 'lest I should be thought extravagant to declare that conception of mine for a rational truth.'

The microscope and its discoveries were the principal theme of her next book, *Observations upon Experimental Philosophy*, published in 1666. She herself recognized to some extent the importance of experiment, as her correspondence with Huygens shows, but she preferred untrammelled speculation, upon which her own philosophy was built. The publication of Robert Hooke's *Micrographia* in 1665 seemed a serious contradiction of her favourite methods. Instead of long disquisitions upon matter and motion and immaterial spirits, Hooke set out precisely the results of his observations through the microscope, illustrating his arguments with startlingly realistic plates. The effect upon Margaret was immediate, and without taking time to digest Hooke's great work, she subjected it to a hostile examination. Her attitude was expressed in a prefatory address to her husband, who had, as she reminded him, ' as many sorts of optic glasses as anyone else ' but who did not busy himself overmuch with ' this brittle art ': ' I confess, I have but little faith in . . . telescopical, microscopical and the like inspections,' she wrote, ' and prefer rational and judicious observations before deluding glasses and experiments.' Her scepticism was expressed even more strongly in the preface: ' The inspection of a bee through a microscope will bring him [man] no more honey, nor the inspection of a grain more corn; neither will the inspection of dusty atoms and reflections of light teach painters how to make and mix colours, although it may perhaps be an advantage to a decayed lady's face, by placing herself in such and such a reflection of light, where the dusty atoms may hide her wrinkles.'

She begins the work by apologizing for the deficiencies of her earlier writings on natural philosophy, which were owing to her lack of education, and takes the opportunity of restating the basic principle of her philosophy, rational, sensitive and inanimate self-moving matter. Turning at length to micrography, she lays it down that as no microscope can discover the ' interior natural motions of any part or creature of nature . . . the best optic is a perfect natural eye, and a regular sensitive perception; and the best judge is reason, and the best study is rational contemplation, joined with the observations of regular sense, but not deluding arts.' She then proceeds to Hooke's observations —on the nettle's sting, on a fly's eye, and on the corn violet's seeds, to choose from among her selected topics. She observes that the nettle's sting cannot contain poison, because the nettle can be eaten young; she doubts if the fly's many-faceted eye is more than a ' glossy and shining globular protuberance '; and she questions if the corn violet's seeds had indeed been properly described. None of her observations shows that she realized at all the full significance of Hooke's method; or if she did, she was determined not to admit it, as being fatal to her own.

Of much greater interest than *Observations upon Experimental Philosophy* itself is the appendix, entitled *The Description of a New Blazing World*. As though she had become restive under the discipline increasingly imposed upon her by natural philosophy, Margaret broke loose into extreme fantasy in this account of a new world. She herself anticipated the surprise the account would give to the reader of her ' serious philosophical contemplations ' and apologized for it in a preface. The reader, she wrote, must not think that she had added the account ' out of a disparagement to philosophy; or out of an opinion, as if this noble study were but a fiction of the mind. . . . Fictions are an issue of man's fancy, framed in his own mind, according as he pleases, without regard whether the thing he fancies be really existent without his mind or not; so that reason searches the depth of nature, and enquires after the true causes of natural effects, but fancy creates of its own accord whatsoever it pleases, and delights in its own work.'

The models for her fantasy were the tales of voyages to a utopia or to the moon, especially Francis Godwin's *Man in the Moone*, published in 1638. A closer resemblance, however, is to her own earlier tales, like that of ' Assaulted and Pursued Chastity '. The fiction begins with the abduction of a young girl of good family by a merchant, but before the villain can consummate the rape, the ship carrying them abroad is driven towards the north pole, where he and all the crew are frozen to death, ' the young lady only, by the light of her beauty, the heat of her youth, and the protection of the gods, remaining alive.' The grim vessel continues on its Coleridgean voyage and sails clean out of this world into another, whose pole adjoins ours. The extraordinary inhabitants of the Blazing World into which the heroine drifts—bear-men, fox-men, goose-men, satyrs and green-coloured men—conduct her to the capital city, Paradise, where she conveniently marries the Emperor and is given ' an absolute power to rule and govern all that world as she pleased.'

Her garb as Empress typifies the wonder and magnificence of her new realm: ' on her head she wore a cap of pearl, and a half-moon of diamonds just before it; on the top of her crown came spreading over a broad carbuncle, cut in the form of the sun; her coat was of pearl, mixed with blue diamonds, and fringed with red ones; her buskins and sandals were of green diamonds.'

Once in power, the Empress sets her subjects to work in teams unravelling the mysteries of the universe, and their reports and her commentaries make up the tedious bulk of the fantasy. Freed from fact at last, Margaret could safely dispense illumination under this disguise without fear of such contradictory witnesses as Hooke. At last the Empress's curiosity reaches so far as the spiritual world and, to aid her in these researches, the soul of the Duchess of Newcastle is fetched from the earth to act as her scribe. The two souls return to the earth together in aerial vehicles and after a trip to the London theatre and a visit to court—which naturally makes a deep impression on the Empress—they arrive at Welbeck. They observe the Duke of Newcastle practising horsemanship and then fencing, ' but the Duchess's soul being troubled that her dear lord and husband used such a violent exercise before meat, for fear of overheating himself, without any consideration of the Empress's soul, left her aerial vehicle and entered into her lord.' The Empress's soul quickly follows and the three souls have so pleasant a conversation ' that it cannot be expressed; for the Duke's soul entertained the Empress's soul with scenes, songs, music, witty discourses, pleasant recreations, and all kinds of harmless sports, so that the time passed away faster than they expected.'

At the beginning of the second part, the Empress's soul has returned to her body in the Blazing World, when she learns that her earthly country of origin is engaged in war. Loyally anxious to help its cause, she consults with the Duchess of Newcastle's soul as to the most effective means. The Duchess advises her to send her mermen to discover a passage into the world and to transport her troops, worm-men and bird-men, in ships devised to act also as submarines. The voyage accomplished, the

Empress compels the whole world to submit to the monarch of her native country by means of firestone, which flames like phosphorus when wetted. The stone is dropped on to cities by the bird-men and is used in mining by the worm-men. Her mission accomplished, the Empress returns triumphantly to the Blazing World, and to her Emperor who has meanwhile emulated the Duke of Newcastle and found happiness in horsemanship. The Duchess of Newcastle's soul completes her mission of making the Emperor and Empress happy by promising to design —oh rare achievement!—a theatre suitable to the production of her own plays. The extraordinary work ends with a brief epilogue to the reader, compounded as usual of arrogance and diffidence.

Few other works of science-fiction can equal the confused ridiculous fantasy of the Blazing World. As either narrative or speculation it is quite hopeless: the absurd action, the ludicrous situations and the tedious quasi-philosophical disquisitions make it unbearably dull; but as an illustration of Margaret's character, of her inordinate ambition, and of her retreat from fact into fiction when once she suspected that fact was becoming intractable, it is invaluable. And there are passages which shine with a poetic phosphorescence, a false light of fancy: ' The bird-men carried her [the Empress] upon their backs into the air, and there she appeared as glorious as the sun. Then she was set down upon the seas again, and presently there was heard the most melodious and sweetest consort of voices as ever was heard out of the seas, which was made by the fish-men; this consort was answered by another, made by the bird-men in the air, so that it seemed as if sea and air had spoke, and answered each other by way of singing-dialogues, or after the manner of those plays that are acted by singing-voices.'

Her suspicions of her own philosophy were deepened by her understanding, however imperfect it may have been, of the real significance of the Royal Society and its work. She may have denounced experimental philosophy in 1666, but her visit to the Society in May 1667, and the conversations which she held with the virtuosi at the time of her stay in London, shook her self-confidence in her own methods. The effect was heightened by her correspondence with Joseph Glanvill and other leading enquirers of the age. Glanvill wrote to her on 13 October 1667 to explain the idea behind the Society. 'We have yet no certain theory of nature,' he began, with little consideration for Margaret's own philosophy; 'and in good earnest, Madam, all that we can hope for, as yet, is but the history of things as they are, but to say how they are, to raise general axioms, and to make hypotheses, must, I think, be the happy privilege of succeeding ages; when they shall have gained a larger account of the phenomena, which are yet too scant and defective to raise theories upon: so that to be ingenuous and confess freely, we have yet no such thing as natural philosophy; natural history is all we can pretend to; and that too, as yet, is but in its rudiments, the advance of it your Grace knows is the design and business of the Royal Society.' [1] In these few honest but tactless sentences Glanvill had overthrown all Margaret's pretensions.

However much her pride may have revolted against the evidence, her common sense admitted it, and her last work of philosophical speculation shows clearly how far she had come towards understanding the weakness of her position. *Grounds of Natural Philosophy*, published in 1668, is in effect a third edition of *Philosophical and Physical Opinions*. She retained her general theories of matter and motion, but abridged them radically and advanced them more tentatively. She was also more careful to avoid controversy. In the earlier work, for example, she had not hesitated to set out her own theory of the loadstone, but now she excised the discussion, simply remarking: 'But, by reason there hath been so many learned men puzzled in their opinions concerning the several effects of the loadstone, I have not ventured to treat of the nature and natural effects of that mineral; neither have I much experience of it.'

She was openly in retreat, and her recognition of the change that had taken place in the climate of opinion since she had

---

[1] *Letters and Poems*, p. 124-5.

wildly speculated as a younger woman is revealed in her altered style. Long before Thomas Sprat had published his *History of the Royal Society* in 1667 and had called for a plain simple prose, suitable to scientific disquisition, similar demands had been made. Walter Charleton's *Ternary of Paradoxes*, published in 1649, was written in a luxurious Latinate prose derived from Sir Thomas Browne, Charleton's acknowledged model. Those 'two heroical wits, the Lord St. Albans, and the now flourishing Dr. Browne,' Charleton averred, had displayed an English style which 'may well serve to stagger that partial axiom of some schoolmen, that the *Latin is the most symphonical and concordant language of the rational soul.*' Charleton was severely criticized for his style and though he protested in his preface to *Deliramenta Catarrhi*, published in the following year, that it could be no crime in him 'to trace the footsteps of those worthies' and to naturalize words fetched home from 'the Greek, Roman, Italian, and French oratories', his style became remarkably simpler in his later works.

Margaret herself had had too little education ever to have adventured upon a Latinate style, and her preference was not 'so much for the eloquence and elegancy of speech, as [for] the natural and most usual way of speaking.'[1] The attraction of her prose at its best is its idiomatic vivacity and spontaneity and its instinctively eloquent rhythms; but as a tool for the discussion of natural philosophy, it suffered from her infatuation for similes. Responding as immediately as she did to the spirit of the age, she grew sensitive to the general change in style, and in the preliminaries to *Philosophical Letters*, she stated portentously that she thought 'it best to avoid metaphorical, similizing and improper expression in natural philosophy as much as one can; for they do rather obscure than explain the truth of nature'—a surprising statement in view of her earlier practice. She went a stage further in *Grounds of Natural Philosophy*, cutting out all the similes which are the delight of the earlier *Philosophical and Physical Opinions* and taming the loose, spirited movement of

[1] *Natures Pictures*, p. c5ᵛ.

the prose. Her style became flatter, cautious and ordinary, and lost its virtue, the earlier compensation for the tedium of much of her thought.

But her fancy was irrepressible: in the conclusion to *Grounds of Natural Philosophy* it revolted as irresponsibly against the discipline she had tried to impose upon it as it had done in the Blazing World. Tired by her attempt to grapple with facts, with matter and motion, microscopes, loadstones and the transfusion of blood, her mind suddenly and incredibly proposed for debate the query, '*Whether there might not be Restoring Beds, as well as Producing Beds, or Breeding Beds?*' Justice cannot be done to the fantastically improbable arguments which ensued between the different parties in her mind over this proposition, but at length it was concluded that if there were such restoring-beds, whereby decayed life was renewed, they must be hung about a creature compounded of ' elemental, animal, mineral and vegetable life ', which could only resemble in shape ' a great and high rock ' and be situated in the very middle of the earth's central sea. And with this last typical gesture, this unwitting gift to the Freudian psychologist, Margaret concluded her final work on her life's passion, Natural Philosophy.

11 Champion of her Sex

I speak of strength to show that women that are bred tender, idle, and ignorant (as I have been) are not likely to have much wit; nor is it fit they should be bred up to masculine actions, yet it were very fit and requisite they should be bred up to masculine understandings.

'I AM, Madam, an admirer of rarities, and your Grace is really so great an one, that I cannot but endeavour some testimony of a proportioned respect and wonder, though perhaps there may be indecorum in the boldness of such unknown addresses.' With this surprisingly frank avowal Joseph Glanvill opened his correspondence with Margaret.[1] The degree of her rarity lay in her sex, and Glanvill defined it when he told her that she had convinced the world, 'by a great instance, that women may be philosophers and, to a degree, fit for the ambitious emulation of the most improved masculine spirits.'

But Glanvill's attitude was unusual; by far the greater number of his contemporaries thought the spectacle of a writing woman, or indeed of a woman practising any arts other than the domestic, highly improper and ridiculous. The famous Anna Schurman wrote to a correspondent in 1639 that 'men of great esteem' beheld with 'evil eyes' anything that tended to the praise of women[2]; and more than thirty years later Anna's English disciple, Bathsua Makin, was even more outspoken in her condemnation of the masculine attitude: 'The barbarous custom to breed women low is grown general amongst us,' she wrote, 'and hath prevailed so far, that it is verily believed (especially amongst a sort of debauched sots) that women are not endued with such reason as men, nor capable of improvement by education, as they are. It is looked upon as a monstrous

[1] *Letters and Poems*, pp. 135-6.
[2] Anna Schurman, *The Learned Maid*, 1659, pp. 38-9.

thing to pretend the contrary. A learned woman is thought to be a comet, that bodes mischief whenever it appears. To offer to the world the liberal education of women is to deface the image of God in man, it will make women so high and men so low; like fire in the house-top, it will set the whole world in a flame.'[1]

Margaret was probably familiar with Anna Schurman's opinions through Anna's English correspondents, but she could not have read her essay proposing a scheme for women's education until 1659, when an English translation from the Latin was published. The appearance of the translation must have been inspired in part by Margaret's own example and by her eloquent defence of the rights of women to education and to a share in the business of the world. Mrs. Makin was certainly Margaret's admirer, and her protestation against the masculine attitude was a less eloquent repetition of Margaret's own splendid attack on the position women were forced to occupy by men.

Before Margaret began to publish she knew that she would meet with opposition from men and from those women, the majority, who had adopted the masculine point of view out of custom. ' I imagine I shall be censured by my own sex,' she wrote in the epistle to ' all noble and worthy ladies ', prefixed to her *Poems, and Fancies*; ' and men will cast a smile of scorn upon my book, because they think thereby women incroach too much upon their prerogatives; for they hold books as their crown and the sword as their sceptre, by which they rule and govern.' But she herself could not have anticipated the strength of the censures made by women like Dorothy Osborne, or the extent of the masculine scorn, shown particularly in the disbelief that she could have written her own books, trenching as they did upon matters closed to women. In the first edition of *Philosophical and Physical Opinions*, published in 1655, she retaliated upon her critics by calling on Newcastle to defend her against the charge of not being her own author, and by presenting in an epistle to the universities of Oxford and Cambridge her view of the subjection in which women were kept.

[1] Makin, p. 3.

The epistle is the most passionate and eloquent statement of the century on the position of women. Margaret's follies, absurdities, and eccentricities may have been many, but they are not of such number that they should be allowed to obscure her genius, and this epistle does much to redeem them, since they can be attributed at large to the very condition which she describes. ' I here present to you this philosophical work,' she began, ' not that I can hope wise schoolmen and industrious laborious students should value it for any worth, but to receive it without scorn for the good encouragement of our sex, lest in time we should grow irrational as idiots by the dejectedness of our spirits, through the careless neglects and despisements of the masculine sex to the female, thinking it impossible we should have either learning or understanding, wit or judgement; as if we had not rational souls as well as men; and we out of a custom of dejectedness think so too, which makes us quit all industry towards profitable knowledge, being employed only in low and petty employments, which take away not only our abilities to-wards arts but higher capacities in speculations; so as we are become like worms that only live in the dull earth of ignorance, winding ourselves sometimes out by the help of some refreshing rain of good education, which seldom is given us; for we are kept like birds in cages, to hop up and down in our houses, not suffered to fly abroad to see the several changes of fortune and the various humours ordained and created by nature; and wanting the experience of nature, we must needs want the under-standing and knowledge, and so consequently prudence and invention of men. Thus by an opinion, which I hope is but an erroneous one, in men, we are shut out of all power and author-ity; by reason we are never employed either in civil or martial affairs, our counsels are despised and laughed at; the best of our actions are trodden down with scorn by the over-weening conceit men have of themselves, and through a despisement of us.'

This moving appeal was reprinted in the second edition of *Philosophical and Physical Opinions*, published in 1663, and although it offered no proposals for the freeing of women from servitude, it could not fail to have some effect. Mrs. Makin's proposed curriculum for women's education, which she attempted to put into practice at the school she kept at Tottenham, closely followed the scheme outlined by Anna Schurman. Mrs. Makin suggested as proper subjects for women, grammar, rhetoric, logic, physic, languages, especially Greek and Latin for 'the better understanding of the Scriptures', mathematics, geography, history and music; painting and poetry, she acknowledged, were 'a great ornament and pleasure.' In practice she inevitably had to compromise, and apart from the usual attainments—music and dancing, etc.—she offered her scholars for an annual fee of £20, Latin and French, and to those who so chose, Greek, Hebrew, Italian, Spanish, astronomy, geography, arithmetic, history and experimental philosophy. Margaret could have had no influence upon Mrs. Makin's curriculum, except perhaps in the election of the several branches of science, which were unmentioned by Anna Schurman, but the spirit of her epistle complaining of the position of women as deeply inspired Mrs. Makin as it did other women later in the century who were struggling against the circumstances of their sex.

As late as 1694, Mary Astell in her influential essay, *A Serious Proposal to the Ladies, for the advancement of their true and greatest Interest*, lamented in words which nearly repeated Margaret's the contempt showed to women by men: 'Were the men as much neglected, and as little care taken to cultivate and improve them, perhaps they would be so far from surpassing those whom they now despise, that they themselves would sink into the greatest stupidity and brutality. The preposterous returns that the most of them make to all the care and pains that is bestowed on them renders this no uncharitable nor improbable conjecture.' But Mary Astell wrote on the eve of change. A few years later Joseph Addison, who never took a step further than informed public opinion allowed, deliberately addressed the *Spectator* papers in large part to his women readers, and attempted in the better interests of society to cultivate their education. Behind this change stood the figure of Margaret Newcastle, who deserves to be remembered, if for nothing else, as the most outspoken and influential feminist of the age.

But Margaret's feminism was not unreasonable; while bitterly complaining about women's lack of education and exclusion from the affairs of the world, she did not pretend that they should be considered on the same footing as men. Their natures and capacities differed: men were the sun and women the moon; or they could be compared to the oak and the willow—'a yielding vegetable, not fit nor proper to build houses and ships as the oak, whose strength can grapple with the greatest winds and plough the furrows in the deep; it is true, the willow may make fine arbours and bowers, winding and twisting its wreathy stalks about, to make a shadow to eclipse the light.'[1] Her reservations about women sprang largely from a contemptuous estimate of the character of the women of the age. As far as she could see, their chief pastime was cards; they had little use for poetry, unless for the verses written in their praise, or for natural philosophy, studying as they did 'no more of nature's works than their faces', or for moral philosophy, which was 'too tedious to learn and too rigid to practise'. The only study of women seemed to be romances, 'wherein reading, they fall in love with the feigned heroes and carpet-knights, with whom their thoughts secretly commit adultery, and in their conversation and manner . . . they imitate the romancy-ladies.'[2]

She would have excepted from her general condemnation of women Mrs. Katherine Philips, the 'matchless Orinda.' Some time before 1664, the year of Mrs. Philips's death, and probably while Margaret was living in London immediately after her return to England, Mrs. Philips made Margaret's acquaintance and initiated her into 'The Society of Friendship', of which she was the centre. The members of this literary coterie took fictitious names and Orinda addressed some complimentary

[1] *Worlds Olio*, p. A4.
[2] *Sociable Letters*, pp. 38–40.

verses to Margaret upon her choosing the name of Polycrite—
the critic of many things:

> That nature in your frame has taken care
> As well your birth as beauty do declare,
> Since we at once discover in your face,
> The lustre of your eyes and of your race:
> And that your shape and fashion does attest,
> So bright a form has yet a brighter guest,
> To future times authentic fame shall bring,
> Historians shall relate, and poets sing.
> But since your boundless mind upon my head,
> Some rays of splendour is content to shed;
> And least I suffer by the great surprize,
> Since you submit to meet me in disguise,
> Can lay aside what dazzles vulgar sight,
> And to *Orinda* can be *Policrite*;
> You must endure my vows and find the way
> To entertain such rites, as I can pay.

But in spite of these verses, Margaret's connection with the Society was of the slightest and her acquaintance with Mrs. Philips did little to modify her scornful attitude towards the character of contemporary women.

She could afford to adopt such an attitude as she herself did not suffer under the great disadvantage entailed on the majority of her sex—the tyranny of an absolute husband. Newcastle loyally and generously encouraged her in her writing and gave her the liberty to publish as she pleased. A character in one of her stories protests that she is determined to live a single life; should she marry, though she might have the time for thought, she might not have her husband's permission to publish, the greater number of husbands always striving, ' if their wives have wit, to obscure it. ' Her own husband not only gave her freedom to print but enhanced her wit by praising it in the commendatory poems he prefixed to her works. She was therefore in a position to regard contemptuously the occupations with which other less fortunate women were forced to idle away their time.

It was no accident that Margaret addressed her epistle on women to the universities of Oxford and Cambridge. As women were excluded from them, the universities became for her symbols of all that she wanted and all that she hoped to attain, and throughout her life she paid assiduous court to them, trying to win their recognition for her own writings. While she was living at Antwerp she persuaded Constantijn Huygens to present her *Philosophical and Physical Opinions* to the library of Leyden University. 'Give me leave to challenge your promise, which was to favour my book, and so me by it,' she wrote to him in 1658, 'so much as to present it to the university library of Leyden; for though my book hath neither wit nor worth enough to deserve a place in that library, yet by the honour that it will receive from your hands it may find a good acceptance.' [1] Huygens was as good as his word and after he had proposed the question to the Rector Magnificus, her gift was accepted. She was so delighted by the courtesy that she presented the library with not one but all her works so far printed, except the diminutive *Philosophicall Fancies*, and had an index in Latin specially printed to accompany the collection.[2]

The Latin index was an attempt to make her works available to Continental scholars. Later she commissioned Walter Charleton to translate her life of her husband into Latin and tried to find a competent scholar to do the same for her philosophical works. Jasper Mayne, the dramatist, a protégé of her husband and a canon of Christ Church, Oxford, was asked in 1663 to find a suitable translator, and he replied on 20 May that he had prevailed on 'an ingenious person of this College to undertake the work', whereby her writings would be 'enabled to travel beyond the seas'. The unfortunate translator soon found himself gravelled by the terminology in her poetry: 'To remove which difficulty,' Mayne wrote on 21 April 1664, 'I

---

[1] *De Briefwisseling van Huygens*, v. 312.

[2] I have seen no copy of the Latin index other than the one in the University Library at Leyden.

have directed him to read Lucretius before he proceed farther; who having softened the most stubborn parts of natural philosophy, by making them run smoothly in his tuneable verses, by an easy imitation will teach him to do the like.'[1] The 'ingenious person' proceeded no further than a reading of Lucretius, and Margaret had to remain content with her philosophy in its native tongue.

When Walter Charleton wrote in 1667 to thank Margaret for a present of her books, he drew a distinction between her and other writers: ' whereas they employ only their wit, labour and time in composing books,' he wrote, ' you bestow also great sums of money in printing yours; and not content to enrich our heads alone with your rare notions, you go higher and adorn our libraries with your elegant volumes.'[2]

The principal recipients of her gifts were the Oxford and Cambridge colleges. Her agent at Oxford was the obsequious Rev. Thomas Barlow, Bodley's librarian, who described himself in a letter to her as ' a poor impertinent thing in black '. As directed, he inscribed and distributed the books to the various colleges. Her courtship of Cambridge, however, was more assiduous and more successful. Oxford accepted her books politely enough but not with that deep gratitude which the other place so eloquently expressed. Of course Oxford may have suspected that as her husband, her father and two of her brothers, Sir Thomas and Sir Charles, had been Cambridge men, it had little more to gain than fresh accessions to its libraries by elaborately thanking her for each of her gifts. Cambridge, lured on by the idea of benefices and benefactions, received every gift with addresses in English and Latin, and exhausted rhetoric in attempting variety. ' Indeed we who wonder that the Ancients should adore the same tutelar goddess both of Arts and Arms,' wrote the Master and Fellows of Trinity in 1663, ' what shall we think of your Excellency, who are both a Minerva and an Athens to yourself, the Muses as well as Helicon,

[1] *Letters and Poems*, pp. 94, 96.
[2] *Ib.*, p. 109.

219

Aristotle as well as his Lyceum?' St. John's, not to be outdone by the rival house, expressed its sentiments more succinctly: 'Ancient Greece itself, the sole governess of all just merits and rewards, in the cause of such unparalleled virtues would have spent herself in ten years' panegyrics.' [1] But rivalry in adulation between the colleges was composed in the several addresses despatched by the Vice-Chancellor and Senate. 'Most excellent Princess, you have unspeakably obliged us all,' that august personage and body wrote on 16 December 1667, thanking her for the gift of the life of her husband, 'but not in this respect alone, for whensoever we find ourselves nonplussed in our studies we repair to you, as to our oracle; if we be to speak, you dictate to us; if we knock at Apollo's door, you alone open to us; if we compose an history, you are the remembrancer; if we be confounded and puzzled among the philosophers, you disentangle us and assoil all our difficulties.' [2]

Cambridge's response may have flattered her pride but it failed to satisfy her deepest ambition, that her philosophical works should be taught in the universities. She would have preferred to expound her writings herself. All the learned heroines of her tales were given the chance of publicly holding forth on the nature of the universe, and she herself longed for such an opportunity. Replying to a correspondent who reported that 'Sir O. B.' had been unable to understand her philosophy, she attributed his difficulty to her inability to teach her opinions in public, as every philosopher of the past had done: 'for it is not proper for my sex to be a public orator, to declare or explain my opinions in schools.' [3] She was no more fortunate in inducing other scholars to speak on her behalf and complained to Walter Charleton on this score. Charleton replied with his customary tact and kindness: 'Nor are you to be discouraged, Madam, if your philosophy have not the fate to be publicly read in all universities of Europe, as your Grace, doubtless out of a most

[1] *Ib.*, pp. 11, 26.
[2] *Ib.*, p. 24.
[3] *Sociable Letters*, p. 298.

heroic ambition to benefit mankind, desires it should.' She had, he continued, sufficiently testified to her good intentions by publishing, and, as he was not a sycophant, he concluded with an observation intended to give her pause: ' Besides, the virtuosi of our English universities have, of late years, proclaimed open war against the tyranny of dogmatizing in any art or science.' [1]

Her ambition was inordinate and ludicrous but it was also so naïve as to be pathetic rather than offensive. ' I wish,' she wrote, ' I had a thousand, or rather ten thousand millions [of readers], nay, that their number were infinite, that the issue of my brain, fame, and name might live to eternity if it were possible.' The Cambridge addresses did not turn her head. They may have allowed her to hold it higher in public but they could not persuade her that she had really achieved her goal. She always suspected that her opinions were not received because they were lacking in substance, and as the suspicion increased her natural diffidence, it compelled her to attitudinize ridiculously. She was in truth humble before the learning which she coveted so wildly, and from which she had been debarred largely on account of her sex: ' if any of your noble profession,' she wrote, addressing herself to all professors of learning and art, ' should humble themselves so low as to read my works, or part of them, I pray consider my sex and breeding, and they will fully excuse those faults which must unavoidably be found in my works.' [2]

Margaret presented her books to individual scholars as freely as to the universities, and they responded as fulsomely. Sir Kenelm Digby told her in 1657 that she was the ornament of the age and would be the envy of future ones; and Thomas Hobbes, after reading her volume of plays, wrote that ' it is filled throughout with more and truer ideas of virtue and honour than any book of morality I have read.' Scholars unknown to her personally were equally complimented, and Henry More was one day surprised to be presented with a collection of her works by

[1] *Letters and Poems*, p. 112.
[2] *Sociable Letters*, pp. 163, b2.

her servant. He may have mocked her to Lady Conway but in his acknowledgement he lauded her and subscribed himself her 'most humble and thankful admirer.' [1]

Such correspondence is a tribute to Margaret's rank rather than to her achievement. As wife of the 'Loyal Duke' she could expect adulation from every quarter to which she applied, and criticism reached her only indirectly. It was quickly understood by everyone that the shortest way to her favour was through praise of her works. Edward and Pleasaunce Oldham, who wrote jointly from Cheshire in 1668 to solicit employment, shrewdly concluded their letter: 'Duchess, your Grace's books have been communicated to several persons of worth of our neighbourhood and are according to their desert greatly approved of, and your Grace highly applauded and admired for writing of them.' [2] Of all her correspondents only Walter Charleton and Joseph Glanvill were at all critical, and they both so genuinely admired her and were so fascinated by her personality that their criticism was too tempered and oblique to counterbalance the lavish praise directed at her from all sides, which encouraged her character to develop in its own extravagant fashion. 'Your fancy is too generous to be restrained, your invention too nimble to be fettered,' wrote Charleton, but the shrewd criticism which he based on this observation was couched in language too courtly to be of effect: 'Hence it is,' he continued, 'that you do not always confine your sense to verse, nor your verses to rhythm, nor your rhythm to the quantity and sounds of syllables.' [3] 'I am not covetous,' Margaret wrote frankly, 'but as ambitious as ever any of my sex was, is, or can be; which is the cause, that though I cannot be Henry the Fifth, or Charles the Second, yet I will endeavour to be Margaret the First.' [4] Can she be blamed for believing at times that she had been elected by popular acclaim?

[1] *Letters and Poems*, pp. 65, 67–8, 91.
[2] Nottingham Univ. Lib., Portland Papers, Cavendish Misc. 60.
[3] *Letters and Poems*, p. 115.
[4] *Blazing World*, p. A4ᵛ.

Among the recipients of her works was the young dramatist, Thomas Shadwell, who was patronized by the Newcastles from the outset of his career. Shadwell had two qualities which were greatly appreciated by Newcastle, a skill in music and a deep admiration for Ben Jonson; and these alone would have been sufficient to endear him. Newcastle's own fondness for music was one of his more noticeable traits, and among the list of his household drawn up immediately after his return to England appears the name of Mr. Young, a violist, who was paid a salary of £30 a year.[1] Of all the poets Newcastle held the name of his friend Ben Jonson in the greatest respect, and as Shadwell pretended to be heir to Jonson's dramatic art, he was certain of Newcastle's admiration for his plays. He was a welcome visitor to Welbeck, the 'sanctuary of the poets', as he put it, and repaid Newcastle's bounty with the dedications which so irritated Dryden. In the dedication to *The Libertine*, 1676, the fourth of his comedies to be inscribed to Newcastle, Shadwell remembered how kindly he had been first received at Welbeck and how much he had enjoyed Newcastle's conversation, which owed to his ability 'to discourse with every man in his own way.'

Shadwell dedicated one comedy, *The Humourists*, to Margaret. He wrote to her and to Newcastle on 20 April 1671 asking permission to dedicate, and in the letter to Newcastle he reminded him that he had seen 'this comedy (before the sting was taken out) and was pleased to approve it.'[2] His panegyric on Margaret conventionally praised her qualities as a lady and a wife, and especially as a writer: 'All our sex have reason to envy you,' he wrote, 'and your own to be proud of you, which by you have obtained an absolute victory over us.' A month after offering the dedication Shadwell was writing to thank her for her present.

Shadwell also played an important part in satisfying Newcastle's own dramatic ambitions. After his return to England, Newcastle prepared for the stage his comedy of *The Humorous Lovers*,

[1] Nottingham Univ. Lib., Portland Papers, Cavendish Misc. 122.
[2] *Letters and Poems*, p. 128.

which he must have begun in exile at Paris. The play was almost entirely his own work, at least it shows no evidence of a skilled hand. Aware of his weakness, or perhaps unwilling as an amateur to devote his whole attention to a play, Newcastle called upon Shadwell, as he had earlier called upon James Shirley, to collaborate in his next comedy, *The Triumphant Widow*. Shadwell later reclaimed the greater part of his share in the play —the waggish coxcombical character of Sir John Noddy, which he renamed Sir Humphrey Noddy—and included it in his own comedy of *Bury Fair*. Newcastle's certain contribution to *The Triumphant Widow* was the character of Footpad, a merry rogue, derived from Shakespeare's Autolycus; and it is some tribute to his dramatic skill that those scenes in which Footpad appears are the pleasantest in the play.[1] Once again Newcastle was able to show his aristocratic and humorous insight into low characters. A second service which Shadwell performed was to write a prologue to Newcastle's earlier comedy of *The Country Captain*, revived in 1661 and again in 1667 and 1668:

> A good play cannot properly be said
> To be revived, because it ne'er was dead:
> Though it seem buried, like the fruitful grain,
> It always rises with increase again.
> So rises this, whose noble author drew
> Such images, so pleasing and so true,
> That after forty years they still are new.[2]

When hostilities broke out between John Dryden and Shadwell after Newcastle's death, Dryden's principal attack on his rival was made in *MacFlecknoe*, the mock-heroic in which Richard Flecknoe appoints Shadwell to succeed him as monarch of the realms of nonsense. Among the advice which Flecknoe imparts to his successor-elect is this on rhetoric:

[1] The scenes in which Footpad appears have been edited from the MS. by Mr. Francis Needham, *A Pleasante & Merrye Humor off A Roge*, Welbeck Miscellany No. 1, 1933.

[2] *Collection of Poems*, ed. Needham, p. 50.

Margaret Daughter
to Tho: Lucas Esq of
Essex 2d wife to Wm
Duke of Newcastle

8. Margaret Cavendish, Duchess of Newcastle. Attributed
to Abraham van Diepenbeke.

And when false flowers of rhetoric thou would'st cull,
Trust nature, do not labour to be dull,
But write thy best, and top; and in each line
Sir Formal's oratory will be thine.
Sir Formal, though unsought, attends thy quill
And does thy northern dedications fill.

The gibe at Shadwell's dedications to the Newcastles was particularly apt since Flecknoe himself had assiduously eulogized
them and dedicated to them. His pastoral tragi-comedy of
Love's Kingdom, 1664, was dedicated to Newcastle alone, and his
comedy of *The Damoiselles à la Mode*, 1667, to both husband
and wife. His intimacy with the Newcastles had begun much
earlier, and that the relation was friendship is shown by
the verses which Newcastle himself wrote to Flecknoe and
which were printed before Flecknoe's *A Relation of Ten Years
Travells*, 1656, and his *Enigmaticall Characters*, 1658, the second
being dedicated to Newcastle. Margaret herself was the sole
dedicatee of *A Farrago of Several Pieces*, published in 1666. 'In
his person there is not much to commend, nor discommend,'
Flecknoe wrote about himself, and much worse might be said of
his poetry. Duller or more gangling verse it would be hard to
imagine, and only friendship and a dropsical thirst for praise could
possibly have made Margaret respond to these verses which
Flecknoe addressed to Newcastle on her biography of him:

Whilst with your noble actions you indite
Unto your lady's pen what she should write,
'T may well be said, as 'twas of Thetis' son,
That you are doubly happy, both to have done
Such famous deeds, and to have had agen
A pen so famous for the writing them. [1]

Dryden might be pleased at connecting Shadwell with his
predecessor on the throne of nonsense as a dedicator to Newcastle, but he himself had also dedicated to him and had been
intimately concerned in his theatrical ambitions. On 16 August

[1] Flecknoe, *Euterpe Revived*, p. 13.

225

1667 Pepys attended the first night at the Duke of York's theatre of *Sir Martin Mar-all*; 'a play made by my Lord Duke of Newcastle,' he noted, 'but, as everybody says, corrected by Dryden.' The comedy was a great success and Pepys expressed the general opinion when he wrote: 'It is the most entire piece of mirth, a complete farce from one end to the other, that certainly was ever writ. I never laughed so in all my life. I laughed till my head ached all the evening and night with the laughing; and at very good wit therein, not fooling.' The play was published anonymously in 1668, but when it was reprinted in 1691 it carried Dryden's name; and there is every reason to suppose that the comedy was almost entirely of his own writing, fathered on Newcastle at the time of its first production in return for some substantial present. The greatest claim that has been made for Newcastle's share is that he provided Dryden with a translation of Molière's *L'Etourdi*, but in fact little in *Sir Martin Mar-all* is derived from the French comedy, and Newcastle's collaboration in it, even allowing for the truth of the assertion, can have been of the slightest.

In the following year Dryden dedicated his comedy of *An Evening's Love* to Newcastle, and the address was a smooth rehearsal of the accepted pattern of his patron's life. His noble birth, his early good fortune, his success in war and his constancy in exile were all eloquently set out in Dryden's best dedicatory style. 'And now you are happily arrived to the evening of a day, as serene as the dawn of it was glorious,' he concluded, 'but such an evening as, I hope, and almost prophesy, is far from night. 'Tis the evening of a summer's sun, which keeps the daylight long within the skies.' He also deftly introduced a panegyric on Margaret: 'lest anything should be wanting to your happiness,' he told Newcastle, 'you have, by a rare effect of fortune found, in the person of your excellent lady, not only a lover, but a partner of your studies; a lady whom our age may justly equal with the Sappho of the Greeks, or the Sulpitia of the Romans, who, by being taken into your bosom, seems to be inspired with your genius; and by writing the history of your life, in so masculine a style, has already placed you in the number of the heroes.' But Dryden's relations with Newcastle were never so close as Shadwell's; none of his correspondence with him seems to have survived, and he did not celebrate Margaret's death in elegy. But it is pleasant that he should have been patronized by the patron of Ben Jonson, and have offered a further reason for styling Newcastle the ' English Maecenas '.

Apart from the drama, Newcastle spent his leisure preparing a second work on horsemanship. *A New and Extraordinary Method to dress Horses*, published in 1667, complements the earlier work by developing certain of its arguments. It was translated into French in 1671 by Monsieur de Solleysel and later into German, and together with the first book it became the authority on manège, perpetuating Newcastle's fame as a master of the art which he so loved.

While Newcastle occupied his old age with these diversions, Margaret was revising and reprinting her earlier works; her last original work was *Grounds of Natural Philosophy*, published in 1668. A third edition of *Poems, and Fancies* appeared in 1668 and second editions of *Natures Pictures* and *The Worlds Olio* in 1671. All three were extensively revised: rhyme and metre, grammar and vocabulary were improved, and many of the more glaring eccentricities were pruned away—an excision to be especially lamented is the loss of the delightful autobiographical fragment appended to the first edition of *Natures Pictures*, removed as unfitted to the dignity of her later character. It is impossible to believe that Margaret undertook the revisions herself, a task so absolutely at variance with her impatient and wandering temperament, and they must have been entrusted to her secretary or to the household chaplain or to one of her dependent men of letters. The new editions were all handsomely printed, and it is a little sad that Margaret, whose expectation of life was so much greater than her husband's, should have unconsciously prepared for an early death by ensuring that in appearance at least her works should be worthy of her life's ambition.

227

12 A Wise, Witty and Learned Lady

And fame is a report that travels far, and many times lives long; and the older it groweth, the more it flourishes, and is the more particularly a man's own than the child of his loins.

On her return to England from exile in 1660, Margaret gladly accompanied her husband into the country when once she had seen that he would not receive the favours and rewards which his loyalty and sufferings had led him to expect. She went the more willingly as she herself preferred retirement in the country to life in the city, provided she could occasionally descend on it to enjoy the effects of her reputation. 'In your last letter you condemn me for living a country life,' she wrote in reply to a correspondent, 'saying, I bury myself whilst I live, and you wonder, that knowing I love glory, I should live so solitary a life as I do; I confess, Madam, both the manner of my life and my ambitious nature, if a solitary life be not to live in a metropolitan city, spread broad with vanity, and almost smothered with crowds of creditors for debts; and as I confess my solitude, so I confess my glory, which is to despise such vanities, as will be rather a reproach to my life than a fame to after ages.' [1] There is no need to question the sincerity of her protestations. She deeply loved the countryside, was well versed in country matters, and enjoyed the company of her contemplations and the pleasures of writing more than all else: 'Wherefore, for my pleasure and delight, my ease and peace, I live a retired life, a home life, free from the entanglements, confused clamours, and rumbling noise of the world, for I by this retirement live in a calm silence, wherein I have my contemplations free from disturbance, and my mind lives in peace, and my thoughts in pleasure.' [2]

[1] *Sociable Letters*, p. 167.
[2] *Ib.*, pp. 56–7.

She was soon to discover, however, that home life was not free from 'entanglements and confused clamours'; for the first time she had to live in close association with her husband's family and to suffer all the suspicions which inevitably fell on a young second wife. Newcastle's children must have been relieved at first by Margaret's childlessness; but as their father declined and showed more clearly the extent to which he was ruled by her, they became alarmed at the possibility of her enriching herself and remarrying in the event of his death. Their alarm seemed to be justified by the generous jointures settled upon her. Newcastle had been unable to make any settlement while in exile, but on 21 October 1662 he provided by indenture that in the event of her outliving him, she should have an annuity of £1,125, charged upon his manors in Northumberland. He also settled upon her for life his manors of Chesterfield, Bolsover and Woodthorpe in Derby, together with Bolsover Castle. [1]

The family's irritation at this provision was further increased by Newcastle's general conduct of his affairs. Immediately upon his return, finding himself caught in the debts contracted during his exile and confronted by a ruined estate, he put the direction of his affairs into the capable hands of Francis Topp, the merchant who had married Margaret's maid-in-waiting, Elizabeth Chaplain. Topp was not restrained in his handling of Newcastle's affairs by any sentimental notion of the easy relations which should subsist between a lord and his tenants and managed them as rigorously as he did his own. His efficiency soon gave rise to complaints, and on 21 February 1666 Sir Thomas Williamson wrote to Andrew Clayton, Newcastle's steward, to tell him of the harsh treatment received by the tenants, 'who indeed have suffered much through the crossness, as I believe, of Mr. Topp, for I perceive my Lord Duke leaves the managing of his concerns chiefly to him.' [2]

The family suspected Topp of serving both his own and

---

[1] For the jointures settled on Margaret see Goulding, p. 20.
[2] Nottingham Univ. Lib., Portland Papers, Cavendish Misc. 60.

Margaret's private interests. They may also have found that his sharp scrutiny of accounts diverted their father's generosity away from themselves; certainly Lord Mansfield had the embarrassment of explaining to his father in 1663 how he came to be £8,000 in debt, £700 of the sum having been spent on two coaches and eight Flanders mares.[1] Topp definitely courted his patron with an eye to advancement, forwarding to him from Bristol as a gift in 1661, for example, the best wines, tobacco and other luxuries that he could obtain. He was particularly anxious to be created a baronet and in July 1667, after several delays, he obtained his wish through Newcastle's influence, and was excused the fine of £1,095 'usually paid for that dignity.'[2] But as Newcastle was able to leave his estates substantially repaired from the ravages of the Civil War, Topp's administration was clearly beneficial and it is very doubtful if he used it to line his pocket.

Topp's baronetcy brought the family's hostility to him to a head and measures were concerted to clip his influence. 'I am most highly pleased with your witty and judicious expression concerning Mr. Topp and his wife,' Lady Jane Cheyne wrote to her sister-in-law, the Countess of Ogle, on 2 July 1668, 'for truly he is no more, though most call him Sir Francis . . . you writ very well in saying you were glad that vanity hath got the better of covetousness; when Mr. Topp was in his coach in Hyde Park, I believe he could have wished I had not seen him there; he reports the thousand pound my father was pleased to give me is not yet due; truly, I expect nothing he can keep from me. I am of your opinion, he intends none of my Lord's children any good, and am very sorry he should so much waste the estate as you mention; methinks there might be some means contrived to hinder him; I would assist in anything I could.'[3] Whatever the scheme contrived among the family against Topp, it seems to have succeeded in part at least, for Lady Armyne wrote to Lady Ogle about this time to congratulate her on

<hr />

[1] *H M C, 13 Rep., Pt. ii*, 1893, ii. 145.
[2] *C S P D, 1667*, 1866, p. 348.
[3] Nottingham Univ. Lib., Portland Papers (uncatalogued).

Elizabeth Topp's departure from Welbeck. It 'will be much to your satisfaction,' she wrote, 'that the Lady Topp and her daughter is gone from Welbeck, I hope never to return thither any more. I hope your Ladyship, my honoured Lord, and all yours will still be more firmly fixed in my Lord Duke's favour and affection.' [1]

Newcastle was well aware of the family's attitude towards Margaret and tactfully tried to restore good relations. Writing to his son on 20 January 1670, he told him that the grandchildren, who were visiting at Welbeck, were all well: 'but Henry,' he continued, 'loves my wife better than anybody, and she him I think.' [2] But such reassurances were insufficient to allay the family's suspicions when only two days later Newcastle increased Margaret's jointure for the third time. On 15 January 1668 he had settled on her for the term of her life the mansion house at Clerkenwell; and on 22 January 1670 he settled on her all the waste ground in Sherwood Forest. Her jointure was yet further increased on 29 October 1670 by the addition of the manor of Sibthorpe and Clipstone Park. These increases so upset Lord Ogle that he wrote to the Earl of Danby on 10 August 1671: 'I am very melancholy, finding my father more persuaded by his wife than I could think possible. . . . I thank God my little family are in health; the joy I take in it cannot be taken away from me by the unkindness to us at Welbeck.' [3]

Margaret can hardly be blamed if she made some provision for the future. Newcastle could not live much longer, in spite of his vigour and temperance, and should she survive him, as she lacked any dowry, she must necessarily depend upon the settlements he could make; and having once enjoyed the state befitting her rank, she was clearly determined not to retire into impoverished obscurity if she could possibly help it. She may also have thought that she deserved some reward for loyally sharing his exile, and such was certainly Newcastle's opinion.

[1] *Ib.*
[2] Quoted by Goulding, p. 20.
[3] Quoted *ib.*, p. 21.

Once the property was settled on her, she handled it with the shrewd practical sense which is the oddest trait of her romantic character. She herself claimed to be able to manage a grange 'indifferently well', and light is thrown on her ability by a letter from William Fuller, Bishop of Lincoln, to Joseph Williamson, written on 12 August 1671, at the time of rumours of a sectarian uprising. Fuller reported that the people of Leicestershire were hurriedly branding their cattle, alarmed by the rumours spread by the sectaries that unbranded cattle would be seized for the King. It 'is reported (how true I know not)', Fuller continued, 'that the Duchess of Newcastle was very severe in punishing those of the Forest in Nottinghamshire, taking away all the cattle that were not branded, as legally they ought to be.' [1]

Margaret's sharpness in managing her affairs, a trait inherited from her mother and encouraged perhaps by Sir Francis Topp's advice, so antagonized Newcastle's household, which was unused to close supervision, that it resulted in 'a horrid conspiracy' against her. [2] When Andrew Clayton, Newcastle's steward, was in Northumberland in 1668, he promised Francis Liddell to persuade Newcastle to pay off a bond for £500, for which Newcastle, along with the late Lord Widdrington and the late Sir William Carnaby, had stood bound to the late Sir Thomas Liddell. Clayton promised in addition to reduce Liddell's rent for the desmesne of Ogle from £180 to £150 a year. In return, Liddell gave Clayton a stoned horse worth £80, a brood mare worth £20, and promised him the best colt 'Black Barb' should get out of a mare that wintered with one Edward Alder. On 29 October 1670 Liddell pressed Clayton to perform his promises as he needed the £500 to begin working a quarry; and as a further inducement, he offered him a fourth share in the quarry for £500, which, he assured him, would be worth £200 a year for twenty-one years. Unfortunately Clayton had to admit

[1] *C S P D, 1671*, 1895, p. 426.
[2] There are two copies of the account of the conspiracy against Margaret —'A true Narrative and Confession'—among the Portland Papers (Cavendish Misc. 9) in Nottingham Univ. Lib. The conspiracy has also been described by Goulding (pp. 21–4).

that he could be of no help to Liddell at the moment, 'for that the Duchess did so narrowly of late inspect his Grace's affairs, as that he could make no alteration of the rental without being discovered; and he also found that she positively obstructed his Grace for paying of that £500 debt.'

Margaret possibly suspected Clayton's intentions. She was well versed in the cheats practised on landlords and had listed a few of them in 'The Tale of a Traveller': 'their reapers steal their sheaves of corn . . . the shepherd steals the twin lamb, the swineherd the tenth pig, the neatherd will mix strange steers in amongst his master's to grass.' The moral of the tale is that constant vigilance is needed if a landlord is to thrive. Clayton cannot have read his mistress's works.

But not only did Clayton accuse Margaret to Liddell and John Booth, another servant involved in the affair, of tiresome vigilance: he also affirmed that she intended making Newcastle's secretary, John Rolleston, draw up new rentals, and that if she succeeded, she 'would break up the family and go to rant at London.' Another charge was that she was determined to get a further jointure of £800 a year, and was enriching herself with a view to marrying again, 'well knowing his Grace could not live long.'

At a second meeting of the three conspirators, held on 30 October, Clayton reported that 'he had studied all ways in the world how to give her Grace a dead blow, and to divert his Grace's affections from her, but he could not find out any person living that would or durst tell his Grace such things as he had to say against her.' After further libelling her character, Clayton asserted that 'it was her Grace's delight to ruin all persons that she had to do with, and that he heard her Grace say the old Countess of Shrewsbury practised the same, and she was a duchess and consequently a greater person than a countess, and would outdo her in that kind.' Booth had been hitherto reluctantly involved in the conspiracy, but Clayton now fetched him over by telling him that Margaret had taken a dislike to him and had ordered his accounts not to be signed or discharged.

In order to benefit their several interests they decided to send an anonymous letter to Newcastle, and met again the following day to draw it up. The letter began by reminding Newcastle of the great honour and esteem in which he had been held by everyone before the Civil War, and then asserted that if he had fallen in the general opinion, the blame was his wife's. But Clayton was dissatisfied with the draft and urged that an accusation of Margaret's misconduct with Sir Francis Topp should be inserted. He was supported by Liddell, who 'added this reason, that one particular instance was of greater force than a hundred generals.' And so the conspirators 'brought in that damned scandal with a long parenthesis.' When the letter was written, they knelt together and gripping it in their right hands, bound themselves to secrecy under 'a curse of damnation, and destruction to their posterities for ever.'

The letter was taken to Grantham and posted from there in order to avoid discovery. On the day of its delivery, 2 November, neither Clayton nor Booth dared stay in the house for fear they should betray themselves; but on their return in the evening, they learnt from Liddell that it had been taken up to Newcastle by John Proctor, his personal servant. While they were at supper, Newcastle sent for Clayton—but the interview must be given in Clayton's words, as they were reported by Booth, who later betrayed the conspiracy:

'He told us his Grace had acquainted him with the receipt of a libel, and further told him he had given it to her Grace, who was somewhat suspicious that he or Gilbert Eagle [another servant], or both of them, had a hand in it; but his Grace said he had satisfied her of their innocence, and that he suspected that acute rascal the parson of Mansfield for it; and if he could find out the author he would have his ears; his Grace further added that the author was both a fool and a knave to think he should be directed by libels.

'Clayton, to colour his ignorance, asked his Grace whether it was in verse or no; and his Grace answered, no, it was a serious thing in prose, and did seem to court him much at the beginning but had abused Peg, as he pleased to call her Grace, abominably.

'Clayton further said that he perceived his Grace did not resent it so highly as he hoped he would have done; yet none knew what effects it might have afterwards, so we all concluded to be secret and to wait the event.'

John Booth, preyed upon by his conscience, determined to betray the secret, and in spite of Clayton's efforts to stop him, made his confession on 30 June 1671, which was duly drawn up in form and witnessed. The truth of the statement was endorsed by Liddell, who probably escaped lightly for his compliance. The punishment meted out to Clayton, the arch-conspirator, is not known.

This domestic drama may suggest a disorganized household, torn by petty dissensions, but the evidence of the chaplain, Clement Ellis, proves the contrary. Ellis was often heard to say, according to his biographer, 'that the greatest personages' belonging to the family 'would suffer themselves to be reproved by him when anything was done or spoken amiss: a freedom rarely to be met with in this licentious age!'[1] Newcastle strongly supported his chaplain, even against his guests. When 'a gentleman of extraordinary note' once uttered some 'profane jests' against Christianity and questioned its truth, Newcastle asked Ellis to answer him and briskly defended him against the gentleman's charge of being 'rude and unmannerly' in his reply. Ellis was rewarded by Newcastle with the rectory of Kirkby in Nottinghamshire.

In spite of 'the horrid conspiracy', Margaret's life proceeded quietly, preoccupied with contemplations. An old friend, Constantijn Huygens, who visited London in 1671 but was unable to extend his tour to Welbeck, wrote on 19 September to remind her of the diversions of her exile. 'I could not forbear to show your Grace by these lines,' he wrote, 'how verily mindful I am of the many favours she hath been pleased to bestow upon me in former times, especially of those favours,

---

[1] Clement Ellis, *The Scripture Catechist*, 1738, pp. xi–xii.

Madam, which I remember did cost you many a white petticoat a week. I make no question but the same noble vein is producing still some new rarities, and pray God it may continue to do so many happy years, to the glory of your name and satisfaction of the world.'[1] New 'rarities' may have been under way, for Mark Anthony Benoist wrote to Newcastle from London on 13 August 1672: 'I have received my Lady Duchess's letter, with the filings of the loadstone, which I intend to show to several persons, to have their opinions whether it be right or no.'[2] But however urgently Margaret may have been questioning nature during these years, it is likely that it replied in the accents of old.

Her relations with her husband's family seem to have been gradually improving and in 1673 she was able to write a perfectly affable letter to Lord Ogle. The letter is worth quoting in its original form to show how little her long practice of writing had improved her spelling or punctuation:

' My lord

I am glad you have resevd such sattesfaction you desir when your lordship was heer at Welbick and I wish with all my sould your lordship may have the fruesion [fruition] of all your good desirs I am allso glad my lord Mansfield [her favourite, Harry] did kindly actseept of my letter but sorry he hath got a knock upon his forhead pray tell his lordship from me if he were a marred man it would be a dangrous bumpe but praying for his happenes as also your lordship

> I am
> my lord
> your lordships humbell sarvant
> M. Newcastle.'[3]

The middle-aged woman writing facetiously to her stepson still scribbled as impetuously and carelessly as she had done as a girl, writing secretly to her lover from St. Germain.

[1] *De Briefwisseling van Huygens*, vi. 293.
[2] Nottingham Univ. Lib., Portland Papers (uncatalogued).
[3] Brit. Mus., Portland MSS. List 1B; Cavendish Papers 1661–95, f. 362.

9. The Duchess of Newcastle. Detail from the monument to the Duke and Duchess in Westminster Abbey.

Newcastle, meanwhile, had begun to prepare for his own death. On 16 May 1671 it was reported that the King had granted him his request for a burying-place in Westminster Abbey, and Newcastle at once asked his old comrade in arms, John Dolben, Bishop of Rochester and Dean of Westminster, to make the necessary arrangements. This commission, Dolben wrote in reply on 2 July, 'made me with great delight employ myself in designing that for your Grace which I should be sorry to live to accomplish, being already unhappy enough in burying too many princes. For the thing itself, I am glad to see the King do that which is so decent and worthy of him, as to order your Grace a tomb among the kings, who have always been so near to him. . . . However, your Grace hath prepared for yourself a more noble and more lasting monument, in the fame of your heroic actions; of some of them I had the happiness to be an eye-witness.'[1]

Margaret must have been glad that she, too, would later be laid beside her husband among the kings. In one of her letters she pretended that she cared little where she was buried, having learnt from the fate of her own family's tombs that such memorials were subject to desecration and destruction in time of war; but as she was so anxious to engage posterity's interest, she cannot have been averse to the idea of a tomb that would also be in effect a public monument. She cannot have imagined that she would precede her husband, so many years her senior, into it; but having undermined her health by her sedentary life and her habit of doctoring herself, she died suddenly at Welbeck on Monday, 15 December 1673, in her fiftieth year.[2]

Newcastle himself was too old to leave Welbeck to attend her funeral, but on 3 January her body, attended by a numerous

[1] *Letters and Poems*, pp. 107–8.
[2] Margaret was survived by three of her sisters: Elizabeth Walter died in 1691, and Catherine Pye—her 'beloved sister'—in 1701; the date of death of Anne, the unmarried sister, is not known. Sir Thomas, her elder brother, had died in 1649, as a result of wounds received in the Civil War, and John, Lord Lucas, in 1671.

retinue of servants, was carried up to London, where it lay in state at Newcastle House in Clerkenwell until Wednesday, 7 January. On the Wednesday evening a solemn procession left Clerkenwell for the Abbey. At the head rode the Earl Marshal's men and Newcastle's servants, wearing long black cloaks, followed by the chaplain to the defunct and four Officers of Arms, one of whom bore the coronet on a black velvet cushion. The coffin, covered in a sheet and a pall of black velvet and adorned with escutcheons of the defunct's arms impaled with those of her husband, was carried in a hearse drawn by six horses. The hearse was also hung with black velvet and adorned with escutcheons in the same style as the coffin itself, and behind it followed the mourning coaches of the relations and of the nobility in order of precedence. Lit by flaring torches, the procession moved slowly through the narrow streets towards Westminster, through Smithfield, the Old Bailey, Fleet Street and the Strand, watched in silence by crowding spectators.

When the procession arrived at the west door of the Abbey, the coffin was lifted from the hearse and carried into the building, preceded by the Officers of Arms, the officer who carried the coronet on its cushion leading. The Dean of Westminster, the prebends and the choir received the coffin and, following the choir, the procession made its way to the vault in the north cross. At Newcastle's 'express desire and direction' the coffin was followed by Lady Pye and Anne Lucas, the sisters of the defunct, the Countess of Ogle, the Countess of Bolingbroke and several other ladies, preceded by a gentleman usher, and behind the women-mourners followed, in order, the Earl of Ogle, the Earl of Norwich, Earl Marshal of England, the Earl of Bridgewater, the Earl of Clare, and many of the nobility and persons of quality. The pall was supported by the Lords Brackley, Lovelace, Byron, and Lucas. The coffin was interred in the vault, and the style of the defunct was pronounced by an Officer of Arms: 'Thus it hath pleased Almighty God to take out of this transitory life to his divine mercy the most high, mighty, and most noble Princess Margaret, Duchess of Newcastle, late wife of the most high, mighty, and most noble prince William, Duke of Newcastle, now living.' [1]

Newcastle was determined that Margaret's death should be commemorated not only by the tomb which he was building in the Abbey but by a memorial typical of her life. He arranged for the publication in 1676 of all the letters and poems which had been written in her praise. *Letters and Poems in honour of the Incomparable Princess, Margaret, Dutchess of Newcastle* included the addresses from Cambridge, the flattering letters of Huygens, Charleton, Glanvill, Hobbes, Digby and others, several adulatory poems, and a group of elegies, to which Thomas Shadwell and Clement Ellis were contributors. But none of the elegists could match the simple eloquence of the epitaph which Newcastle wrote to grace the tomb where he himself was to be interred on 22 January 1676, and where he and Margaret are still to be seen in effigy lying side by side:

' Here lyes the Loyall Duke of Newcastle and his Dutches, his second wife, by whome he had noe issue; her name was Margarett Lucas, youngest sister to the Lord Lucas of Colchester; a noble familie, for all the Brothers were Valiant and all the Sisters virtuous. This Dutches was a wise, wittie and learned Lady, which her many Bookes do well testifie; she was a most Virtuous and a Loving and carefull wife, and was with her Lord all the time of his banishment and miseries, and when he came home never parted from him in his solitary retirements.'

---

[1] This account of Margaret's funeral is taken from the Funeral Certificate in the College of Arms. Sir Edward Walker, Garter King of Arms, received £40 in fees for directing the ceremony, and the three heralds £30 apiece (Brit. Mus., Add. MSS. 12, 514, f. 290).

CHECK-LIST OF THE WORKS OF
MARGARET CAVENDISH

[All the works are in folio unless otherwise stated]

Poems, and Fancies: Written by the Right Honourable, the Lady Margaret Countesse of Newcastle. London, Printed by T. R. for J. Martin, and J. Allestrye at the Bell in Saint Pauls Church Yard, 1653.
(The title-page of another issue reads: *Poems, and Fancies: Written by the Right Honourable, the Lady Newcastle*, etc.)

Philosophicall Fancies. Written by the Right Honourable, the Lady Newcastle. London, Printed by Tho: Roycroft, for J. Martin, and J. Allestrye, at the Bell in St. Pauls Church-yard, 1653. (12mo.)

The Worlds Olio. Written by the Most Excellent Lady the Lady M. of Newcastle. London Printed for J. Martin and J. Allestrye at the Bell in St. Pauls Church-Yard 1655.

The Philosophical and Physical Opinions, Written by her Excellency, The Lady Marchionesse of Newcastle. London Printed for J. Martin and J. Allestrye at the Bell in St. Pauls Church-Yard 1655.

Natures Pictures drawn by Fancies Pencil to the Life. Written by the thrice Noble, Illustrious, and Excellent Princess, the Lady Marchioness of Newcastle. In this volume there are several feigned Stories of Natural Descriptions, as Comical, Tragical, and Tragi-Comical, Poetical, Romancical, Philosophical, and Historical, both in Prose and Verse, some all Verse, some all Prose, some mixt, partly Prose, and partly Verse. Also, there are some Morals, and some Dialogues; but they are as the Advantage Loaves of Bread to a Bakers dozen; and a true Story at the latter end, wherein there is no Feignings. London, Printed for J. Martin, and J. Allestrye, at the Bell in Saint Paul's Church-yard. 1656.

Playes written by the thrice Noble, Illustrious and Excellent Princess, the Lady Marchioness of Newcastle. London, Printed by A. Warren, for John Martyn, James Allestry, and Tho. Dicas, at the Bell in Saint Pauls Church Yard, 1662.

Orations of Divers Sorts, Accomodated to Divers Places. Written by the thrice Noble, Illustrious and Excellent Princess, the Lady Marchioness of Newcastle. London, Printed Anno Dom. 1662.
(The title-page of another issue is dated 1663.)

Philosophical and Physical Opinions. Written by the thrice Noble, Illustrious, and Excellent Princess, the Lady Marchioness of Newcastle. London, Printed by William Wilson, Anno Dom. M.DC.LXIII.

CCXI. *Sociable Letters, Written by the thrice Noble, Illustrious, and Excellent Princess, the Lady Marchioness of Newcastle.* London, Printed by William Wilson, Anno Dom. M.DC.LXIV.

Philosophical Letters: or, Modest Reflections upon some Opinions in Natural Philosophy, maintained by several famous and learned Authors of this Age, expressed by way of Letters : By the thrice Noble, Illustrious, and Excellent Princess, the Lady Marchioness of Newcastle. London, Printed in the Year, 1664.

Poems, and Phancies, Written by the thrice Noble, Illustrious, and Excellent Princess the Lady Marchioness of Newcastle. The Second Impression, much altered and corrected. London, Printed by William Wilson, Anno Dom. M.DC.LXIV.

Observations upon Experimental Philosophy. To which is added, The Description of a new Blazing World. Written by the thrice Noble, Illustrious, and Excellent Princesse, the Duchess of Newcastle. London, Printed by A. Maxwell, in the Year, 1666.

The Life of the thrice Noble, High and Puissant Prince William Cavendishe, Duke, Marquess, and Earl of Newcastle; Earl of Ogle; Viscount Mansfield; and Baron of Bolsover, of Ogle, Bothal and Hepple; Gentleman of his Majesties Bed-chamber; one of his Majesties most honourable Privy-Councel; Knight of the most Noble Order of the Garter; his Majesties Lieutenant of the County and Town of Nottingham; and Justice in Ayre Trent-North: who had the honour to be Governour to our most Glorious King, and Gracious Soveraign, in his Youth, when he was Prince of Wales; and soon after was made Captain General of all the Provinces beyond the River of Trent, and other parts of the Kingdom of England, with power, by a special commission, to make Knights. Written by the thrice Noble, Illustrious, and Excellent Princess, Margaret, Duchess of Newcastle, his wife. London, Printed by A. Maxwell, in the Year 1667.

(A second edition, in 4to, was published in 1675.)

De Vita et Rebus Gestis Nobilissimi Illustrissimique Principis, Guilielmi Ducis Novo-castrensis, commentarii. Ab Excellentissima Principe, Margareta ipsius uxore sanctissima conscripti. Et ex Anglico in Latinum conversi. London, Excudebat T. M. MDCLXVIII.

Grounds of Natural Philosophy: Divided into thirteen Parts: with an Appendix containing five Parts. The Second Edition, much altered from the First, which went under the name of Philosophical and Physical Opinions. Written by the thrice Noble, Illustrious, and Excellent Princess, the Duchess of Newcastle. London, Printed by A. Maxwell, in the Year 1668.

Observations upon Experimental Philosophy: To which is added, The

Description of a new Blazing World. Written by the thrice Noble, Illustrious, and Excellent Princesse, the Duchess of Newcastle. The Second Edition. London, Printed by A. Maxwell, in the Year, 1668.

The Description of a New World, called the Blazing-World. Written by the thrice Noble, Illustrious, and Excellent Princesse, the Duchess of Newcastle. London, Printed by A. Maxwell, in the Year M.DC.LX.VIII.

Plays, never before Printed. Written by the thrice Noble, Illustrious, and Excellent Princesse, the Duchess of Newcastle. London, Printed by A. Maxwell, in the Year M.DC.LX.VIII.

Poems, or, Several Fancies in Verse: with the Animal Parliament, in Prose. Written by the thrice Noble, Illustrious, and Excellent Princess, the Duchess of Newcastle. The Third Edition. London, Printed by A. Maxwell, in the Year 1668.

Orations of Divers Sorts, Accomodated to Divers Places. Written by the thrice Noble, Illustrious, and Excellent Princess, the Duchess of Newcastle. The Second Edition. London, Printed by A. Maxwell, in the Year 1668.

Natures Pictures drawn by Fancies Pencil to the Life. Being several feigned Stories, Comical, Tragical, Tragi-comical, Poetical, Romancical, Philosophical, Historical, and Moral: Some in Verse, some in Prose; some mixt, and some by Dialogues. Written by the thrice Noble, Illustrious, and most Excellent Princess, the Duchess of Newcastle. The Second Edition. London, Printed by A. Maxwell, in the Year 1671.

The Worlds Olio. Written by the thrice Noble, Illustrious, and most Excellent Princess, the Duchess of Newcastle. The Second Edition. London, Printed by A. Maxwell, in the Year 1671.

Index

shot, 101; poems to brother's memory, 101; moves to Antwerp, 102; ill health, 103; prescribes for herself, 103–4; doctors prescribe for, 104–5; exercise and diet, 105; sent to England to claim for N.'s estate, 107; sails for England, 108; reunited with family, 108; petitioner before Committee, 108–9; life in London, 110; extravagance of dress, 110; begins writing for publication, 110; on poetry, 110–11; publishes poems, 111; on her writing, spelling, and grammar, 112; manner of composing, 113; her reading, 113; her criticism of writers, 113–5; her criticism of Shakespeare, 114–5; transcription of her poems, 115–6; M. C.'s 'atoms', 116–7; poems quoted, 116–7; on magnets, 117; fairy poems, 118–20; her best known poem, 120; 'dialogue' praised in *Connoisseur*, 121; anticipates Thomson, 122; nature poems, 122–4; 'Fancies', 124–6; Marvell and M. C. compared, 125–6; *Poems, and Fancies* published, 126; Dorothy Osborne on, 126; excuse of 'false printing', 127; many prefaces, 128; dedication to Sir C. Cavendish, 128; modest of poetic talents, 129; Waller's 'adulation' of, 129; Westmoreland's poem to, 129–30; *Philosophicall Fancies* published, 130; tedious months in England, 131; sees N.'s property sold, 131; writes on Sir C. Cavendish and Bolsover, 131; rejoins N., 132; Sir C. Cavendish's death, 132; Antwerp home, 134; pleasure in Antwerp, 135; makes the 'tour', 135; fondness for ballads, 136–7; music at Duarti's, 136–7; hard weather and amusements in Antwerp, 137–8; shrovetide fairs, 138; riots, 138–9; neighbour's jealous wife, 139; maids' idleness, 139–40; resumes *Worlds Olio*, 140–1; defends cosmetics, 141–2; N.'s introduction to *Worlds Olio*, 142; M. C.'s portrait, 142–3; publishes *Philosophical Opinions*, 143; another portrait of, 143; N.'s verses on portrait, 143; Flecknoes' verses on M. C., 143; introductions to *Opinions*, 144; N.'s

defence of M. C., 144–5; dedicates *Opinions* to universities, 145; on natural philosophy, 145–6; on N.'s love of horses, 146; her depression chided by N., 148; portrait with N.'s family, 151; title-page of *Natures Pictures*, 151; portraits described, 151–2; verses describing frontispiece to *Natures Pictures*, 152; dislike of reading 'romances', 157; ms. of plays lost at sea, 159; publication of plays, 160; on benefits of public theatres, 160; plays impossible to perform, 161; prologue to plays, 163; exhaustion of ideas, 164; orations suggested as next work, 164; on orators, 164; publication of *Orations*, 165; *Orations* discussed, 165–7; *Sociable Letters* published, 167; *Letters* discussed, 167–9; condemnation of gambling, etc., 169; on passage of time, 169; suspects that N. might lose rewards for loyalty, 172; holds banquet and ball for Court, 173–4; N. on M. C. as wife, 175; M. C.'s distrust, of N.'s ship, 175–6; on N.'s return to England, 176; 'in pawn' at Antwerp, 177; practicality of, 177; sets out for Flushing, 177; travels in Dutch man-of-war to England, 177–8; disappointments in London, 178; country retirement, 178–9; her summary of N.'s losses in Civil War, 181; N.'s peerage, 183; visit to London and Court, 183–4; eccentric behaviour of, 184; begins *Life* of N., 184–5; on writing history, 185; criticisms of *Life*, 186; dedicates *Life* to Charles II, 186, 191; method in *Life*, 186–7; familiar touches in *Life*, 187–8; N.'s encouragement of M. C.'s writings, 188; *Life* published, 188; Pepys and Lamb on *Life*, 188–9; *Life* compared with Hutchinson's and Fanshawe's, 189–90; *Life's* handsome appearance, 190–1; 'the spirit of the age' and M. C., 192; watches metamorphosis of butterfly, 193; meets Huygens, 193; corresponds with Huygens on 'Rupert's drops', 194–5; unable to experiment, 195–6; on dissection, 196; theory of atomic nature, 196; on natural philosophy, 197–201; on

249

INDEX

Printed by The Whitefriars Press Ltd., London and Tonbridge.